Your Beautiful Life

LESSONS FROM AN ANCIENT MASTER

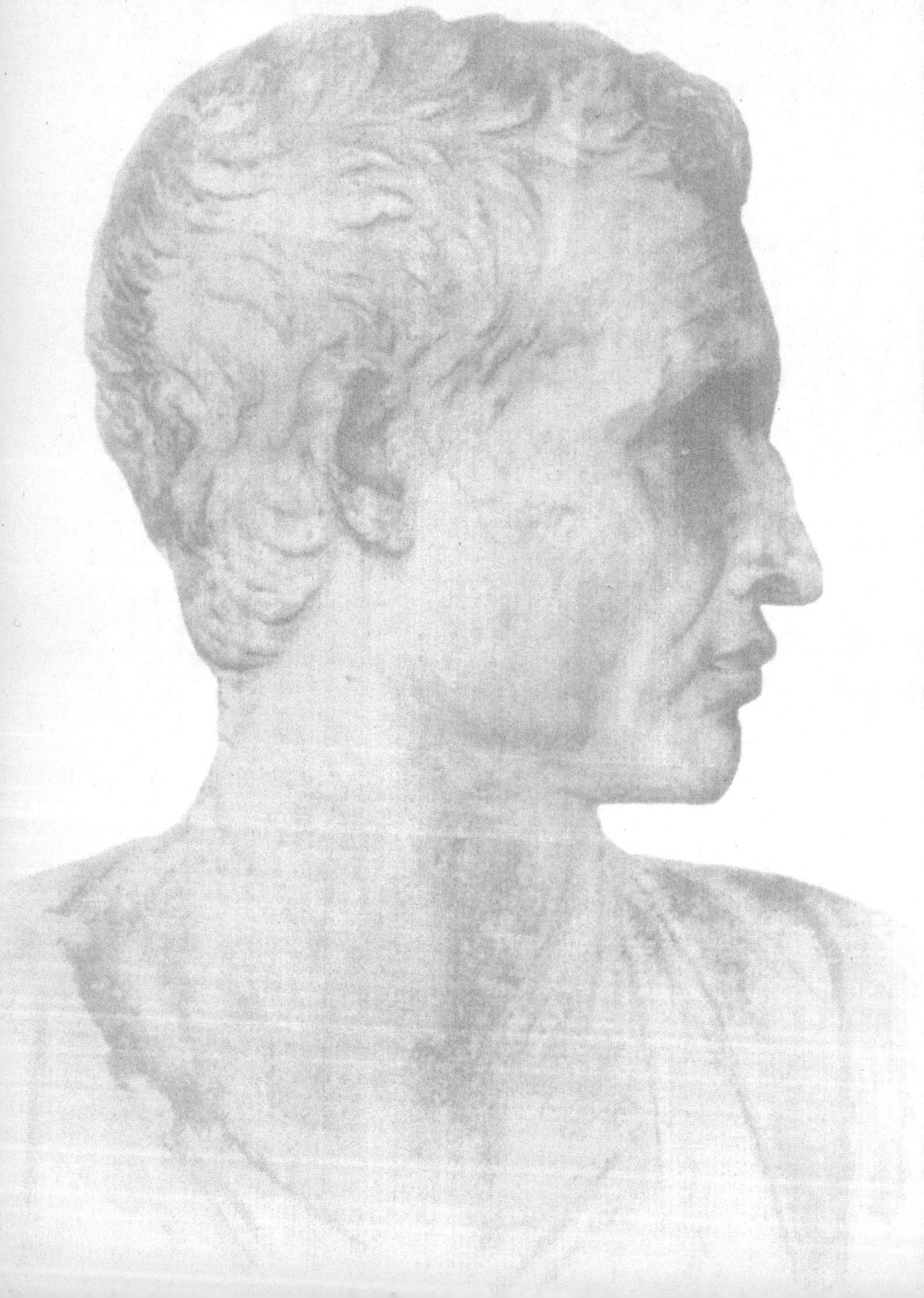

Your Beautiful Life

LESSONS FROM AN ANCIENT MASTER

Sally Mackay & Susie Trumble

BDP
BARKER DEANE PUBLISHING

Your Beautiful Life:
Lessons From an Ancient Master
By Sally Mackay & Susie Trumble
www.yourbeautifullife.com.au

Published by Barker Deane Publishing
44, 23-25 Bunney Road, Oakleigh South
Victoria 3167, AUSTRALIA
www.barkerdeanepublishing.com.au

First published by Barker Deane Publishing in 2011

Image of Virgil reproduced with permission from the Hector Berlioz Website (www.hberlioz.com)

National Library of Australia Cataloguing in Publication Data:
Your Beautiful Life: Lessons from an Ancient Master
3rd Edition (2013)
ISBN: 978-0-9808795-4-4

Cover design by Darren Cotzabuyucas and type setting by Andrew Morgan

Acknowledgements

Susie and I express our heartfelt love and gratitude to our husbands, Mark and Pete, for their unfailing support through our many years working with this book. Our life partners have traversed alongside us through many personal challenges that emerged as we set about anchoring Virgil's teachings in our lives. They have shared our growth and expansion and at times picked up the pieces of our shattered dreams.

Pete had been involved since inception, contributing insights and countless hours of editing that have been blended anonymously into the chapters. Sometimes, when I was ready to give up, his enthusiasm for Virgil's work and my channelling provided the motivation for me to keep moving forward. Thanks for believing, even through the veils of my own self doubt.

Mark has worked on all I.T. matters in support of bringing our vision to life. When Susie and I saw no avenue open to expand the book's influence, Mark's efforts in bringing the website to life filled that void. He hasn't always understood Susie's passion for Virgil's work, nor my channelling, but he has been unshakeable in his support. Thank you.

Thank you to my childhood friend Carol for sharing her artistic graphic skills for the website and for always holding a high vision of me through all my imperfections.

To our gorgeous children: Teah, Maya, Christian, Oliver, and Luca. You keep us grounded and focused and bring so much love, blessings, and at times, challenges. We love you dearly.

We wish to thank our 'Spiritual Group' friends: Ange, Beck, Deb, Elisabeth, Vicki, Juliet, Kim, Tim and Fiona. They were the first to 'road test' Virgil's course and their faith in our trinity was the catalyst that enabled our original, intimate channelling sessions to evolve into a genuine course. They have grounded these teachings in their daily lives and have never wavered from their belief that our work was important and that we should take it to the world. You are our great friends.

To Fern, Nikki, Bronwyn, Libby, Vicki, Lou, and Andrew who were the first to journey the course outside of our formal sessions. Their individual process demonstrated that a physical mentor was not a prerequisite for success. Thank you for assisting us to expand our reach.

We wish to acknowledge our spiritual teachers who have enriched our lives over the years. Johanna for providing a solid foundation that has seen me through so many challenges and changes. Your love and support has meant so much over the years. To Noreen, for introducing me to the concept of feeling consciousness. To Nadine, for facilitating my opening to channel, for supporting its anchoring, and for providing the venue where Susie and I first met. To my most recent teacher Annie, for coming in when I believed I didn't need an Earth teacher and for supporting my rebirth process into service. You are all wonderful people, thank you so much.

To our parents Arthur and Shirley, and Noel and Vera. Before we became so involved in spirituality, you had already taught us the importance of personal integrity, hard work, and service. You have held the highest vision of us as individuals; a vision we have always strived to sustain amid your love and support. To my mother-in-law Margaret, for standing by me and opening to spirit through her interest in what I do - you are amazing.

To all our family members, Rob, Debbie, Deb, Andrew, Mish, Pauline, Ian, Ant and Liz. You represent all the beauty, safety and love that characterises family. We love you dearly, thank you for loving us and always wishing us the best.

Finally, to our publishers Derek and Natalie, graphic designer Darren and our editors Suzan and Ilana. Our gratitude to you for seeing us at that deeper level of Spirit, and for trusting our joint process so completely. Meeting you has been a truly guided experience of impeccable timing. We feel so fortunate to have found you and look forward to our future work together.

Sally and Susie March 2011

Dedication

The descent to the infernal regions is easy enough, but to retrace one's steps, and reach the air above, there's the rub. Virgil 19 BC

The descent to ego consciousness is easy enough, but to retrace one's steps, and ascend to feeling awareness above, there's the rub. Virgil 2011 AD

Dedicated to all of us now making that ascent....

Dear Reader:

Each chapter contains a lesson which we recommend you follow for a week or thereabouts. There are fourteen lessons in all. Try not to judge whether you are 'doing it right' or 'getting it' as there are no right or wrongs within this course, it is ***your*** *unique journey. If you begin feeling as though you are lost, don't give up, persevere- but do journal it – that is all that is required; the rest will unravel.*

Table of Contents

Meet Virgil, The Guide

"If you live your life responding only half the time from Soul and the other half from ego, then you will always manifest resistance in order to move forward"...Virgil.

Greetings and welcome to those of you who are about to undertake this adventure inward - an adventure less about learning and more about awakening. The self that you identify with now is a portion of your total being, which is indeed great. You have lived more lives than you know, accumulated more talents, skills and fears than you yet realise. You contain experiences that are right now unconscious, but influence your daily life in significant ways. Your primary relationships contain a richer tapestry than you realise, with many encounters charged with meaning. The deeper nuances of your life can be known to you right now, but you must seek this meaning in the light of Soul, via the inner planes. Do not be discouraged or apprehensive. At present all that seems unknown within is already reflected all around you in the physical- in your life. We will bridge your understanding between the world of spirit and the world of matter, as it relates directly to your own unique experience. I look forward to being your guide through this beautiful transition from unknowing to knowing.

It is fair to say that presently your true grace is unknown to you, not because it is hidden or you are unworthy, but merely because you do not recognise it. You are simply so ensconced in your mortal ego existence that you have temporarily thrown a cloak over these other portions of self. Yet, it is this unrecognised portion of self that contains the answers you seek. These answers are not worn spiritual doctrine, but instead are completely unique and original to you and the remarkable Soul journey you are on. You created the questions, because within, you already contain the answers and you are now ready to bring them forth.

Many of you understand such concepts and refer to this as 'separation', where the ego and higher self interact unconsciously with each other. Further, you are so well versed in this notion of separation that you actually accept the condition as an aspect of physical existence. This 'fact' then generates feelings of powerlessness or futility of never experiencing the true light of Soul and creating a supportive, loving environment. I am here to tell you that separation is not a natural state in earthly reality. Through the pages of this text I will prove this to you.

It is no cosmic accident that you are present in this now, on the Earth plane. Irrespective of your level of spiritual achievement, you are here to learn. The Earth plane, for the open ego and willing participant, is a grand teacher. For the closed ego, devoid of conscious connection to spirit, it can become a very difficult master indeed. Let me be clear; you are not here to master the Earth plane as an entity in any way, but neither is it intended to be your master. Earth is on her own journey of discovery and evolution and works in unfailing cooperation with all energy forms. You are here only to master the self and all that you experience is trying to turn your awareness inward to this fact.

In less dense realities, manifestation from thought to form is much faster. On Earth, it takes a great deal of charged feeling energy to catapult thoughts into the world of matter and more time for the energy to coalesce into form. Still, time is evolving too and you have probably noticed that manifestation is speeding up. How often do you hear people comment that they should be careful of what they wish for? In the wake of the energy of higher consciousness, matter is infused with light and therefore becomes less dense. This rise in vibration means that less energy is required to form matter. You are presently confronted in the physical, with the consequences of your inner thoughts more rapidly and fully than ever before. The time ahead will be much easier for those in cooperation with their inner dialogue and who understand their own part and responsibility for manifestation. This will be your greatest gift to yourself – sovereignty over your life.

Know that right now, you, regardless of physical circumstances, are the perfect creator of your experiences. You unconsciously work within the laws of manifestation, not because they are absolute, but because you agreed to them before you became physical. This enables you to witness your inner realm made 'real' via the rich and colourful canvas of matter. For most of you, your outer reflections are far more compelling than your inner dialogue, so the physical outcomes get far more of your attention than their inner source. This leads you to believe that things happen to you which effectively hands your power of creation over to a force outside of yourself. For these people, Earth and society have become painful masters, but this need not be the case.

The Earth plane is your ally. It provides the means for you to explore your inner realm in living colour, so to speak. It manifests reality through you, directed by your inner beliefs, charged in feeling. Therefore, any difficulties you experience as well as any joys, must spring forth from your own inner creativity. Your true nature is creative, not good or evil, right or wrong, and your environment is not staid and fixed, but a living extension of the evolving self. As I guide you through this learning, the depth of your awakening will be of your own making. But know this – with the help of Sally and Susie, we will be supporting all and any action that will draw you back to love, to wholeness and the experience of self.

Some of you will relate easily to this text, and the exercises given, while some may struggle with the concepts introduced. All of you however, have the ability to witness the truth of this work in your lives and therefore truly ground the awareness that we are seeking to impart. Consistent focus is all that is required, no acting needy or craving after specific outcomes. You need to allow your natural creative processes to automatically manifest your focus in the 'real' world of your physical life. You will truly touch, feel and experience the wisdom and truth of this text, via your physical life. When this happens consciously, the realms of Spirit and Earth unite and the growth is truly unassailable. Throughout this process, allow yourself the freedom of expression that is unique to you and try to avoid making yourself 'right' or 'wrong'.

The Channel, Sally, would like me to reveal a little of myself to the reader at this point. I identify with 'myself' in vastly different terms than you identify with 'yourself,' as I do not have the distraction of a physical ego and all the limiting beliefs that usually characterise it. I have no first-hand experience of earthly life in this present now to draw on- although I have a glimpse of it from my own previous Earth existences and via the intuition, feelings and intellect of The Channel.

Essentially I exist beyond the physical realm in a state of pure energy, in touch with my multidimensional state, of which Sally and Susie are a part. I flow in the light of creation and evolution, just as you do, but with one marked difference- I do so in full conscious awareness, whereas you waiver between the conscious and unconscious. You do this because you have set up an artificial but extremely compelling barrier within the self. It is time to take it down. The Channel is intimately connected with me and our highest purpose essentially aligns, meaning she is predisposed to understand the concepts that I impart. Together, we engage the essence of my experience as it exists in pure energy, and then draw on our own unique perspectives to translate it through the dimensional layers into the world of matter. This process, often referred to as 'channelling', is the means by which my experience as a multi-dimensional being can be transformed into something meaningful in terms of the physical now you are experiencing. Your and my spiritual experience is not as different as you may think. Within our individual feeling essence lays our unique and unassailable kindred brotherhood. Further, all physical manifestation, in all its vast expression, also shares this common feeling essence. Throughout all of earthly history, there is but one driver at the source of such varied physical expression. Individually and collectively you strive to **achieve conscious self-actualisation. In other words; to know thy self and take responsibility for consciousness.**

You may ask, 'what makes me able to assist you bridge the seeming abyss between the unconscious and conscious mind?' In simple terms: it is my Soul's work, and every existence I have lived has been toward engaging this aspect. I have lived a full reincarnation cycle upon this planet, with experiences ranging from spirit medium European cave dweller to an applauded and, in your terms, famous Roman poet. It is from the latter life that I take the name Virgil. Not because I am attempting to 'reinvent' that life frame, but because it was my most recent earthly experience and one where The Channel and I were connected - to an extent physically, but more so from a Soul's purpose. We set the foundations, if you like, for the co-creation of this course. Most importantly, my Virgil experience was immersed within a time frame where the roots of your current society took hold on the planet. My writings in the past influenced Roman Society and therefore the mass consciousness of the day. It could be said that I had an influence on the cradle of your current civilisation.

It should not surprise anyone that I still seek to positively influence society's evolution at this time of profound change. I need to draw on my experience as Virgil to have some measure of understanding for the day and age you now dwell. You could argue that the physical manifestations of the times are vastly different (and you would be right), the foundations of your society, and many of its social mores and assumptions, can be traced back to Roman heritage. Therein lays our common ground. When I commune with The Channel, the life experience of Virgil is the 'bridge', if you like, between my multidimensional self and The Channel's experience, as she is immersed in now time. Therefore, it is critical to my ability to 'speak' to The Channel that I bring forward the essence of the Virgil life frame.

When one completes a reincarnation cycle on Earth as I did, and you all will, many opportunities arise in which to share the hard-earned wisdom that the realm affords. My speciality revolves around the collective consciousness and the extraordinary cooperation of energy that gives it life. The collective consciousness can only be evolved by those people that are immersed in it. Without consciousness to accept, and ground, all the love energy that is presently focussed in your direction, it will 'return to sender'- so to speak. It is projected again in your direction, until you finally accept it. To assist this acceptance, the collective needs to be evolved one mind at a time. This is the larger purpose of my work.

I truly love this planet and the human condition - both are at crossroads in their evolutionary path. Even that which would seem destructive, is still sourced from soul essence and therefore can be used to trigger love and peace at any time of your choosing. We refer to this notion as **essence over**

form. Essence is gleaned only from the inner planes of awareness and is a much more reliable ally than the judgement of physical form. Understanding your life essentially, rather than according to physical outcomes, will open you up to love and acceptance. This will in turn, have a positive effect on the collective and therefore, the entire evolutionary phase. It is an important time for all.

Please take the time to open yourself to the learning you are about to undertake. Open your mind and heart and hear the call within; the call to awaken. Know that my own essence is within every channelled word you read. Never forget that you have found this work for a purpose and that in truth, this purpose will always revolve around the self. The journey will be uniquely your own, as it must be, and is beyond judgement. You have never been alone on this earthly journey, no matter what you may think, and I hope that in the weeks ahead you will recognise this. You are about to allow, in your daily life, an opportunity to learn how to recognise the language of Soul – that has always been present, yet ignored. I look forward to being witness to the positive change your Soul's love, when recognised, will have on your own life and on the life of the collective dream.

Be Blessed. Virgil

Meet Sally, The Channel

Before you begin your journey, I would like share some background information on myself, Sally, otherwise known as 'The Channel'. I'm not psychic, clairvoyant or even a medium. I've never predicted anything of note. My spirit guides don't whisper in my ear, giving me advance notice on events, although I wish they did – don't we all? I have spent twenty years in the pursuit of 'spirituality'- whatever that means- in its many guises, searching for my niche. Along the way I learned to channel my spirit guides and the most predominant of these entities is the one who calls himself Virgil. An ancient and gifted philosopher, Virgil is now so much a part of my life that I can feel his presence even in my ordinary day-to-day existence. It has not always been that way. He is clearly the most highly evolved guide I have with me and generally supervises all my channelling activities. He has enriched not only my life, but also the lives of anyone who has been called to sit in his space. He is someone really worth knowing. I'll tell you our story of coming together. This has culminated in the birthing of this wonderful course.

As a child I never felt destined to do anything in particular when I grew up. I liked the idea of teaching children, but really I think it was because I liked the sound of my own voice, rather than a genuine calling. I was a day dreamer and I remember toying with questions of an afterlife from a very young age. My earliest recollection is of trying to imagine death as a state of nothingness. I tried to imagine what nothing would look and feel like. Even with my childish reasoning, I could not accept that such a state actually existed. That, coupled with a feeling, or perhaps hope, that there was something inside of me that could never be extinguished, led me to seek answers to the bigger questions of life. I never wavered from my feeling –or perhaps fear – that there had to be more to life than death, so I set out to discover what it was.

My family was in no way traditionally religious. We never discussed faith, never went to church and I was not christened, therefore I had not inherited a spiritual identity. My independent exploration of religious doctrine began when I was eight years old where I participated in Christianity through Sunday school classes. The elderly teacher was aghast that I was not christened and in her words, 'Not a child of God', and quickly had me fearing that I was damned to hell. This affected me deeply as I felt victimised by God himself and disconnected from the Christian teachings I had learnt so well. This was the first time that I felt alone and abandoned by spirit – unfortunately it would not be the last. At about age 13, my fears of abandonment were so prevalent that I (along with my sister) asked our parents to arrange a traditional church christening. My brother, Robert, who is seven years older, thought we were both idiots. Standing up there on the dais, a teenager, being christened with all the babies in their frilly gowns was (up to that point) one of the most embarrassing moments of my life- so I think he was right.

Now that I was a 'child of God', my fears were alleviated somewhat. The sense of safety that ensued allowed me to explore many traditional western religious theologies throughout my adolescence. To my dismay, the more I immersed myself in seeking answers, the more questions, inconsistencies and judgements I found. I never felt the sense of belonging and connection to spirit that I longed for. As a young adult, I vigorously investigated several lesser known Eastern doctrines, eagerly exploring Soul consciousness for the first time. Despite my serious dedication however, the answers to those bigger questions of life continued to elude me. I believed in my heart that religion was something concrete and real and was more than blind faith and modelling behaviour. I began to despair that I would never experience true consciousness. The immersion in eastern philosophy had certainly provided me with a glimpse of the potential of Soul union – so I yearned for answers more than ever and still hoped to find my spiritual home.

Fortunately I 'accidentally' came across new and different doctrines. I had my astrology chart professionally done first and played with numerology for a while. This led me to future gazing and soon I started to see psychics, tarot readers and clairvoyants. At first, I didn't perceive in any way that these people could provide me with the spiritual connection I sought. I didn't go for insights into the meaning of life – I went to get predictions concerning the usual areas of marriage, children and career. I didn't know how to discern a good spiritual reader from a bad one in those days, and I just took as gospel everything I was told, with occasional awful consequences. I quickly learned that there was a vast array of people calling themselves 'spiritual', 'psychic' and 'clairvoyant', who represented the full spectrum of integrity (or lack thereof) and abilities. It was a lesson in the meaning of discernment that helped me understand that I needed to narrow who I would allow to show me the way into this new world, for I genuinely wished to pursue my search in integrity.

Right on time, I met someone who appeared in direct contact with the spirit world and who was more concerned with my spiritual development, rather than my marriage prospects. She appeared to speak to something over my shoulder and I, more than once, turned my head expecting to see someone standing behind me. It was a little disconcerting. The personal information that the reader knew was so accurate that it dispelled my fears sufficiently and enabled me to open up and really listen. She revealed that a brand new guide had just joined me and was standing behind me. She said his name was Virgil and that he was a philosopher, here to teach me all about the spirit world. She added that he was a strong, powerful energy and because his form was tall, he looked imposing. She cautioned me not to be scared if I ran into him, as he was highly evolved and of the light (whaaaat????). I had a vague sensation of a presence behind me, but quickly rationalised it away as imagination or the power of suggestion. I was, quite in awe of the reader and the things she knew about my deepest self, as well as the prospect of guides assisting us in our lives.

In the midst of that reading, my relationship to spiritual pursuits altered forever. I was less concerned about getting the lifestyle predictions and instead began quizzing the reader as to how she could do what she did and see what she saw. I was truly fascinated and remarked how much I wished I had her gift. 'Oh, it's not a gift', she told me, 'It's your birth right. Anyone can do it if they want to'. Those words were to change my life. The hairs on the back of my neck were standing up. I suddenly wanted to see this Virgil for myself. I'd seen the movie, The Exorcist, and it had terrified me. I didn't want to conjure up anything dark or evil. Séances or the like were never my thing. Even as a child playing with friends using an upturned glass around a circle of childishly scrawled letters, gave me the 'heebee geebies'. I was excited, but such a novice that I also felt a little uneasy, even scared.

For weeks following the reading, I remember being quite anxious that I might actually see this spirit called Virgil. In my mind I asked him not to startle me if he was going to 'pop in'. He occupied a great deal of my thoughts and I began searching bookshops for reading material of a spiritual nature. I thought he would materialise and just sit on the couch and chat about everything he knew about his world – such was my naivety in the ways of spirit. He never did materialise so I just went about my daily life, although for some reason I knew he was real. It was only a subtle feeling at that stage of our relationship. I can't ever remember doubting his existence, even from the outset when I had no logical reason to be so sure.

Soon after this encounter my life changed in a profound way. I met a talented spiritual healer named Johanna who invited me to join her beginner's psychic group. For the first time, I felt like I had found a theology that gave me answers to every question I had and backed the theories with real experiences. I remained under the tutelage of Johanna for over a year. It was an amazing time for me and I soaked up as much information as I could. Johanna offered to help me learn everything - past life therapy, psychic development, psychometry, crystals, meditation, healing massage and more. She was a Reiki Master. She cleansed homes of negative energies and could see auras and guides. She was everything I wanted to be. I had a go at most things, but never really succeeded in anything. I found myself once again feeling abandoned by spirit. I so loved what I was learning, the potential of what was possible, and yet it never seemed to happen for me. It was a great time, but it was a difficult time as I started to play with my new spiritual knowledge. I watched it work and transform my daily life in small ways which was very exciting, though I was frustrated by my lack of concrete spiritual success, which I equated to my failure to see and hear the other world.

My initial joy at finding such a loving, exciting environment began to wane as I questioned my apparent lack of abilities. Where were the grand visions, the profound messages, the life altering moments where spirit obviously intervened? The more I yearned for these things, the further away they seemed. Sometimes, sitting in circle, Johanna would tell me she could see Virgil was present and that he had a message for the group to be delivered via me. For the life of me I couldn't hear what he was saying. I knew he was close because I would sweat and my heart would palpitate, but I didn't hear or see anything. Johanna would try many tactics to get me to open my mouth, from gentle encouragement to a firm dressing down. Nothing worked. I could never consciously connect with Virgil in that environment, despite how completely supportive it was. Over time, from sitting in those circles, the idea that I would channel a book directly from Virgil began to grow. I imagined I would sit down and take dictation and 'voila', a book would be birthed. My expectation couldn't have been further from the truth. I still had a lot to learn.

Soon, a new teacher named Noreen entered my life. Noreen was completely different to Johanna in every way. There was nothing concrete about what Noreen taught. Her lessons were based only in energy work, including the notion of feeling body, which meant nothing to me at the time. Noreen was a walking contradiction. She spoke of self sovereignty, yet had many 'hangers on'. Her own life was an open book and it was messy, yet she held no judgement of self and others. She would frequently talk of concepts and ideas that were 'out there' and would sometimes leave me uneasy. She was at times brilliant and amazingly honest. Strong one minute and utterly fragile and flawed the next. She would frequently check out my energy through squinted eyes, warning me that she had to 'smash that intellect, girl'. - I loved the attention. I didn't really understand what she meant by that concept or whether I really believed it to be true. Still, she never stopped playfully berating me for my many questions. She always engaged me and mostly made sense. She would simply smile knowingly and tell me to let it go and get out of my head and into my feelings.

In the early days of working with Noreen I was enraptured, even though I thought she was perhaps a little strange. Essentially she provided the first place I felt I really belonged. Her house was open and we basked in her light, and she equally basked in being our spiritual touchstone. For a while, my feelings of abandonment went away and I glowed. It wouldn't last though. It took me some time to realise, but it was a co-dependent relationship. Inevitably it was time to pry myself loose and it wasn't easy. It took me a while to appreciate the valuable lessons Noreen had given me, not only around the dangers of co-dependence, but more importantly, the concept of feeling as a way of moving through the spiritual world. She showed me an alternative to all the new age stereotypes that abounded in the books I read. My expectations had always been in visualisations or hearing voices and I had never had any of that. I always felt things. When Virgil was close, I could feel him, physically as well as emotionally. Little did I know this would be the way he and I would communicate. So, without Noreen, I might still be trying to see or hear Virgil speak to me and be berating myself for my failure to do so.

By now several years had passed and I had been concentrating nearly all my free time in the pursuit of 'spiritual growth'. I had read all the 'in' literature on the subject and participated in nearly every course around. Despite grounding small and occasionally significant insights into myself, I still felt on the whole let down by spirit. I tried very hard to follow all the rules yet remained stuck in old habits and a demanding but unfulfilling career. I dreamed of channelling and read many instruction books trying to learn to connect with the higher realms- Virgil in particular. Nothing seemed to happen. Eventually, when I had all but given up, I met a woman who facilitated channelling workshops. I knew as soon as I spoke to her that she would be able to help me. Her name was Nadine.

Before we were to begin, Nadine suggested that I should experience her channelling her own guide Ki, in order to demystify the channelling process. There was no doubt in my mind that Nadine was truly channelling when I first met her guide Ki; the presence of his personality and the energy of the room were palpable. More convincing than this was the accuracy and potency of the things that the guide spoke to me about. Ki, through Nadine, shed sense and light on some deeply personal issues that were uniquely my own. It was like he spoke to the deepest part of my being, that aspect that is often denied even by the self. Truth rushed in to me in one of those 'of course' moments of clarity; everything fit. I often refer to 'you had to be there', when someone doesn't quite 'get' an event I am trying to explain. Perhaps that moment with Ki was a 'you had to live in my skin' moment in order to 'get' it so there is no point in elaborating further. Suffice to say that I was completely sure that I was working with a teacher of integrity.

Very satisfied with Nadine's ability to channel, I looked forward to undertaking her course. She was different to the teachers I'd had before; she was like an Earth mother and was very grounded. She didn't see auras or guides. She immersed her life in spirit nonetheless, via the shamanic rites of the Native American Sioux. It was exciting for me to meet someone who also didn't see or hear the spirit world, yet was working in a meaningful way on a seemingly enlightened pathway. I was hoping maybe I had found my niche. The first channelling lesson involved the theory of how the connection occurs energetically, where the guide steps down in energy while I reach up. I knew the theory well, but had yet to experience it as real. I remember we had several sessions, over a few weeks, where we prepared the mind and body before we actually tried to bring Virgil through.

Preparation involved intent via meditative work, the clearing and daily activating of the chakras using the Soul Star, and might have included a mantra of sorts. My favourite preparation task was recording on paper all the qualities I hoped for in a guide. It was the ultimate wish list and something I took very seriously. I had to recite that passage so many times over the fortnight, but all I can remember is, 'I call to myself a guide who is gentle, loving and wise'. In essence I wanted a high level guide who could assist with my own evolution as well as that of the planet and the collective. Of course the guide who answered my call was Virgil. From that day forward a new spiritual journey had begun for me.

I was sitting in Nadine's channelling chair as she took me through a visualisation designed to raise my vibration to the point where I could mentally invite the guide in. He, of course, would then need to lower his vibration and hopefully we would connect somewhere in the middle. I can still recall the feelings of our initial connection and they were distinctly uncomfortable. My heart raced and thumped and my breathing was shallow and fast. I felt a physical heaviness, yet an inner lightness overlaying my entire body. It was like I was suspended and unable to move. I felt like I didn't have any control and I was starting to panic. Nadine gently spoke to the guide, which enabled me to discern his presence as distinct from my own self. This in turn assisted me in allowing him through.

Virgil seized his opportunity and briefly spoke of the notion of karma, challenging our ideas of it being a linear cause and effect. He referred to the power of the moment where our focus should lie. I was fascinated, but had had enough of the physical sensations so the energy withdrew immediately. My body returned to normal almost straight away and I wondered what I had been so worried about. In that one moment I knew I could trust this guide and although my body felt like it was being controlled, I knew that it was more about my surrendering it than the guide taking it. So much was communicated in that moment, not in words, but in feeling and knowledge.

I emerged from the experience positive that I would never be harmed and that nothing would ever happen against my will. I was disappointed that I had panicked and couldn't wait until the next try. I didn't have to wait long. Nadine offered me a space in a weekly group she held specifically for graduates of her channelling course. When I joined, there were six would-be channels all working towards developing their abilities in a non-threatening environment. It was both supportive and enlightening working in that group and we all enjoyed being in the space with so many guides present. I lived for the channelling group, and was a dedicated participant for quite a while.

It seemed a natural progression to look at the other things that Nadine offered. I participated in many of her other courses and workshops including Shamanic groups. I enjoyed my foray into the Native American culture immensely and it is a love that has never left me, even now. I enjoy its beauty and its simplicity. It is perhaps even more relevant to me now, having undertaken Virgil's course, as it reminds me that I am human and of the natural Earth. One of the most enduring rituals from this time is the burning of dried sage as a cleansing agent for the body, mind and especially the soul. I, and others from that group, simply could not contemplate undertaking any spiritual practise without the smell of the pungent smoke filling the room. It is both uplifting and reassuring to me.

My experience into the Shamanic ways culminated on a weekend retreat, under the guide of Nadine. A small group immersed ourselves in nature, participated in medicine wheels, a sweat lodge, journeyed to drums, and more. A few days before, I had completed an inner child workshop with Nadine, and had finally freed myself from the bonds of my crying, six-year-old self and all the pain that was harboured there. I remember this period as probably the most profound of my spiritual journey to that point. It is not surprising therefore that I met my eventual book partner Susie on that amazing weekend. I was very introspective as I tried to ground the profound impact of the inner child healing. This coupled with the full workshop agenda of activities, meant that Susie and I never had the opportunity to connect in a meaningful way. As is the way of spirit, one Shamanic ritual had to be rescheduled to a later date and Susie and I met again in a more relaxed environment, where we had the chance to talk.

Susie, I soon learned, was a channelling groupie. The only spiritual books she had ever read were channelled and she couldn't get enough of it. Susie is a very easy person to like - fun, kind and generous - and when she learned I was a channel, she asked if she could participate in a session. We started meeting at her home that she shared with her partner, Mark. After relegating him to his bedroom, we would channel for hours about a huge range of topics. Susie learned to hold the space while I channelled and this coupled with our regular sessions meant my skills were being developed. I now had someone who would hear me channel as often as I could keep it going and she wasn't at all intimidated by the strength of Virgil's energy as some people could be. Susie has the ability to draw more out of Virgil than anyone else. There is a bond and connection there that transcends this life. We are a true trinity, with each one important to the whole. In time, we began our own 'group' of like minded friends who each brought their own unique talents and perspectives to our sessions. It was a thoroughly liberating time as we began to be responsible for our own learning under the direction of our guides. We set our own agendas and began to take responsibility for our channelling processes. We had fun as we played with our guides and soon we were more connected than ever.

As delightful as this time was, there was one prevailing expectation I continued to flounder with. I still longed to write books with Virgil and really had no idea even where to begin. Virgil and I continued, with Susie's unfailing support and encouragement, to deliver more and more complex theories. It became easier to trust that I was definitely channelling a separate entity and not my own ego. Still, I lacked the confidence to begin the seemingly complex task of producing a book. I channelled and transcribed information on a huge range of topics from those practice days, yet the book never seemed to materialise. I was disappointed and felt entirely powerless and once again, abandoned by spirit.

Despite this, a great deal of growth and happiness characterised this phase. Susie, Virgil and I had developed a genuine and intimate friendship. We always loved connecting together and Susie and I were consistently empowered by his messages and the new slant he was able to put on old theories. He was always unfailingly loving, supportive and gentle. My channelling was now cemented in my life, going from strength to strength with new energies joining us, each with their unique message and perspective. Ventril and Eurana, who also call themselves, Twin Flame, originate from the Pleiades and have a deep sense of fun coupled with a fascination and love of observing our nature. Red Wolf, a Native American Indian who is quiet and reserved, yet profound, also joined us. On one hand the channelling was expanding which was positive, yet at the same time it seemed to stagnate, as it remained within the confines of a small group of supportive and willing friends. This was not my highest aim for my spiritual work. I continued to wait without a plan or concrete direction.

Throughout this time many changes continued to occur in our day-to-day physical lives. Susie and her partner Mark had a baby boy, and a few years later my partner Pete and I too became parents. Despite the demands of relationships and parenting, Susie and I continued to nurture our spiritual focus and together still managed to take the odd spiritual course. Susie was desperate to heal a physical rash which had troubled her for many years, while I was dreaming of a career in spirituality based around channelling.

Neither of us had any success at creating these ideals despite our persistence, and it seemed we had tried every course around.

We took a break for a while from pursuing new courses and settled into our domestic challenges, while still attempting to view our ordinary day-to-day lives with a spiritual focus. Then Pete, our two year old daughter and I moved to our new home, which was 45 minutes from the suburbs. This made it difficult for Susie and I to connect, so our sessions ceased altogether. Eventually Susie, the channelling groupie, decided enough was enough and began making the journey to our home on a weekly basis to restart our channelling focus. We had no grand plan in mind, no agenda we wanted met. It was more to embrace and return to the fore of our spiritual connection which we had neglected, due to the 'business' of living our normal daily lives.

Susie and I went through our usual rituals before we began to channel. We lit candles, got ourselves physically comfortable and burnt sage until the smoke filled the room and we could feel the cleansing properties work their magic. The more smoke we made, the more clear our intentions became. We discussed our joys, our fears and the spiritual journey of our unfolding lives. In a short time we knew a theme had emerged from our discussions and we were keen to hear Virgil's views. Essentially we were sick and tired of the physical lives we were living, despite our spiritual dedication and focus; things were not going well for either of us. Since the foundation of spirituality is that we create our own realities, up until that point we always measured our spiritual growth according to the events we experienced in our physical lives. The challenges and pain we saw as our lessons. The good times we saw as being in the flow. We would always intellectually reconcile the bad things after the event, analysing why it was necessary and what growth it gave us. The problem was we were living our lives in hindsight, analysing events after they had occurred, rather than consciously creating them in the moment. Of course, we couldn't articulate it in this way at the time. Instead we vented frustration and anger at rarely being able to create what we wanted. We were sick of dedicating our lives to spirit only to have a shitty time of it.

On this first occasion back after quite a long break, Virgil did not want to discuss actual events, rather he pursued a theory. He urged us to measure our life not in events, but in our feelings. He spoke clearly, yet conversationally, in a relaxed manner and gave Susie an exercise to do during the week. She was to record her ego thoughts in a journal and see what transpired. We were intrigued and had no idea where it was going to lead. The act of completing the task diligently gave rise to a great deal of insight for Susie. The next week, Virgil channelled a consuming session offering explanations for the insights Susie had gained. As my ego was totally removed from the process he was able to slip a small, yet hugely significant comment under my guard. 'Congratulations, you have started the book; last week was the first lesson in what will become a course.'

Virgil really is an amazing guide. After so many years of dreaming of success and blaming myself for the lack of it; just like that, he began, when Susie and I couldn't have been expecting it less. We were thrilled, especially to be doing it together. It was an amazing time in our lives and it continues to influence us all these years afterward. I hope you are able to grow from participating in this course, with the same lasting depth that we have so far achieved. We thank you for joining us.

Sally

Meet Susie, A Fellow Traveller

Susie is not a fictional character, (although some of the dramas she creates might lead you to think otherwise). She is I - a normal, everyday wife and mother with a unique connection to a wonderful guide called Virgil. I ask myself frequently, how on earth I became the 'test case' in the course that Virgil has so brilliantly constructed. As you will see, I was often haunted by my fear of not being up to the task before me. Succeed I did – and still continue to, for the course is not a destination, but a new way of life.

Like many people, a large part of my young adulthood had been spent investigating the notion of higher consciousness. As a result, I immersed myself in many New Age methodologies. Although I couldn't articulate it at the time, I now know I was searching for meaning as well as release from the anomaly that was my life – that is, despite a supported and loving environment, an ever present inner discord coloured every aspect of my being. This inner turmoil was seeking acknowledgement and in finding no answers outside of myself, I was eventually led to an inner search. I was absolutely captivated by spiritual theories that espoused I could create anything I wanted and whole-heartedly learned as much as I could. I reasoned that when my perfect physical life emerged, that the bad feelings I carried would just disappear.

Despite my considerable efforts, my perfect life failed to materialise and so my inner angst just continued to grow. It was at this time that Virgil took me aside and attempted to show me a new way to perceive my existence. That journey became this book, Your Beautiful Life, which contains the course you are about to undertake, with me as a very human reference point. Before you begin your own journey and in the process get to know me, warts and all, I have provided you with some specific background information about myself. This introduction that follows will explain the significance of many of the situations that occur in my life throughout the course.

I am an Aquarian born in 1968 in Melbourne, Australia. I grew up in a family of four, with one younger brother, in a house in the suburbs. I was in a very loving family, with supportive parents and was given every opportunity with which to lead a successful life. My childhood was happy and aside from some of the usual teenage issues, mainly problem free. I had a life filled with activities and friends with whom to divert my attention. I was very sporty, focusing particularly on a tennis career. Unfortunately this never eventuated to the levels which I dreamt, but which successfully exhausted the over abundance of energy I contained.

Despite having a lovely childhood, it did not translate into a strong sense of self. Over time, I managed to layer feelings of inadequacy, which I consistently blamed on my physical circumstances. I had insecurities about my appearance, like many young girls I suppose, which were grounded further by my attendance at an elite, all-girls private school. I found it difficult being surrounded by so much "achievement and beauty"- qualities I considered I most definitely didn't possess. I became entirely intrigued with the fantasy of not being in my body and trying to 'will' myself to be someone else. It was a feeling that went beyond merely wishing I was someone who was taller or prettier or smarter – those concepts I recognised even at a young age, would not make me happy. It was a deeper feeling that I could never put my finger on, one that was blind to me, until I completed this course.

I grew up in a family with no spiritual framework, aside from visits to the Catholic Church which I was forced to endure. However, I soon realised that this provided me with the opportunity to attend Blue Light Discos and meet boys. To one attending an all girl's school, this was really very exciting. My parents used to chuckle at my interest in the Christian Youth Group my neighbour ran, accusing me of being there for the social aspect as opposed to the religious one (of course they were right). I really questioned very little while growing up about my life and the world around me.

There was never a time when I wasn't going to become a primary school teacher; I simply never considered another career. I adored playing with and babysitting other people's children and fantasised about the twelve kids I was going to have in my life. In fact, all I wanted to do when I grew up was to have children. I envisaged a very simple life for myself. I perceived, like many people, that this kind of life would sustain me and that there would be nothing that would occur that I could not fix in some way. I was not one to daydream at all about my future, in terms of what I was going to do with my life; I just presumed it would all fall into place. Of course, this was far from the reality of what was to become and frankly the road I have travelled so far has never ceased to surprise me. Thank Goodness I didn't create all of those twelve kids!

Things really changed quite a bit for me when I moved out of home after I finished school. I was at College gaining my Primary School Teaching degree and supporting myself with three part time jobs. Despite all the physical hardships, living with my friends and having my independence was the greatest feeling for me. I was having so much fun despite the fact that after moving out of home an unusual rash appeared on my face. Doctors didn't know what it was or what had caused it, but a good cortisone cream fixed it temporarily. Over a number of years though this rash got far worse and reared its ugly head more frequently, not just on my face but on large areas of my body. I saw every dermatologist recommended to me. I was desensitised against everything I reacted to in allergy tests (which was most things). I used cortisone cream daily, I had anti dust mite bedding, I would sit in rooms with ionisers - really the list goes on. I honestly feared I was becoming one of those people allergic to the 20th Century. I saw naturopaths, homeopaths, Chinese healers, and tried everything recommended. Being a school teacher by this time, teaching among Asian and Greek students, I also tried out all of their cultural, ancient remedies. None of these worked. It was very hard to simply put on a brave face and get on with my life, despite the fact that my friends and family would continually assure me I didn't look that bad.

As the rash got worse over the years, so did the feelings I had about myself. Of course there were many opportunities to cover up these feelings and life wasn't all bad. I met a wonderful partner, Mark, and was surrounded by loving and supportive family and friends. Despite this I was finding it more and more difficult to get through each day. These feelings at the time would have been explained as very low self-esteem, lack of self-worth, etc., I would say, in hindsight, that I experienced depression. I remember these feelings clearly and how absolutely disgusting they were. I would look in the mirror and perceive myself as grossly ugly. I would go to bed every night and will myself not to wake up. I simply hated being in my skin. I would have quite literally 'sold my soul' to be someone else or to not even be here at all. I was medically incurable. I could not conceive a future, especially a happy one, with this rash. It was time to take action.

I walked into a large new-age shop one day and came across the book, 'Bringers of the Dawn: Teachings from the Pleiadians'. It was a channelled book which, like most people, I thought was completely 'kooky', but I still had a strong attraction to it. The Pleiadians discussed that if you were reading this book then you were a member of the 'Family of Light'. This resonated with me even though it was a new concept in my life. It was not what I would call a spiritual beginner's book in any way, yet it was the start of my spiritual journey. I loved it, despite the fact that the second I started reading it I had a strong allergic reaction. Along with the continual rashes, my whole face literally swelled to the size of a basketball. I was distressed beyond belief as I thought I was going to explode. Clearly a new phase was beginning.

Soon, I became obsessed with all that the Pleiadians spoke of and began purchasing every book containing channelled material, of which there were many. I particularly enjoyed the 'question/answer' format many of these books used, where people would ask a myriad of questions about their lives and planetary events which would then be answered beautifully by the guides. My curiosity about the occurrences on this planet in the past, present and in the future was insatiable. How often I wished it was me asking the questions! These books became my bibles and I would quite literally carry them around with me during the day, in case I needed to refer to them at any point. I was mostly excited about prospects that I had not considered before – there is life beyond this planet; our Soul has a journey; our life does have meaning; we are part of a mass consciousness; we are living in unique times of profound energetic change; and many other concepts. I developed an extensive intellectual understanding of many of the spiritual theories and practices. The channelled entities in these books came through in such unique and beautiful ways. I felt so guided and loved while reading these books. I started to accept that we are indeed not alone on our pathways and that there is a wide range of assistance available to us.

All of these books were fabulous at the time and many talked about the fact that we were living in a unique planetary age. This age would culminate around the year 2012 in an event called 'The Ascension'. To my delight, I suddenly had my ticket out of here. All I had to do was hang around till then and I could just disappear as part of a wave of higher consciousness. I had handbooks that instructed me on how to prepare for 'The Ascension'. I had special meditations to do (mind you I was particularly unsuccessful in this area), I would clean my chakras daily, I would say prayers and invocations ... frankly there was not much I wouldn't do to be a part of this.

None of my favourite books were practical or earth-based, as fun as they were to read. Many talked about physical changes occurring in our bodies as a result of the changes happening on the planet. For me this became the reason I was experiencing the skin condition. It was nothing to do with 'me'. It was simply beyond my control. It was an exciting phase as it was a respite from the way I felt about myself and the life I was experiencing. Despite the fact that my primary reason for entering into spirituality was a physical one, I have still, to this day, never read a Louise Hay book, (certainly the most well known author of books concerned with healing problems within your body). They held little appeal to me. I was not interested in pursuing spirituality in order to get to know myself better, or to 'love my disease' as I was often advised to do in order to cure it. I was only interested in just barely 'hanging in there' until the all powerful Universe ran out of tests for me and all my issues were dealt with. There would come a time when it would all go away and then my life would be perfect. I became very entrenched in all the New Age theories and was extremely diligent at following all the rules. Naturally, I also adopted the flowing velvet outfits that were fashionable for one on a spiritual pathway at that time!

I was fortunate during this phase though to come across many talented healers. The first person I chose to see was a healer/channel called Nadine, who has already been mentioned by Sally. Of course it was her channelling talent that I initially called upon, as I had no concept of being 'healed' as such. I went with a friend as I was very nervous. I had no idea what it would be like talking to her guide, and I most definitely expected her to trance channel. I was pretty much only there to see a channel in action as opposed to learning about 'me'. The only thing I wanted to know about my life was why I was experiencing the rashes, but I had a list of twenty or so other questions ranging from: 'Do animals have souls?' to 'Was I anyone famous in a past life?' I was so fearful of finding out something bad about myself that not a single question I asked was about anything personal. The guide at the end of the channel, however, did mention out of the blue that the skin condition I was currently experiencing was as a result of building prisons around myself in this life and that it was time to take a leap of faith and start exploring my inner self.

So I immediately enrolled in a beginner's spiritual growth course, also run by Nadine. After several years of intellectual exploration this really was the beginning of starting to explore my issues and peeling away some of the layers. Believe me there were many...even just having the confidence to speak up in a group situation with strangers was a big hurdle to overcome. Over a number of years, up to the start of our work on this book, I explored a great deal of the personal growth options that were around. I never felt particularly good at anything spiritual. I was always that annoying person who, if with a friend, would get the giggles when the meditation began or would rudely sit in the back row whispering about other things. I had few spiritual talents...I wasn't psychic, I couldn't channel, I never 'got' anything in readings. I would become embarrassed at other people's displays of emotion which I would always be able to contain. If I had ever been issued with a report card I would have probably failed. Despite this, whatever I was into at the time in spirituality permeated every aspect of my life. It would be the framework with which I would analyse, judge and measure up whatever was occurring.

I saw many healers which, for me, were always a more preferable option than doing a course, because I wouldn't have to put myself 'out there' in front of other people. I had become quite house bound, at times for weeks on end, if my face looked particularly bad. I was most certainly building more prisons around myself. Nevertheless, I cleansed myself of habits that no longer served me. I worked through many inner child issues, healers cleared the blocks present in my body and I would experience past life regressions. I particularly loved purchasing crystals and surrounding myself in their energy. While I was always very interested in what I would learn about myself, I would classify few of these experiences as being profound. None of them healed my skin, which was really the only thing I wanted. As spirituality for me, was about having the perfect ego life, my progress always measured up drastically short.

The course that was to change my life forever, in an unexpected way, was the Shamanic Workshop weekend away. While the course had a very primal effect on Sally at a spiritual level, I enjoyed the connection with nature but I mainly remember the delicious food we ate. Again, as was characteristic of me at that time, I revealed little of myself over the weekend to strangers, but thoroughly enjoyed listening to everyone else's journeys. It was in the final hour on the final day walking back to our tents that I struck up an individual conversation with Sally, knowing she was a channel. I was extremely excited but didn't want to appear desperate, as I quizzed her about her channelling. Let's just say, I was far less interested in her 'inner six-year-old child's journey!'

As already mentioned by Sally, it wasn't until sometime later that we struck up not only a friendship, but a relationship based around channelling and spiritual growth. I was absolutely in my element as I had found something in the spiritual realm that I was good at – questioning Virgil. It came as no surprise to my friends and family that 'having a chat' was to eventually become my pathway. The great man himself, Virgil, also loves a chat as you will soon discover. We quite quickly struck up what I would term a strong friendship, albeit a unique one. I would quite literally count down the days until we did our next channel. I was always like a child 'hanging out for Christmas'.

I loved the whole process of channelling: the beautiful space we would charge up with sage, the anticipation before the guide came in, the information we would receive and the joy of basking in all that energy. I still to this day love watching Sally as she begins to channel as I can always tell the moment Virgil enters by the beaming smile on her face and I, too, experience physical sensations in my body. He is a beautiful energy, very masculine yet very tender and loving. He quite distinctly makes his presence known. With Sally's assistance, he has been my salvation. I always remember reading in my books that 'when the student is ready the teacher will come along', and this has been absolutely true in my case. From the very first channel I experienced, there was not a doubt in my mind about the very powerful connection he has with Sally, based mainly around the love and shared purpose he has for and with her.

I have watched Sally's channelling evolve over the years from the humble beginnings when she would often take some time to establish the connection and when the circumstances would have to be exactly right (in our terms, not necessarily his) for him to come through. These days I often wonder whether it is Sally or Virgil I am speaking to, as she offers her many wise words....their energy is that interconnected. From our perspective we have always treated the connection we have with Virgil as being sacred and have considered ourselves extremely lucky and honoured. Neither of us knew anything about the life he led as 'Virgil the poet' on this planet, thankfully because I may have been too much in awe to talk to him. To this day I have never researched his life here, nor read any of his ancient writings. Much to our delight and surprise however, through our open conversations with him, aspects of his past life have been revealed to us. As we would channel together and question him, we would gradually discover that he was a much higher entity in the spirit world than we had originally presumed. He went from being a lovely guide who assisted us in our daily lives, to clearly someone who had a message of significance to impart.

Thankfully meeting Sally served a dual purpose: being introduced to some of her friends, and joining what we still to this day call 'Group'. What had been missing from my life up until that point was the journey with like-minded friends. For me that has been fundamental to my experience. It was in Group one night that Sally and I both understood that our pathways would be in-

trinsically linked together. There were four of us present and we were holding a special ceremony to honour ourselves and each other. We had to buy each person a gift to be presented at the end of the evening. I spent a long time in a New Age shop choosing my gifts and chose Sally a ceramic rune-stone necklace with engraved markings representing 'the victory rune of the spiritual warrior'. I opened my gift from Sally first and was astounded when inside the wrapping was the identical rune-stone necklace that I had bought for her. There was no criteria given for the gift, so what were the chances that not only would we choose the same gift for each other, but also out of the twenty-five rune-stones, we would select the one with the same inscription. I had to wait some time for Sally to open her present from me and by then I was giggling like a madwoman; I was bursting by that stage. Sally still laughs at how she thought I was an idiot as she watched my over-reaction to her modest gift. When she got to open her gift from me and revealed the same necklace, she was equally amazed and joined in my laughter. We still have those necklaces, more precious than diamonds, as they remind us not only of our connection, but also the magic messages of spirit during those early days.

Other members were to join Group over the years. One theme that was present for many of us was how 'religious experience' had always eluded us on our spiritual pathways. For all the journeys we had completed, separately and together, we would still sit around bemoaning our plight and waiting for that event which would categorically prove not just the existence of spirituality, but of it actually working in our lives. We never felt as if we had a true gauge of our growth. Years rolled by. Despite all of our so-called spiritual progress, based around the healers we would see and the courses we would do, we would occasionally admit that, we still felt the same disempowered way about ourselves and our lives. That was a pretty big thing for us to admit, as none of us ever doubted we were on the right pathway.

For several years, my life was very entrenched in a cycle where everything would be fine, in spite of the rashes, and then out of the blue, something bad would happen to frankly rock my world. Funnily enough, this would prove to me that Spirit was actually working in my life. As I emerged from the difficult situation, I would always feel like I had peeled away another layer. In time, I perfected the art of working out the intellectual spiritual justification for whatever was occurring and therefore everything in my ego world 'meant' something at a spiritual level. I had little concept of the big picture emerging in my life or of the feelings and issues that were the basis of the creation of my experiences.

While I would openly espouse the theory that we created of our lives, I did not own that concept. I blamed myself for everything 'bad' that happened and patted myself on the back when something 'good' happened. I seemingly had no control over my life. I frequently questioned Virgil on the mundane aspects of my life, because all I wanted from him was 'the' formula which would make everything better. I would bottle anything he said in the moment and make it my new rule for how I was going to live. Then, everything that occurred would be measured against my new rule and judged accordingly. Of course the one problem with this was that the rules kept changing.

It is only now, with hindsight and from working through this book, that I can understand why Virgil could not simply fix my life and tell me what would solve all of my problems. I was frequently very frustrated and troubled while speaking with him yet he would always respond with love and never gave up on me. Still, I just did not understand why these situations still occurred in my life.

A perfect example of this type of situation was the birth of my first child Christian. I worked long and hard on empowering myself to create the best possible circumstances for my pregnancy and his birth. I read all the appropriate books, did many mother-child meditations and focused on visualising my ideal, drug-free labour in a birth centre surrounded by crystals and mellow music. Much to my surprise the complete opposite occurred. I had an amniotic fluid condition where my uterus swelled to a size I thought it incapable of (my friends still laugh at how huge I was). I was fourteen days overdue so I was induced and ended up being on every drug available until an emergency caesarean was finally performed. I had a very big, healthy baby and of course was delighted with the result. Yet again, I believed I had failed, not so much in a physical sense but in a spiritual sense. While I understood birth was a co-creation, things did not go according to my plan in any way. As was my cycle, I felt the need to consult a number of healers to deal with the issues surrounding the birth and why it had occurred. I was on a constant roller coaster dealing with situations only after the event and trying to reconcile them with hindsight. It was costing me a fortune!

There was one such event when I had simply had enough. I was pregnant, this time with my second child and experienced a miscarriage. I was absolutely devastated but also shocked to the very core of my existence. It shook the foundations of my spirituality at every level. Naturally I consulted a healer and felt I had 'dealt' with the situation, but I was still very uneasy with myself. Sally had by this stage left the Group a few years earlier and moved to the mountains. We now tended to catch up as family get togethers rather than channel. I missed our shared focus on spirituality, let alone my chats with Virgil. She, too, missed her channelling, which was usually done in my presence, so we decided to start meeting once a week for this purpose.

We shared a channel and for the first time I was given a task to undertake the following week. Following this, he informed me that the miscarriage had simply put me in my 'feeling body', which was a necessary state for us to begin the book. Despite being at my lowest point and still recovering from my ordeal, I cannot tell you how relieved, surprised and delighted I was to begin this new phase. I was in a state where I was so tired of my pathway and the events that occurred in my life. I simply did not think that I could cope with another 'band-aid' solution. Not after experiencing so many disappointments with my spiritual pathway and all the things it promised. Really this had to be 'it.'

It was the format the book was going to take which most excited me – the fact it was going to be a course based on a combination of real life experience with channelled material. I knew from my own journeying that it was this inner grounding of spiritual theory that was missing from my life. Though I 'acted and behaved' in a spiritual manner, I still did not 'feel' it in my life. I marvelled at the perfection of this format and in fact still do to this day. As you will read, I was a very willing, yet insecure, subject. I was continually amazed at how I got myself into the position I was in – being part of this book. I could not identify with my ego self as being anything special or significant and felt many times quite undeserving of the attention I was getting from Virgil. I was curious about what I would uncover about myself. This would explain why I was involved in this journey. It was only that I trusted Virgil implicitly to guide me along this pathway, that I eventually made it through.

It was at times a difficult journey, as it will be for you, but do not give up. What I found the hardest was that I had no idea where the journey was going. I had no safety net and nowhere to hide. My only option was to surrender to myself...eventually. What I gained at the conclusion of the course has set me free. Upon reflection, what amazes me most about anyone's spiritual journey is just how guided it actually is. I went through a phase of thinking that everything I had done with the spiritual ilk prior to completing this course, had been a waste of time. Now I know how wrong that was. Everything has been perfect and has played a part in the bigger picture of who I am and what I am here to do. This is just as significant as who you are and what you are here to do. It is important for you to remember and focus on the fact that this is about getting to know who you truly are and if you need assistance on this pathway, ask for it. It will be there in abundance, though as we know, may not come in the form you expect. Trust me, you will be so relieved and amazed at the conclusion (or should I say, new beginning) that you will absolutely have considered this journey worthwhile.

I wish you all the love, joy, and support in the world!

Susie

CHAPTER 1
Your Journey Begins

Thank you for beginning this journey with us. As we revealed in our introductions, the course began most unexpectedly when Susie and I decided to get together to rekindle our spiritual focus and reconnect with Virgil, following several months break from channelling. It is interesting to reflect though, that at the time, our lives were in turmoil. Both of us felt very frustrated by the fact that, despite all our spiritual understanding, we had no clue as to why we were manifesting difficult lives, much less how to change them. In fact, only days prior, Susie had suffered a miscarriage, which of course shook her to the core. As she went through the process of mourning her loss, a sense of unease began to emerge that perhaps the true source of her pain went deeper and was not just related to the miscarriage. So it was with a degree of trepidation that we began to delve into those deeper feelings, in the hope that we would then receive more profound guidance from Virgil.

Essentially, we were tired, exhausted perhaps, of trying to live by the 'spiritual rules' we had been taught. We were disappointed by our lack of success in creating satisfying, nurturing realities, while our growth seemed to revolve around hard lessons grounded in hindsight. We wondered if we actually understood spirituality at all and whether we would ever be able to master growth without pain. At our core, we were feeling let down and abandoned by Spirit - as though we had been left to flounder alone. Despite this, we supported each other in expressing our fears. We were both tired of wallowing in failure; we eagerly awaited Virgil's presence that evening.

Susie and I prepared ourselves physically and energetically in a specially designated room that had been nick-named the 'chanting room' (by my partner Pete's unbelieving but humorous brother). It was adorned with spiritual power objects from many cultures ranging from Thai Buddhism to Native American Indian. Crystals and candles dominated the centre of our small circle. The savouring smell of burnt sage enveloped us. I finally wrenched the smudge bowl out of Susie's grasp (known as 'The Sage Hog'), and passed the smoke over my space. We drew on the smoke to cleanse our mind, body and spirit as well as focus our highest intentions in readiness for the work we were to undertake.

As the energy vibration heightened in the room, we could feel our negativity dissolve, and soon I felt the need to beam an unbelievably wide grin and utter that wonderful and familiar sentence that let us both know Virgil was with us; "Good evening my friends." After such a long time without him, it was like welcoming back an old, beloved friend. Virgil spoke at length concerning our spiritual and physical journeys. He urged us to begin to pay less attention to the physical and instead put more energy into experiencing the inner feeling of our lives. Toward the end of the channel, despite Susie avoiding the issue, Virgil brought up the subject of her miscarriage. He told us how it had well and truly put her in touch with her feeling body – in other words, it had prepared her for this new focus he was espousing.

For the first time in all our years of speaking with him, Virgil then introduced a focus that was to be taken away from the safety of our sessions and placed into the journey that was our lives. (This task will be revealed to you at the end of this chapter.) He then added that I, too, was in denial of my true feelings. The trying circumstances of my deteriorating relationship, coupled with a feeling of spiritual helplessness, had also put me in my feeling body.

If you too sense that your feelings are bubbling under the surface, seeking release, know that you are in the perfect space to commence the new focus you are about to undertake.

This book is the culmination for Susie and me, in actually learning to walk, not just talk, our spirituality. Since that first session, we and many others have grounded this course into our daily lives in our own unique way. Right from the outset you, the reader must accept that there is no right or wrong in the process about to be revealed to you. Participate with an open mind, and an open heart. Take what you will out into the journey that is your life - just as we all have done.

During this course, I will offer you an insight into what was occurring for us, as participants, via a short preamble to each chapter. For the most part, my narration relates to Susie or myself. However, we have run many courses since then, and I have included the experiences of other participants where they are particularly relevant. I now hand you over to Virgil. Know that you are welcome in joining our extended family of participants and therefore as he is talking to us, he is of course, including you.

Sally...

Good evening, my friends, Virgil is with you. Welcome to the first lesson of our wonderful course.

Thank you for coming through so quickly Virgil.

Indeed, it is much easier to connect when the energy is as vibrant and welcoming as you have made it this evening. I thank you for your open focus and for your very clear intentions. This has raised the group energy of the room to a heightened vibration. This means that you have reached up to me, and therefore, I do not have to lower my vibration to a large extent. Maintain your open focus and we should have a very powerful connection. I welcome you all here and give you my blessings. I understand the reasons that drive you to attend this course. I ask that you trust me to guide you through whatever manifests, while you are entrenched in it. You see, my friends, I see before me energies so beautiful, energies not hidden by the mask of ego, but instead dancing in the knowledge of their own light. I see wisdom, and a collective urge to move through the physical density with the light of Soul. However, as I move my energy to match the vibration in which you tackle your day to day world, I see what you would refer to as blocks. These prevent you from seeing and more importantly, **experiencing who you truly are.** Your own inner light seeks to guide you. I will take on this role for a short time and be the bridge between your normal ego awareness and the higher aspects of your own self. Soon, you will recognise your own light and will no longer need me, the bridge, so to speak.

You have a deep feeling tone that pervades your life. This feeling tone is calling to you in a gentle, rhythmic fashion. It is never needy or desperate, just present, patient and real. It is so subtle that you hardly recognise it, but in your heart, you all know that it exists. You call it by many names, perhaps God, The higher self, or Soul to name a few. The terms are basically meaningless, for there is no separation to the self. You are familiar with these terms, so we use them here to assist in the communication process. Whatever name you call this feeling tone, this ever present connection to source, know that it is real in your life and that through it, I have a wish for you to find your way home. Patience and perseverance are what are called for here. I know that you are up to the challenge.

To begin, we need to expose all that you would accept as fact about this reality and particularly your self image within it. We then need to undo all that which is not aligned to the reality of Soul - your true nature. This undoing can be done in a moment, but so dense are the barriers you have built around yourself, for most, it must be undertaken as a process. This is where I am to assist you. I have designed the process to speak to you where you are right now, then slowly draw your focus away from ego awareness and into your own light. Your light is the key here, not the light of mine or others, but an acknowledgement and acceptance of the powerful light that you contain.

Through your spiritual classes you have been told of the capability of union with your Soul reality and to heal the apparent separation would reveal a 'Nirvana'. You have all at one time or another aspired to experience this union, yet despite your considerable efforts, it never seems to materialise. All the guides and teachers tell you that it is possible and this is the truth. The state of knowing cannot be provided to you; instead you must open your eyes and recognise this as a place within. You need to seize it as your own and you need to reflect it all about you. This is what we will be trying to achieve over the next weeks.

You all feel prepared to participate fully in this journey, for which I am pleased and excited. I will be here to support you along every step of the way within each course meeting. You can also call on me at any time and I will be present to influence and assist. Understand though, I will only be available via your feelings, for this is the foundation of your own innate wisdom.

You all understand the intellectual concept of creating your own reality, yet consistently things appear in your reality that you disown. Circumstances occur, which you believe you could not have possibly created by your own thoughts. Make no mistake; all things that appear within your reality are part of who you are, at this point in time. The first step in understanding their meaning is to embrace them as your own creations and then to show them the light that is within. For they are protecting what is you; that beauty, that spark, that inner feeling tone.

Presently, through positive affirmation and kind action and thought, you hope that one day you will have the life that you desire. Yet somehow 'unwanted' events occur that you seem to have no hand in creating. I will teach you that it is indeed your hand, which paints your environment. You will learn how to trace the source of your physical circumstances back to the inner tone where you can heal it. This is our greatest hope for you. **Thought alone, positive or otherwise, does not create your reality.** If this were the case, can you imagine how even more chaotic your life would be? Thoughts are but one, albeit significant, aspect of the miracle of manifestation. At its very basic level and what energises those thoughts, is your own unique feeling self.

The theory of creating a wonderful reality appears complex. Many of you have been attempting to understand and master the rules of manifesting for some time now. As you have learned and tried to obey the myriad of spiritual 'rules' that abound, one cannot help but be more confused when events are birthed that are seemingly the opposite of your intention and effort. This course will lead you beyond the intellectual mire and into true spiritual knowing, whilst at all times respecting and loving your unique humanity. It is through your feeling tone that your reality stems and grows upwards through the layers. At any point you can either; recognise and listen to the inner, or you can ignore it; soon it will be projected outward. Having ignored the inner roots that gave the projection life, it appears foreign to you and it is therefore disowned. Anything that you project outward, even that which you consider ugly, is an aspect of self that you have considered ugly and consequently will not embrace. You understand these concepts intellectually, but still this knowledge does not urge your focus inward, so there is no change afoot and the cycle continues. **We will teach you to no longer understand the spiritual nature of this world intellectually, but to know it, because you are it.**

You are intrinsically connected to all things and to know this is the critical aspect of moving forward. What you have done, up until this point, is trained the conscious mind (or ego) in the nature of spiritual theory. The ego is a clever tool, but a servant to your current beliefs, therefore it has adapted its behaviour to suit – just as when you were a child you adapted your behaviour to suit the demands of your parents. As the course progresses, you will be consistently confronted with the choice of continuing to operate from a level of intellectual knowledge, or to move into the feeling body- where you operate from a level of just knowing. An easy choice in theory, but you will learn, this takes courage.

Your ego thoughts, in this day and age, tend to be what directs your world. You follow them at whim and often you will lose your true self for a time. This is not the true order of your existence. The ego's function is valid, but it is not equipped to take on the role of leader, its vision is not whole. For example, your eyes are the lens by which you view the physical world. The physical eye does not make a decision about which direction you should take, it is merely the means by which you view the surroundings. You can receive and interpret data, which then allows you to overcome or avoid any obstacles. Similarly, the ego was designed to be the lens by which you viewed your conscious and unconscious world, bridging the two and providing each with a reference point. The ego was never meant to make decisions about the direction your life should take as a result of its observations, any more than the physical eye can decide your physical direction. The ego was designed to gather and interpret information derived from this physical environment and turn it inward, so the Soul self can comprehend the experience of life on this Earth plane. The ego was then meant to await feedback from the inner that would influence its ultimate decision. Therefore, the ego self is an open-ended system designed to seek information from both within and without. In this day and age, it appears to be especially biased toward the events without.

Your Soul self in its natural state is so magnificent that its high, fine vibration can not incarnate fully within the dense physical flesh. It therefore creates a portion of itself that rises up to take on the challenge of physical existence. This portion is often referred to as 'ego' or 'personality self'. Its nature changes as your conscious and unconscious thoughts change. It interprets all psychological events and physical objects of this realm; returning the information to the Soul for the greatest growth and learning. The ego allows all that is foreign to the Soul's realm to be experienced, so without the ego's skill, physical existence would be without purpose. Therefore, the ego is the bridge that heals the concept of separation, not the cause of it. It feels alone and abandoned because it has been hypnotised by the physical realm and has forgotten to look inward.

Many of you have heard variations of this separation concept before – it is not new. What we are intending to do in this process, is to return the ego to its rightful place - to allow it to be guided from the higher self. In this way, rather than make decisions at whim, based on the intellectual beliefs of the ego, your life can be guided at a conscious level from within. Then, you can interpret the events that occur in your lives and move through them with greater clarity and love. Within this clarity, an assuredness will emerge that the events, in physical terms, are meaningless except for how they affect you and your own internal feeling environment. These are concepts that you will probably have no difficulty in understanding intellectually. **Our challenge is to remove the intellectual understanding and create an inner knowing.**

At this point, I would ask if you have any questions.

Virgil, I just don't understand about how the Soul self is only a portion of ourselves and how the ego is feeling separate and abandoned.

The Soul self is an energy of such a fine vibration that it cannot possibly be fully incarnate in this physical reality. The denseness of this matter in your earthly plane could never contain it. In order to experience this dense physical reality, the Soul sends what you would refer to as a portion of itself forward in time and space to engage here. It creates an aspect of itself and endows it with special skills to enable it to adapt here. When I refer to a 'portion', I do not mean it as truly separate. If you like, imagine a star sending out light in many different directions. There is no real separation of the light points of that star as they are emanating from a common source. Yet, if the light only focuses outward, there is only darkness and aloneness before it and its fellow beams look distinct and apart from it. If, the focus is turned inward, then it would see its own core shining so brilliantly and recognise it as the source of its power. It would also recognise all the other, apparently separate light beams, as being derived from the same shining source. The ego is an extension of your Soul self in the same way.

The ego's nature and beliefs change according to the prevailing attitudes of the conscious mind. The conscious mind deals directly with the mental environment of this plane. The ego is the 'lens' by which the conscious mind is able to interpret conscious, unconscious and physical data. It is highly attuned to this physical environment, so much so, that it feels most comfortable within limitation and rules. The ego is essential to your Soul's purpose in this physical environment, for the Soul could not experience any physical events without it. The ego allows you to do things - it is the physical specialist. For example, it allows you to manipulate the body. It has so highly refined this task that at times it believes that this is its only function. This feeling of separation, this conscious mind versus Soul, was never meant to be the case. The ego has always had the ability to look outward as well as inward, but at this point, it has forgotten to look inward. We want to tune and refocus its vision so it seeks expression and guidance from the inner, rather than feeling alone in a series of seeming random physical and psychological events. Once it peers inward it will understand the source of its life and the love that is within.

Virgil, why does the Soul self seek expression in this physical reality?

This is a grand question. This physical reality you are experiencing is dominated and tainted with the notion of polarities; that is one of opposite forces. Your ego especially feels comfortable with these 'facts'; it has been specifically designed to operate within these rules and boundaries. Extremes of hot and cold, up and down, male and female are unquestionably 'fact'. Overlaying this is that all things in this reality appear as separate and are seemingly temporary. This reality allows an expression of Soul, of consciousness. That is unlike any reality that exists anywhere else, even other realities that are physical. This reality represents all that is foreign to the true nature of Soul and therefore it is a grand experience.

You are immersed in the challenge of creating wholeness which is your natural state and therefore unassailable. At the same time you are experiencing a polarity which is especially convincing. It is a dense reality – being foreign to your natural state, many become distracted by its beauty and terror. The reason this reality must be so dense and therefore difficult to navigate, is that it can only be created upon a solid foundation of judgement categorised by the notions of negative and positive. Judgement does not exist in the less dense planes, yet it is a prerequisite of ego consciousness or you would not be able to discern this reality at all.

Judgement need not be a dirty word for it is the foundation of the notion of polarity and therefore this entire physical plane. Judgement only becomes tainted when it is wielded either against others, through projection, or against yourself, through suppression. This will become of greater significance to you as the course progresses. So to answer your question: you seek expression in this physical reality to evolve consciousness, thereby adding another level of experience to the Soul self - that of polarity; yet simultaneously maintain your natural state of union.

I will move on at this point to your task for the week. This is what I would refer to as the beginning of your processes and the importance of your journaling. Many of you have jobs, families, and daily lives that require your utmost attention. This is used as a convenient reason to focus predominately in the physical area. I understand these pressures. However, you create your own reality. You need to take responsibility for the fact that you are creating these pressures that draw your energy into one specific area. You need to make room in your reality for yourself and for your Soul self to have its expression. You need to carry your journal with you wherever you go, in case you need to use it. Now I am not saying that you should cease talking on the phone to an important client because he or she insults you and you need to journal it. What I am saying, is that if you are still hurting or seething later, you journal those thoughts honestly and allow them to flow and expand. I am asking you to make a conscious choice to actively record the contents of your conscious mind and ego self consistently for an entire week. This is an important part of this initial process.

So for the next week, I want you to record your ego thoughts with the same diligence that you would if I were to say to you, "If you think a person dead, it shall happen in an instant." If you really believed your thoughts were this powerful, you would work hard to be more aware and conscientious of what you were putting out. I do not want you to manipulate your thoughts and I do not want you to push them down or create only good things by sheer will. I want you to allow **all** thoughts freedom in their natural state, but I want you to be aware of them. Do not attempt to draw conclusions from this process – at this point you only need to be aware of what you are putting out there. And please make the time to journal. Are there any questions?

Regarding keeping a record of every thought and allowing them to come through – when we write them down, do we need to then go in and explore the thoughts further, or do we just express them on the paper, leave it at that and move on?

You don't even need to record every single thought. All I'm asking of you is to allow your natural mind chatter to emerge, without manipulation, and to actually notice it. Before we can begin to retune the ego focus, we need to ascertain and acknowledge its current direction. Conscious awareness of your present reality, through journaling the ego thoughts, is step one in a process that will evolve. It is not an end in itself. It is a critical step, because I cannot assist you in changing what you are doing until you first become aware that you are even doing it. It is experiential – not something you intellectualise, but something you are to experience. This is all that I am seeking in the first week from you.

Virgil, how do I know what's an ego thought and what's something else?

Journal whatever comes to the surface – do not attempt to categorise your mind's contents in this way.

If I have a thought about something I'd like to be doing, is that necessarily ego?

Indeed. These are clues that we will expand upon later. It is a good point that you bring up, not all ego thoughts are going to be bad.

Are we to record thoughts or events that may trigger reactions from us or stir something up inside as well?

Indeed. Anything that you feel needs to be recorded should be recorded. It is not a test and it is largely for your own eyes, so do not feel inhibited. Record what is important to **you**, what pushes **your** buttons at that time. Done with diligence, this exercise will assist you greatly - not only this week, but in future weeks. You may rely on it as a way to overcome the mind confusion and blaze a trail into the heart and Soul of the matter confronting you. There is no need in me defining the exercise further, as it is foremost a tool to reveal your own process. I want you to become aware of what lies within your conscious mind, as opposed to just hearing yourself without listening. Record whatever you like. At this point I would like to conclude as it is critical that we move into next week with as little mind clutter as possible. Just focus on the task for the task's sake, without any attachment to outcomes.

Thank you very much for coming through this evening and I'm sure we'll look forward to speaking with you next week.

I wish you well.

Be blessed.

Thank you, Virgil.

Lesson One

Journal your ego thoughts - diligently and without expectation.

CHAPTER 2
Your Ego Thoughts

We had all spent a week journaling, to some degree. Some participants were prolific in their writing, whilst others were more sporadic. It is wise to consider right from the outset how strong your commitment to this week's task was and why. Journaling is an important tool that greatly supports Virgil's lessons. It facilitates the process of self discovery. No one else can tell you who you are - you have to reach your own conclusions. If you have been diligent, try to continue that strategy. If you have been inconsistent, please make a decision to more fully engage in journaling your outcomes. Whatever your level of commitment, that in itself should give you an insight into an aspect of self. The reasons you have for avoiding the task should also be noted and recorded in your journals next week. These justifications are most certainly ego thoughts.

Without exception, those who wrote more consistently moved through to the essence of their natures faster than those who did not. Fortunately, even if you have not been wholly committed to the process this week, you are still able to move on to the next lesson. There were no right or wrong outcomes for Lesson One and your individual experiences and reactions provide you with unique insights and are perfectly valid. However, in future weeks you may have to repeat lessons before moving on, if you chose not to fully immerse yourself in the tasks. Your success lies in your own hands, but that is really no surprise, is it?

Everyone found recording their ego thoughts a most revealing exercise. The revelations were definitely unique to each individual. One person, who followed a 'spiritual' pathway in words and action, found there was a great deal of negative, even brutal, mind chatter under the surface. It was initially difficult for her to accept. It was in direct contrast to her surface self-image of love and light, but because it was written down, she could no longer ignore or suppress or really justify the thoughts away.

Others found that when difficulties arose they turned to a victimhood mentality. They blamed others, their childhoods, or their lack of something for their present dilemma. Although the notion of victimhood was not new to them, especially in a spiritual sense, the extent to which it dominated their personal lives and relationships was a realisation. Again, because it was exposed on page after page of their writing it could no longer be denied.

A few participants revealed that they couldn't find time to journal consistently and were already tired of the process. This led some to a realisation that they spent a great deal of energy avoiding commitment. One participant, who had identified commitment issues dominating her ego chatter, actually got trapped in a faulty lift as she was leaving work to attend the course. The time it took for a technician to rescue her meant she was unable to attend the second week. She was the first person to manifest the outcomes of the course lessons into her physical environment – she was definitely not the last. Some who chose not to journal consistently did so because they could not see the benefit. They were so attached to analysing and justifying everything via the intellect that they were incapable of committing to a task, merely for the task's sake, without searching for meaning. Lack of commitment is a common issue following week one, however, the source of it is as varied as the individuals concerned. Each week this course will assist you in uncovering your own unique reason for manifesting these general themes.

Some of the quieter participants felt that they didn't do the task correctly because they didn't experience any 'flash of insight' and consequently felt they were a failure. Their insight, of course, lay in the fact that there were no rules, no correct answers, and only general instructions; they had concluded themselves a failure before the course had even really begun. They too waxed and waned in commitment depending on how successful they felt.

Hopefully, as a result of recording your ego thoughts last week, you are also forming a general theme or hue threading through the barrage of surface chatter. Even if you have only arrived at the conclusion that there is a great deal going on that previously you had not noticed, then this in itself, is an important step forward. If you have managed an insight into the ego's world; even better. If you have been able to identify an ego pattern, try to remain mindful of it as you progress through each new lesson. This pattern will continue its dominance in the short term, but the manner in which it plays out in the physical might be a surprise. As you progress, continued journaling will ensure you expose all of your ego chatter, enabling you to move through it. The following text will help you to understand, that even when we do get a handle on our patterns, the ego illusion does not just lie down and behave.

The insights Virgil provides this week, coupled with your new found or continued diligence, will ensure you are equipped to recognise your ego, thus enabling you to begin to straighten its vision. You are now ready to begin Lesson Two. As always Virgil will be represented by standard text. Remember, to make the most of the essence of his channelling. Prepare yourself in a spiritual sense. Imagine you are part of the group, joining us in a dimly lit, warm space full of support and love.

Sally...

Good evening my friends. It is a pleasure as always and I welcome you to Lesson Two.

Thank you, Virgil.

Last week you asked us to consider our thoughts- to treat them as if they may one day have the power to strike someone down in an instant. Since then I have found myself drawn to the conclusion that my thoughts are not really who I am. I don't like the things I think a lot of the time. For instance, where people or situations hurt me, I was shocked at the attack thoughts I would entertain and how fully I would go with them. Later, even after the dust had settled, I'd find myself thinking the same negative and graphic thoughts – and that really bothered me. I've come to the conclusion that I feel quite weak sometimes. I think it's because I'm scared to know my own thoughts, maybe because I don't know to what extent they're attached to my feelings. I sense I'm really scared to express my feelings - in fact, I haven't expressed my feelings pretty much my whole life. Would you like to comment on this?

Indeed Susie. The fact you are experiencing these attack thoughts is a sure sign that you are not experiencing your feelings. These attack thoughts are your protection from painful feelings; they are created by you and projected outward in an attempt to mask the pain and obliterate it from your reality. What you perceive as anger, is in fact a **feeling** that if experienced in the moment, would lead to an awareness of an aspect of self that requires healing, an aspect that is seeking your attention. Rather than embrace true feeling, you contrive anger towards another person or event. You dwell in your thoughts, concerning how or why they made you 'feel' a certain way. These thoughts leave you as negative energy, not because they are 'bad', but because they are sourced from the lower vibration you exude in a state of ego consciousness. They will return to you in a different form containing an identical essence, because like vibrations naturally attract.

It is important to acknowledge the thought on a conscious level in order to validate it, but know it is hiding a deeper essence and ask for it to be revealed. The thought just needs to move aside from your conscious focus, so that you can experience the true nature of your feeling. If someone has hurt you, it is only because you believe in your own so-called, imperfections. The ego does not believe that you are whole and complete right now. Unconsciously it perceives certain events as validation of its own faulty world view. When you seem under attack from another person, consider them as the fearful person they are, not in arrogance, but in empathy. You are both experiencing, in your own way, a lack of love and compensating for this by producing ego thoughts. Despite constantly perceiving imperfection, the ego still fights to mask the feelings that invalidate it. It does this by projecting them outward and therefore the pain is perceived as sourced outside of itself, even though your heart still aches.

Virgil, I'd like to ask you whether you could take me through any exercises that would enable me to get to what's behind my anger thoughts – or is it best left to be experienced in the moment.

It is a matter of **intention** to access the feeling underlying the thoughts, more than anything else. You must accept that there is actually nothing hidden from your perception, yet it appears as though you cannot see the forest for the trees. While most of your conscious attention continues to be focused in the mind, this is what will continue to be the filter through which you view and engage your physical lives. The filter of ego is so limited that you literally perceive yourself and others, in only a shadow of true awareness. Presently, this ego focus dominates the way in which most people meet the world. Its perceptions are in no way representative of your entire reality. Aligning with the ego creates a smoke screen that masks your true nature. Your intention to see through the ego illusion can be actualised via the training I will lay down in this course; it is a process of not so much becoming, as homecoming.

To begin, the only requirement is of directing your conscious awareness to recognise that feeling underlies thought. You are very much in tune with your mental body and physical body, but you need to fine tune your response to the emotional body. Once you achieve this, you will understand how they are intrinsically related. It is not necessary to understand the mechanics of how to 'switch' focus, for there is no separation. It is simply a matter of tuning in, and allowance. The means to enable you to learn of your true essence already exists in the unique events unfolding in your lives. You, my friend, will create the perfect circumstances. When aligned with my lessons, this will facilitate the opening of self awareness that you so seek. You must trust your life circumstances. They are a reflection of the perfection of your own innate wisdom and creativity.

We have spoken before of the foundation of polarity on which this earthly reality has been constructed. All of your surface 'feelings', despite their considerable variations, can actually be divided into either fear or love. Love is easy to allow and expand. Fear tends to make us suppress and contract. Truthfully, all feeling experience should be allowed life and expansion, since all feeling is valid and potentially healing. Emotion will rise to the surface if you allow it. You should avoid any attempt to label the feeling, such as "this is hurt" or "this is anger". Such labels are ego constructs used in an attempt to understand what is foreign to the intellect i.e. true feeling. Should you require assistance in bringing feelings to the surface you can simply try to **breathe** them through. Imagine as you breathe deep into your diaphragm that you are breathing in white light. As you exhale, you are releasing whatever emotion is being masked by your negative thought. Try to run away with the feeling, rather than the thoughts or events that generated it. These small steps will assist in aligning your focus and are not ends in themselves.

As you become better observers of your ego realm, you will have an idea of its motivations or in higher terms - the feelings that underpin its actions. For instance, an event in your life may trigger a feeling of inferiority to another. You could quickly suppress (build up your own ego) or project (make yourself a victim of another's arrogance) such a feeling via mental rationalisation, yet still be left feeling vulnerable or uncomfortable. This discomfort would influence your immediate behaviour. Perhaps you might consciously or unconsciously seek validation from others, to make yourself 'feel' better. In this way, you may have suppressed and missed the feeling in the moment. However, you can observe it play out in your life, in an attempt to get your attention. All the frantic seeking of reassurance could be avoided if you just payed attention at the outset and allowed the feeling expansion, rather than focussed on the physical event that triggered it. In time, you will sense a familiar unidentified element colouring events where feeling is first denied or projected. Allow such a process to unfold through ongoing immersion in this course and avoid any further intellectual approach to your issues. Affirm that you are supported in your own processes. Know that you will create the time and space to fully experience what is required. At this point this is all you need to know. Do not let others or indeed your own past experiences colour your present. Once you have experienced this on a number of occasions we will expand on this further.

So being in your feelings can be achieved through practice?

Indeed. Feeling is your natural state. Children are especially feeling focussed, yet they are taught to suppress through various methods of control. We want to expose the elements of control and allow emotion to come forth as it is required. You will find yourself experiencing a greater level of empathy for other people. You will better understand why their judgements are coming towards you. In this understanding lies the key to transmute negative thought into positive energy. It is not sufficient to catch a negative thought and then, through the mind, mould it into something else through sheer will alone. Emotion is the creative essence of all life on this planet. Although you can recite by rote a positive affirmation via the mind, it is a very long and protracted way of achieving anything. It is through the intensity of feeling, converted to conscious thought that our reality emerges. This is why I say to you to watch those negative thoughts. For I know that any strong thoughts are driven outward by emotion, which makes them much more powerful than your idle day dreams.

Virgil, I noticed in my journaling how I was able to justify my anger thoughts by rationalising them against many surface reasons. Now I can see that it was all mind play and that deep down the feelings are still there. I think that these feelings stem from my childhood. I think as a child I always wanted to be popular and I wasn't. I always seemed to just have one friend who I'd eventually fall out with and then find someone else. Would it be best to experience those anger thoughts from that level?

It is not appropriate to rationalise it in the way that you have - by following your intellectual cause and effect process in terms of the inner child reacting in a certain way. The ego has been trained in many spiritual terms and uses them to its advantage. When negative attack thoughts emerge, you can often recognise that a person is 'pushing your buttons', as you relate the feelings to a past event. This can lead you to intellectualise the whole process according to what you have been taught and to invalidate the feeling as something unreal from the past. For example, you may recognise your contribution in any drama by understanding your motives for attacking another as being based on events of your childhood. Perhaps you are even able to identify your behaviour as a learned response or a defence mechanism and somehow you think that this awareness heals you. All this does is neatly categorise the judgement and keep you firmly entrenched in intellectual play. This does access the feeling, as the identical emotion leads you back to a physical 'event' of the past. However, it does not access the feeling body and therefore does not allow you to shed light on the true source of such pain.

This is the point where many have left their spiritual development, in this day and age. Many are aware of their judgements and hurts as they arise and recognise them as emerging from inner child dramas. They therefore don't act them out. They also don't heal them from within. Conscious recognition of your unique 'issues' is an essential start; however this alone cannot heal you. Generally this leads to further suppression of feeling, not through denial, but through intellectualising it and assuming these feelings were imposed on you by events of childhood. **You create your own reality by the parents/circumstances etc. that you attract as a child – in other words these childhood events are designed to bring into the physical what you already contain within – not the other way round.**

Let me attempt to illustrate a point. The Channel once witnessed a mother standing in a supermarket queue with her ten-year-old son who wanted an ice-cream. The mother was openly hostile and rude in the way she spoke to the child, despite his apparent even-tempered behaviour and told him he was getting nothing. She then proceeded to purchase for herself an expensive packet of cigarettes, while continuing to humiliate her son. The Channel felt the negative judgement rise in her, towards this woman, and caught it. Then in her mind she mentally dealt with the situation. She talked through and rationalised it using all the 'new age' clichés she has learned. Some examples were: it's a co-creation, they each have their own lessons, they've attracted the circumstances, and I'm feeling this way because this is my issue, not theirs etc. She believed her conscious rationalising of the circumstance indicated how evolved she had become in being able to rise above her judgement. However, The Channel was actually empathising with the child and wanted to attack the mother – so attack thoughts definitely went out, even though they were quickly caught.

The intellect had played a little game but nothing had been achieved, for The Channel hadn't reconciled **why** she automatically felt empathy with the child and focused on the 'terrible' mother. She quickly recognised that her feelings stemmed back to her own childhood feelings - of unfairness, powerlessness, and the inequity of being a child. Having recognised their apparent source, she pushed them aside as mere outcomes of the past, not something to be experienced in the moment. The 'justifications' of the judgement were really ego games to prevent her from experiencing the feelings that were emerging. A more honest response would have been to act out rather than suppress.

Act out in what way?

To actually stand up with courage for the child. That would have been a greater act of experiencing the emotion, rather than to rationalise it out of existence. As a child, The Channel could not act out her emotions and therefore had to rationalise the feelings away by pretending and fantasising. Different mind control but the same result – an absence of feeling. What I am trying to convey here is that it is the same response or outcome that she had used as a child. Now wrapped up in a spiritual equation it seemed different, evolved and therefore justified. A response that would have been honouring the soul would have been to allow the emotion to rise up and out, even if necessary to tell the woman what she **thought** of her and to accept the consequences. Let me qualify that statement by assuring you it is not the most appropriate or indeed ideal response. Certainly a more **honest** one would at least allow the emotion to be released.

So had she reacted in that way, the next time she saw a similar scene would she feel less of a reaction and then maybe a few times down the track would she be able to send genuine love to the mother and the child?

Not necessarily. There are in fact three reactions and only one will lead you to healing. The first is what The Channel did, which was to intellectualise the process framed in spiritual language. Although it seems very 'spiritual', it still suppresses the emotion, which means it can't be healed. For this reason, physical events will continue to transpire to trigger this emotion so that it can be healed. The second is to experience the emotion, then project it quickly in either silent judgement or verbal attack. Most choose the former and judge themselves superior to those who would act out, but energetically they are the same thing. Because the feeling is projected or 'disowned' then of course it cannot be healed. The most appropriate response would be to allow the emotion to rise and be fully experienced consciously in the moment. Sitting in the apparent judgement of that event, she would eventually connect it with her own source of pain, as opposed to a mere outcome of a past circumstance.

This connection would ensure she owned the entire episode as an experience of her own feelings, period, rather than an experience of a childhood trigger. This might then lead her to own the feelings rather than continue to assume that they were something imposed on her by childhood events. She could then realise that the boy is a kindred spirit, and their commonalities lie in essence and not form. Perhaps she would send love to him rather than attack thoughts to the mother. Can you understand the difference in focus here?

To access and heal that emotion, the best reaction would be to send love and light to the child, for a future where things are different, where you have your rights and feelings respected. Not via a forcing of 'right' thinking, but in a knowing that is generated only from feeling body consciousness. This is a loving response to the same issue. Compare this to the initial reaction which was still considered to be a 'spiritual' outcome, which is not the case. It is true to not judge the judgement, however it is not appropriate to intellectualise the feeling and therefore block the emotion that is driving these thoughts upwards.

It's very confusing. I've studied spirituality for years and your explanation of this scenario makes it more confusing. My intellect knows the correct way to respond to that situation and I could quite easily send love to the child and probably to the mother. Am I faking it?

It depends. We are talking about The Channel's experience in our example. There will be an initial response that you need to be aware of. If that response is negative, but is what triggers the sending of love thoughts, then you are doing so in judgement rather than through a genuine feeling connection. **It is the difference between sending love thoughts contrived by the mind and sending genuine love as an expression of how you feel.**

So, if we send surface level love thoughts, they're generally in fear of our true feelings?

Indeed, or in denial of true feeling. Your aim is to respond to the feeling body. Allow the mind to attend to its role, which is to manipulate the physical environment, not to manipulate your life and your relationships. You need to be constantly reminding the conscious self to direct its awareness to your feeling body. It's not as though the ego can act independently of you. It is just where your focus is currently trained. The ego has been thrust out into taking control through our many years of conditioning. It is useful to affirm to yourself - 'I choose to be in my feeling body' - and this will direct the conscious awareness.

Whenever you react strongly in any situation, in anger or love, pay attention to the initial feeling. Often, you only become aware of what you're feeling when it is triggered in the physical and then enters the conscious mind. However, if you focus on the event, then you will interpret the feeling according to it, rather than as an expression of self. That external focus will thwart the Soul's attempt to initiate an expansion of the feeling, since your response is always coloured by so much past conditioning. Try to take a step back from the events and consider your initial response as the trigger, instead of being carried away by the feelings that are attached to it. As your awareness is trained into the feeling body, you will become more conscious of that initial feeling and the events will reveal their true gifts to you.

Avoid spending too much time on the menial, as over-analysing can lead you to create unnecessary dramas. You can spend much of your life analysing the mundane with little result. Attempt to put any event which is causing emotional angst into perspective. What aspect is ego drama and what aspect is genuine feeling? Are you creating more drama to avoid experiencing genuine feeling? Allow your ego to deal with your physical environment, such as the workplace, for this is its speciality and it is highly skilled at it. You will not manifest any circumstance that is outside of your abilities to cope. Distractions and annoyances will draw your energy if you allow them to. The events themselves are not important. Only your response in dealing with them is worthy of your time. If you are choosing ego dramas over genuine feeling, this is often only a distraction created to keep you occupied so you can avoid your inner world. Be conscious of what you are co-creating.

To recap: Lesson One was to become aware of your thoughts. That was a critical step in tuning your consciousness into them. You have related to me what you achieved from this exercise. The supermarket incident is a powerful example of how the ego twists spiritual knowledge to its own ends and how we can intellectualise our learning away. So now you understand that we must experience the emotion that is driving these thoughts upward.

During the coming week, actively participate in the following affirmation: 'I choose to be in my feeling body'. This will assist your consciousness tuning in, so you can experience feelings as they arise rather than focusing on the thoughts of ego. When you experience negative thoughts instead of feeling, you are to acknowledge them. Appreciate them, knowing they are misguided forms of protection and then begin to delve into the emotion driving these thoughts upwards. You do this by focusing on the affirmation and allowing your own process to unfold, which will be unique to each individual. You may choose to breathe through them as earlier discussed – intention and awareness are the keys. Remember, we are undertaking a process here, do not allow expectation to colour your unique experiences. Record in your journals, once again, your thoughts and feelings.

It is always a great pleasure to be in your energy and I am deeply grateful for your support of The Channel in these processes and for your enthusiasm.

Be blessed
Thank you so much for your message.

Lesson Two

I choose to be in my feeling body.

CHAPTER 3
Your Feeling Body

By this time, Virgil's theory had begun to infiltrate our daily lives. Circumstances arose that supported his teachings and made it real for us. We started to get inklings that something significant was occurring and for this reason, week three is one of my favourite chapters - both as a participant in the original course and later as a joint facilitator with Susie. The previous lesson of affirming our feeling body really started to shake the veils of illusion we had been working with all our lives, by providing an insight into our ego games. Grounding or accepting what was being revealed to us was proving difficult, because we were still approaching everything from an intellectual perspective. We loved receiving Virgil's explanations and our excitement outweighed our frustrations somewhat and inspired us to continue.

Looking back at these times with the advantage of hindsight, I believe that the source of our frustration stemmed predominately from expectation. You will see that Virgil alludes to this on more than one occasion. We immersed ourselves in the exercises and in both Susie's and my case, began waiting for an epiphany that would change our lives. Of course, we didn't articulate it in those terms, but you definitely get a sense of our mounting impatience throughout this chapter and those that follow. After so many years of participating in various spiritual practises and modalities, yet experiencing little in return, we were waiting for the visions and magic to happen that would make our progress real. Others – even you – may also have a sense that your expectations are not being met. However, the reality is that each participant is completely unique and therefore the outcomes of your journey will unfold in a completely original manner. There can be no expected results. The key lies in knowing this and allowing your life to manifest without judgement.

The course is designed to be a week-to-week proposition with little formal structure, based on getting to know your response to your life as it manifests in each present moment. It might feel as though you are flying blind on trust, but as it is a journey of your own making, the question must be one of self trust. How you feel about trusting your own inner creativity to show you the way forward can be very revealing. Each new exercise is designed to build upon the other and expose a greater aspect of the ego's conscious world. Initially, this is all Virgil is trying to achieve. In the beginning, we behaved as though each week was an end in itself and contained a desired outcome that we had to achieve or else! I caution you not to be preoccupied with grandeur, as we were. Generally your expectation is driven by ego and the ego only needs to be recognised.

Virgil's explanations in the following chapter are wonderful, although, at first glance there are aspects which seem 'deep' or on the surface complicated. You might be tempted to mull them over intellectually in an attempt to grasp them more fully. Believe me, this is not the aim or purpose of Virgil's teachings. Living your life in light of what is revealed, will facilitate an understanding of Virgil's concepts more readily than any amount of mind analysis. The goal of each lesson is to focus on the new task, while remembering what you have noticed about yourself from past weeks. To ensure that you have a solid foundation of where you are before you begin a new level, we suggest that you read your notes from the preceding week before you commence a new chapter.

To begin to build your foundation this week, consider what you have learned about yourself from the lessons so far. Imagine that you have to summarise your findings to a group of fellow participants - what would you say? Irrespective of what you have uncovered about yourself, allow and accept it for what it is. You are experiencing what you are supposed to – be it confusion, anger, apathy, frustration or anything else. Much of what you are going through now will make sense in time and even be expanded on as the course progresses.

For us, at this point of the course, feelings that we had previously only recognised on a mere surface level, were now acutely felt. For example, it is one thing to intellectualise the notion of being a victim or a failure, but it is another to start to feel it. All of us inadvertently set up defences against these feelings, but for the first time, we all recognised we were actually doing it.

This recognition came in hindsight, so we were unable to cease our defensive stance. Nonetheless it was still quite a revelation and a positive step forward.

These defences were as varied as the individuals concerned. Some sought their defence in attack and were shocked at how 'bitchy' they were capable of being, but then remarked how brilliantly they justified their stance based on ego logic. Another admitted to being empowered by attack – which was a surprise to her, given her surface abhorrence for such anti-social behaviour. Others drew their attack inward against themselves as they collapsed more fully into their victimhood beliefs. In their own words, they didn't get anywhere because 'they just couldn't do it'. Some even thought they'd be kicked out of the group for being too incapable. They automatically thought themselves failures, even though there was nothing to do except affirm to be in their feeling body, which they did anyway. So you can see that the exercise somehow does expose the ego's beliefs and illustrates how strongly some of us hang on to its doctrine of limitation.

Others remained firmly enchanted by the channelled material trying to make it all fit their current beliefs by just mulling it over and over. Yet all this does is contradict the affirmation - I choose to be in my feeling body. The entire aim is to redirect focus away from the intellect. Nevertheless it did reveal where this person thought their true power lay – in the intellect. On the surface and in the doctrine they espoused to the world that they believed true power lay in spirit. It exposed therefore that their surface thoughts were very well practiced, but it was not what they truly believed deep inside. Interestingly, this person led a life that was seemingly difficult in many areas and one that could be construed as unsupported in a spiritual sense.

The point is that no matter what conclusions you are able to learn from last week's task, there must be more of the ego's paradigm exposed. Accept your insights and allow them to be, then continue with diligence and you will eventually expose it all to the light.

I now hand you over to Virgil and trust that the following text prepares you for the upcoming challenges and insights your life presents.

Sally...

Good evening my friends and welcome to Lesson Three. The energy is much lighter and joyful tonight.

Hello Virgil. You came through very quickly tonight – we must be doing something right.

(Grins) Indeed you are Susie. Your feeling focus is raising the vibration to a higher level and so we align more easily as a result.

Wonderful. I've been affirming all week 'I choose to be in my feeling body', which has been really exciting to do. Something I've realised though is that what I thought was a thin veil of illusion, now actually feels like it's three feet deep. It's been a very difficult week.

The veil of illusion has not changed. What has altered however is your perception of it. You now have an inkling that this illusion is neither imposed upon you, nor an undeniable aspect of physical consciousness. Instead you are beginning to understand that it is actually sourced from within. It must follow then, that the 'battle' you have been waging via the events of your life is a battle with the self. This is an important realisation to enable you to begin to free yourself from limitation and fear. You now understand where the power to do so lies. What you are experiencing is a duality of consciousness and motive. On one hand, you feel excited by the prospect that this course will free you from your binds. The ego joins in your enthusiasm, courting you and is prepared to follow, but can only do so to the point that its limitation and fear will allow it. It cannot help this; it merely knows only its own reality which is limited. On the other hand, there are underlying feelings that are seeking expression, but which you have not yet accessed. You have completely neglected to delve into the shadow side, where the key to these inner feelings reside. The ego is not yet equipped to fathom their true significance, but in time it will be.

There is an aspect of you that fears this physical existence. The ego has kept your focus away from this secret, despite its apparent enthusiasm to embrace the lessons and outcomes. This recognition is a positive step, as this is how we become more familiar with our ego self. The ego is focusing on the outcome once again – some future destination it believes remains just out of your reach. It is not willing to walk with you while you move through the various layers required to open the doorway to inner mastery. It is to explore the seeming 'dark' side of venturing into your feeling body and allow these feelings and fears to come forward. What is it that you would fear most if you allow yourself to think about entering into your feeling body? What fears, what notions come forward at this time? Can you answer this or do you need some time?

I'm not sure. Maybe I fear who I truly am.

That notion is critical to this process; who you are, is greater than the sum of both your personality and your ego self. The ego fears that allowing the higher self to come forward it will be smothered by something greater and will cease to exist altogether. To this end, the great paradox is born. The aspect of self that can actually liberate you is your inner wisdom and knowing. When viewed from ego limitation, this equates to its demise. This is obviously an untenable situation and one that you must expose and heal. The ego avoids confronting its fears by focussing anywhere but in the present. It dreams of the future, bemoans its past, but will not look in the now - for fear it will encounter demons, when in fact it will encounter clarity.

The Soul self is coming forth to embrace the ego and allow it to take its proper place safely in the physical environment. You have been taught that the Soul, or the higher self, can only be experienced in death or in altered states of consciousness. Therefore, the ego feels less important. It can accept the Soul at any time as the soul is constantly communicating at a higher frequency. Given our beliefs in separation and higher and lower self, no wonder the ego senses the finer frequency and turns its attention outward.

When the ego learns to turn its focus inward and embrace the reality of its soul lineage, it actually becomes greater. It will open to receive and ground more of its source. It may feel like it is collapsing inward, but it will rise again, infinitely more equipped to deal with this physical reality. Of course the ego will rise altered, but presently it does not understand that its integrity continues. For example, consider how your intellect grapples with the theory of reincarnation. Try to envisage the concept of participating in different bodies, sexes, colours, abilities and creeds while all the while maintaining the integrity and consistency of self. A difficult concept to understand from your current vantage, but it is utterly true. The integrity of the Soul through countless incarnations is never compromised or separated. This concept, on an unconscious versus conscious basis, is what the ego struggles with. The point is spiritual truth can only be fully grounded through experience, not in the weight of arguments and theories. This is why you must ground the lessons as you immerse yourself in your daily life, so that you can experience your own spiritual truth.

Virgil, I remember you telling me on another occasion, that for many, the 'in' thing in spirituality was to view ego in a negative light, which is incorrect. You said that we potentially brush off a lot of our negative traits, our competitiveness, a lot of our shadow as being merely ego and not worth considering. You also said that we should avoid separating our ego and view it as a little child to be nurtured. I sense that I might be actually reinforcing separation and I don't want to do this.

Indeed Susie. The ego needs to be embraced in allowance not discarded or dismissed as less, via judgement. The ego cannot experience the power of its greater self without the perception of death, destruction, and rebirth. It fears for its own safety, which it equates with your safety. Rebirth is a natural function of ego, it is not meant to be a staid, fixed object. Without the urgings from the inner, your dreams, aspirations and skills would never change. For example, you can and do constantly make decisions in your life that you know are going to change who you are. These changes are initiated because the ego is constantly receiving feedback from the Soul, which is urging it in different directions. Presently however this feedback is not conscious. We are seeking to change that awareness.

In sleep, the ego falls back into its source and is renewed and reborn. It has no conscious awareness of this process, as the integrity and continuity of self remains intact. This is a constant, natural process and whether you believe it or not, it will continue. Consider yourself at age eight. There is no question that you are the same person, despite the fact that you are now very different both physically and psychologically. Time is simultaneous. Linear counting, the way that you mark your physical age, has no bearing on your evolution. The influence for your changes has been this rhythmic return to source and the following rebirth into a new now moment. You have already experienced many deaths and rebirths, with each creating a change in perception. The process of maintenance of the self is so complete and seamless that it is easy to deny that it even occurs. We need to train the ego to pursue this inspiration and feedback, consciously and with love. Teach it to look inward as well as outward and to understand from where its true direction is sourced.

The ego is so fearful of embracing the higher self that it will desperately manipulate its environment to avoid looking inward. It is not as though it is 'evil' and deliberately trying to keep you in fear – quite the opposite. It believes it is fighting the good fight to keep you safe. Because it has ceased looking inward it has a very limited understanding of what life is. It plays only within the limited reality of its own world view and has no conscious experience of the safety that lies beyond itself. Think of the myriad of games you played as a child, within the reference of a child's understanding, with no concept or idea of what the true picture of what a 'grown up' reality was.

So how do we teach the ego to look inward?

It is a process. The ego is seeking rules to abide by so that it can create the illusion of pursuing union with Soul. All the time your focus is actually on the ego, which keeps you from this union. The natural state of ego is open-ended; it can look inward and outward simultaneously. Therefore we are undertaking a course that will **undo what is unnatural.** This undoing will automatically return the ego to its natural state. **It is ego that believes you have to learn things – Soul understands that all is already there if you would just recognise and embrace it.**

Understand that in no way am I aiming to further separate the ego or make it unworthy. I am merely providing an overview of the prevailing ego reality at this time. I am trying to illustrate that whilst you try to manipulate your ego focus, you are playing in the realm of ego which is limited. It is not wrong or bad, it is merely limited. You need to remove the intellectual focus and stop trying to analyse the impossible, the unlimited in terms of the limited. Just allow the true self to step forward and you will grow with grace. Once the ego experiences this true self, it will understand that it can exist as one, in a safer, nurturing environment. It will not fight once it understands its true nature – just as you will not fight a nightmare once you awaken and realise that it is just an illusion. It is the same for your ego. You need to show it the light by experiencing the feeling body and allowing the Soul to come through.

So is that how you perceive us – as our true selves?

Yes, as your entire self.

This week, while regularly affirming my feeling body focus, I experienced unusual reactions to my feelings. I tried the breathing exercise to bring the feelings up but they just felt fleeting, like heaviness on my heart for a few seconds. I think what bothered me was actually the absence of feeling. I was hoping to breathe the feelings through, but I quickly switched into my head space questioning why nothing was coming up. It was a battle to maintain any kind of feeling.

Your ego expectation of what **should** occur is what kept you in your head space. This lesson is a good training process for you, not a destination. As you continually affirm to be in your feeling body, you direct your focus to where it should be. At this point this is all we are trying to achieve. Undertake the exercises for their own sake, not because you want a certain outcome. This outcome or expectation by its very nature is contrived by the ego's limited concepts. Our aim is to cease limitation, not reinforce it. The ego is seeking results so it can move on and be safe. It is keen to evolve, but only within its own limited terms. This is all it knows and is its only current point of reference.

Affirmation can work in this instance because we are using it to check in and correct our focus, not to achieve an end in itself. Soon you will get an idea or picture of how your feelings wax and wane throughout any given period. Your ego has been taught in the past of the validity of calming your emotions and seeking harmony in the feeling body. You therefore, have some intellectual training and consequently ego expectation of what this means. This limited expectation versus the larger reality is what is causing a degree of angst for you. This reaches out and affects your auric field, which in turn affects your conscious thoughts - although you generally have no concept of where these thoughts are coming from. **You may attract incidents to yourself that appear to the ego as the cause of your angst, but understand this is not the case. The incidents are outcomes of your unchecked feelings, not the cause of them.** You are having difficulty in holding these emotions because you have had no training or practise in actually owning them. Negative feelings have been considered an outcome of your failings and therefore avoided, instead of something to be embraced and validated.

For many years you have been working conscientiously on training the mind to acquiesce to the spiritual doctrines you have been taught. You have tried to 'think' like someone of higher awareness, based on learning, rather than as an expression of self. Many have tried affirmation to will an outcome. For us, affirmation is an initial training period in focus, not in manifestation. A degree of confusion is perfectly normal for someone who is attempting to reframe their idea of reality from the inside out. You need to maintain feeling awareness and stringently avoid judgement of one emotion being a more desirable emotion than another. You need to observe your inner dialogue and affirm that you choose to be in your feeling body and simply allow all experience to flow. Eventually you will be as familiar with your emotional body as you are with your mental body.

When you talk about emotions and feelings are you implying that they are the same thing?

They are so closely aligned that they can be considered the same thing. Again it is your ego that seeks this neat clarification and labelling. Feeling, not validated, drives forth as emotion so you can notice it at an ego conscious level. I would say to you that one is the left and one is the right hand. Both are just part of the layer coming forward.

I'm just thinking about a friend of mine who was bothered recently about a war overseas. She has a friend who is a great spiritual teacher and told him that she was really affected by the fighting. He told her, 'to get out of her emotional body as it's taking her away.' He implied she should be above being affected by this situation.

I say that the emotional body was leading her to an opportunity to access and heal a fear and a deep insecurity. Her ego perceives the dramas occurring outside of it and is living in fear – fear that this could also be her reality. This shows that the ego feels abandoned and a victim of random events. It may **think** it creates its own reality, but it doesn't really **believe** it or it would not be so fearful. It would know the source of its own life and reality, if it would look inward. We may colour our perceptions by claiming our feelings of pain are for the poor people caught up in war. However, communion with our own Soul would afford us the unique understanding and knowing of the larger reality and we would not question such events in terms of ego judgement. We identify with the people involved for many reasons. Ultimately we must consider; why them and not me. Validating her emotions could have led her to a place within, that revealed a basic insecurity and lack of safety for self. Once exposed it can be healed.

So our emotional body doesn't necessarily carry us away?

No. It is the ego trying to understand and intellectualise the emotions that carries you away on tangents. Through the subtle feeling body the Soul self seeks expression. Its presence comes up through the layers until it finally registers in the conscious mind. We can either choose to rationalise the feelings away, or we can choose to experience them fully and flow with them back to the source. So when I say to you 'choose to be in your feeling body', this is to actually **feel** the emotion of any situation.

It feels very vulnerable. It almost scares me.

Indeed, it is a vulnerable place for those who feel they have something to lose by exposing their true self. For those who experience and understand the true nature of the Soul, this is a place of great strength.

There is a vulnerability stemming from what you perceive in yourself as weakness. This is the ego self making judgements based on its limited world view. It examines the physical environment, then your response to it and concludes that you are weak and alone. It has no concept of the depth of where these feelings come from, nor their true purpose. Feeling should not be divided into good and bad or right and wrong, for all polarity is illusion. In the experience of ego vulnerability, is an acknowledgement of the strength of Soul. As the ego sees itself as separate, it concludes that vulnerability is a weakness.

The ego will buy into dramas and defend its position, rather than be genuinely vulnerable. To 'hold your light amidst chaos' can be equated to holding your Soul vibration amidst ego drama. The lower vibrations you exude in a state of ego consciousness need to be allowed so they can take you on a journey to uncover the true feeling essence of any situation. This is why I say to you that mere thought affirmations are insufficient to create change because it is not solely with the power of thought that we create. **The key to creation lies in the feelings.** Within feeling is true intent, the paradigm of self you are working with in this lifetime. For example, if you have a basic belief that you are unworthy, no matter how many times you affirm otherwise, the basic belief will materialise in the end as it sits on the foundation of all your creations. It therefore will seep into all of your relationships for it is the way in which **you** meet the world. Following the feelings back to the source, no matter how they have manifested physically, will uncover this basic belief and enable you to heal it. The condition for healing faulty beliefs lies only in the experience of your true self.

If you created merely by conscious thought you would find that society in itself would be remarkably different. For example, if you surveyed the population, the majority of people would consider that they are caring, generous, giving and tolerant. Yet, they are involved in co-creating a reality that globally reflects chaos, indifference and intolerance. This occurs because present Earth feeling energy is couched in fear – your fear. While buried or ignored, fears such as lack, difference, mortality and more give rise to fearful creations. These basic fears, which are actually only faulty beliefs about reality, need to be healed. You refuse to acknowledge their presence internally, so they must birth into physical reality as objects and events to get your attention, as your attention is almost always focused outwardly.

So how do we heal these global fears so that we no longer have to manifest them?

The only way to heal the collective consciousness is from the inside out. Each person must begin by bringing light to their inner realm and heal their own life. When this is done you will effortlessly affect the collective, as your inner light joins with others of like vibration to manifest your group reality. Within the next cycle of 1000 years, all will abandon fear and create from a source of love as the ascension process fulfils its purpose.

It sounds wonderful Virgil and something worth working towards. Sometimes I feel emotions and judgements that just won't clear. I'm angry or upset over something for a long time and I feel unable to move on from the situation.

When strong emotions won't clear, where you feel that you are obsessing and are unbalanced, then this is a strong indication that you are approaching the situation from a lower vantage point. For example, say you have been wronged by a friend. You might mull over how awful the other party is and how you didn't deserve the treatment. This takes you off on tangents, thinking about what you would like say to them, perhaps replaying events in your mind and feeling victimised and mistreated. Rarely do you get past the physical event or trigger and really delve into the underlying feelings bubbling away. At these times, know that there is something arising that is uniquely yours to learn. It is distinct from the rights and wrongs of the physical interaction and there needs to be a focus of intention. You need to pull the feelings, no matter how uncomfortable, around you like a blanket and just be in the experience. With perseverance, the light will reveal the true essence of the trigger.

If you have tried the breathing exercise, with an intention for the real message to rise with each breath, then rest assured that you will manifest opportunities to see the situation clearly. Following the breathing, attempt to clear the ego chatter (or ranting). Your journal is particularly useful at these times. The ego is accustomed to being heard virtually unchallenged, judging the self and others. You won't change this imbalance overnight. You must validate the ego's stance - you do this by allowing all the judgement and pain to come into the physical. It is more preferable to write it down in private than act it out irrationally in public. When the ego has been heard, it will quieten down sufficiently so that you will be able to experience, to some degree, your own inner awareness and 'hear' its higher perspective. Journaling also assists you to review your progress as we proceed further and deeper. In this way, the ego joins the journey with you and assists you to appreciate its true validity and expertise. The more familiar you become with the way the ego functions, the more adept you will become at placating and reassuring it, so it will eventually willingly surrender control. Let the ego be heard; it has valuable insights in respect of the physical arena which we still need to consider in the whole picture. It is not necessary to suppress ego, but it is necessary to balance its perceptions with the inner knowing of Soul.

That's interesting, because this week I had several phone calls from my friends in various states of crisis. I noticed myself immediately analysing their situations, as I would normally do. However, because of the feeling body focus, I concluded that they should just feel in general and breathe it through. So, is this correct? When we are at the point of high emotion, we just need to feel and experience it?

Exactly. When you find that you are at the point of emotional despair it is generally because the ego has tried the intellectual analysis, without relief and now has nowhere to turn. This causes panic and it draws on all that emotion it has been avoiding, which allows it to come to the surface consciousness. The ego cannot abide a lack of power or control. If it cannot save itself, then who will? It will then project its own lack of ability to cope outward into its surroundings and identify something outside of itself as the cause of its trouble. It will usually then attempt to deal with the physical aspect and may even relieve its burden for a time. However, if the inner is ignored, soon other situations will manifest to draw this feeling energy up again, until it is finally recognised and worked with at a deeper level. You can avoid blindly navigating this cycle by consciously acknowledging and working with the feelings initially - a process that I will teach you in the next weeks of the course. Once again, allow the ego to be heard, but use the journal to clear the chatter and avoid acting out in crisis.

Yes, I see how that's a good way of looking at it. I was a bit worried that we'd all be walking around telling everybody exactly how we felt about them, which of course would be very destructive.

Indeed Susie. One does not need to share your feelings with everyone in order to allow them expression and validity. Even people who consider themselves highly spiritual and of the highest motives, have said awful things, then attempted to justify them in the name of honesty and validation. Just because, from their view 'it needed to be said,' does not mean that it needed to be heard. These people fail to understand that they are merely placating their own egos by clearing their own chatter, which can be done as I have indicated, without the need to wound others.

Spiritual honesty and integrity does not necessarily mean you must truthfully engage others in the nature of your ego thoughts. The whole point of the Lesson One exercise was to illustrate how contradictory and misguided these random thoughts are. Integrity can mean being silent, turning the other cheek or taking action when appropriate. The key lies in knowing what is most appropriate in any given situation and then to act accordingly. The Soul's response will always honour all involved. The ego's response will generally honour your own stance and that of anyone else who shares your position.

This knowing how to respond is evidence of the true mastery that you seek and cannot be achieved naturally and with grace from the vantage of ego. Ego will always seek to judge and categorise everything it comes across based solely on the sum of its past experience, for that is its only reference. Its entire picture and image of life is based totally on what it has learned in this world, since it is the only reality it acknowledges. This is a very limited view for two reasons. Firstly, in terms of the nature of this earthly reality, given the different cultures and experiences of the planet. Secondly, from the aspect of your greater spiritual reality – that there is more to life and to the self than this physical body and ego.

The majority of people on this planet have not moved beyond the ego level of awareness, let alone extending it to encompass a spiritual perspective. Moving beyond ego limitation is a necessary state to facilitate a positive experience of Earth changes. More and more people will be drawn to respond to the feeling body and a quickening of events will ensue that will indicate clearly whether you are operating from an ego or soul focus. It is actually only a change in focus – it is not as difficult as you would think.

I have noticed that females enjoy talking about how they feel rather than feeling it.

Indeed, or talking about how others make us feel.

Yes, good point. Can the feeling of a moment be returned to?

It can, but we need to focus on the now.

I sometimes feel a flutter in the heart. Is that being in the feeling body? And if so, do I work on the flutter being longer?

Your ego is seeking a formula again, something it can implement by will and discipline to achieve your desired expectations or outcomes. If you work on making the flutter longer you will be working within the mind, judging that longer is better. It is the intensity or the knowing gained from the experience in that moment, irrespective of the time frame that is important.

Well I could probably talk forever, but I think it's time to move on to what you'd like us to do this week?

Yes my friend it is time, for The Channel is becoming weary. Lesson One was a simple task of focusing on your thoughts. This was to help you become familiar with and understand your own dialogue. To facilitate an awareness that, despite the fact that you walk a spiritual path, you can and do exude negative or even destructive thoughts. Following on from this was the affirmation to be in your feeling body. This change in focus enabled you to begin to accept that your thoughts are not random, but are instead forms of protection against feeling the shadow side of your own self. We now understand that in order to avoid acknowledging our inner pain, we turn to remedies such as attack and projection, or judgement and suppression. Most of you will have an inkling of your preferred defence against feeling and you must take that awareness into the coming week and continue with the affirmation; 'I choose to be in my feeling body'.

You may question why we are continuing with an extension of last week's focus. The truth of the matter is that this initial phase is designed only to bring you in closer contact with your own unique paradigm. We have achieved the first layer of this awareness last week in that you will have recognised that you do respond to your life in a learned manner. Some will have even identified a reliable pattern such as victimhood or attack, colouring their dialogue. That very awareness will enable you to get beneath the patterns of response and therefore blaze a trail to the feelings driving them forth. Essentially, the awareness of your patterns will enable you to cease being a slave to them and therefore free you to hold a higher and stronger awareness of self going forward. The affirmation focus will be easier to maintain. As a result, more of the inner self will be revealed to you. Be aware of calming the emotions so that you can listen to the self that is perpetually calm. To this end I would like you to document quite clearly the outcomes of these events.

O.K. Thank-you.

(Virgil senses something amiss) Do you understand your task? This is important for me.

I don't think I do, entirely.

What element requires clarification?

Well, I've scribbled down a few things. I need to remove the expectation I have applied to the affirmation. I need to be aware of calming the emotions. It's those areas where I feel as though I will still be in my headspace, and then I'll start getting all confused, questioning where my focus is.

Do you mean you have difficulty in trying to determine whether you are in your head or in your true feelings?

Virgil, I'm always in my headspace.

That's a strong belief and one that will be competing with our new affirmation. This is why the observance of conscious thoughts was such an important exercise in the first week. Susie, you have been training the intellect for such a long time in spiritual theory that I know the task of correcting negative self thoughts should come fairly easily to you. The thoughts are emerging from the feelings of inadequacy which translates via the ego to fearful negative self talk. All these feelings emerge and are judged negative and weak and are used against you. **There is no right or wrong to this process, there is no better or worse. All that is required of you is to affirm 'I choose to be in my feeling body'. In reality, this translates as choosing to experience your feeling without expectation or judgement.**

As you were talking then, I decided I'm not going to worry about this. I'll just do the affirmations.

Exactly. Allow it to come forward. If you find yourself negatively talking about others or about yourself, just stop, then immediately affirm, 'I choose to be in my feeling body' and see what messages come forth with the feeling.

Yes I've noticed through doing all the writing and observing just how much I talk about other people.

It's a fine distraction. This week, try to bring the feeling body more fully to conscious awareness. Remember to just experience and journal and the foundations of the process will be laid. We can expand in future weeks. I look forward with great anticipation as we move through these lessons.

Be blessed.

Thank you.

Lesson Three

I choose to be in my feeling body – strive for greater awareness.

CHAPTER 4
Feeling Body - Further Explored

We looked forward to this week's channel with great anticipation. All of us had managed to consistently apply the affirmation of feeling body awareness and furthermore, had even managed to maintain it as a genuine focus in our daily lives. The problem was, instead of making us more loving, calm, and focused, as we had anticipated; it gave rise to a dominant, somewhat self absorbed ego. We were all experiencing annoyances within our various working or family relationships, that pushed our buttons and reflected our worst weaknesses. The situations and dramas were as varied as the people concerned. The common thread was that the situations appeared to be outside of our control and we felt powerless to influence them. We concluded with some regret, that the level of drama in our lives proved that we just weren't getting it. Some blamed themselves, their relationships, even Virgil and the lessons. In hindsight, it was once again our inability to drop our expectations around the particular lesson that gave rise to our frustrations. We thought we were supposed to be evolving a greater spiritual consciousness. We anticipated certain stereotypical behaviours that should occur and which we were, of course, incapable of maintaining. Despite our frustrations, we continued to look forward to Virgil's channelling. Everything was unfolding in the perfect manner for our greatest learning, but in the midst of our life's' circumstances, we found it difficult to see this perfection.

In keeping with our dominant ego chatter and scattered energy, we had numerous problems and significant interruptions that preceded this channel. Our young daughter would not settle to sleep, and our normally quiet mountain home was suddenly noisy. The tape broke, the recorder made a continuous mechanical noise which dominated all the sound recording and finally I, The Channel, had trouble even 'feeling' Virgil's presence. It took a long time to deal with the physical interruptions and even longer for me to reach that space of clarity and calmness that allowed a strong connection with Virgil. We were especially frustrated with the problems manifesting around the channelling, because of all the situations in our lives, this was one where our commitment was absolute and our intentions always crystal clear. If this was going awry, then we held little hope for the other aspects of our lives that we put far less conscious attention to. Surely these difficulties could not be our creation!

Virgil immediately had a message for us which we have included here because it illustrates his teachings beautifully. It shows how our lives mirrored the lessons and reminds you that if you are struggling at this point then you are certainly not alone.

Sally...

Good Evening my friends and welcome to Lesson Four.

I would like to open tonight with a statement in relation to the objects and events that have brought us difficulties this evening. There is, of course, a higher purpose at play. More often than not, demonstrations work more quickly and more profoundly than words alone; in fact your life is a continual demonstration of your inner state. This evening's events conspire to represent a microcosm of how the process of publishing this book will become, should your energy remain so scattered. There are a number of ways in which you can move forward at this time and each choice that you make will determine, of course, the future reality and integrity of the book.

The Channel has a surface conscious intention and expectation to move forward with utmost integrity and commitment. Present circumstances mean that her energy is required in many directions and not all of them align with this solid intention. She uses these circumstances as the physical reasons she is unable to fulfil her surface goals in relation to the book work. Further, she sees them as direct evidence that she is unsupported in her deepest desires and dreams. The fact is however, that these physical difficulties are not imposed upon her, but are instead sourced from within. Fears around putting herself out there, for example, give rise to circumstances which prevent it from happening. This is how your unchecked fears can thwart your clearest of intentions and how it then appears as though your dreams are not supported by the Universe. At such times, the ego becomes incredibly frustrated because it is obeying the manifesting 'rules' it has been taught with determination, but its process is seemingly unsupported.

This is again evidence of **how we create our own reality from an emotional core** and the beliefs that exist there are unrecognised. When we don't face our internal fears and don't feel them, they will manifest in ways that the mind cannot rationalise. For example, The Channel lays the blame for her lack of progress in working spiritually firmly at the feet of her need to engage regular full time work. She is, of course, reliant on the income and so cannot leave her employment. If she (in her terms) would 'take a leap of faith' and leave her job, hoping that something more supportive would come in to replace it, she would most certainly create the lack she so fears. It has not really been faced. Acting on a 'leap of faith' supporting a premise that you have been taught, as opposed to how you really feel, is tantamount to acting on a dare. Critically, this act would not alter the original fear of putting herself out there because it actually works with the symptom or outcome of that fear, instead of the cause. To this end, spiritual progress would not be made since the source of the difficulty is not addressed.

The fact is this, attempting to 'fix' your life via working on the physical with an expectation that this will make you feel better internally, is like trying to fix a poor cake mix once the cake has been baked. Furthermore, working outside in instead of inside out usually exposes the ego to greater confusion, as it adds fear and uncertainty to the fray. Tonight's relatively minor mishaps illustrate how this level of reasoning will impact on your broader life if allowed to run free without examination. Everything in your life could be solved by observing and acting on the smaller inconveniences. If ignored though, you open the way for it to escalate in importance - to get your attention. So I leave you with those words and I would ask that you sort through these issues of commitment and make your choices... let us begin.

Virgil, I found that most of the week I was in quite a dreadful state. To begin with, armed with the new knowledge you have given us, I suddenly thought I had the spiritual tools to negate every other person's position. I felt like lashing out at spiritual teachers, I found friends annoyed me. Then, on the other hand, if that wasn't ego enough, I also began to feel dreadfully insecure about my role in this book - that perhaps I wasn't up to the task. I've been trying to access what is below these thoughts and all I could come up with was anger. As I journaled, it occurred to me how well I've picked up your teachings and turned them into a new attack against both my environment and myself. It concerned me and I reached the conclusion that I needed to drop all this analysis. Do you have any comments?

You are doing very well in this process, Susie. You have actually experienced one feeling essence expressing itself simultaneously in seemingly opposite ends of the polarity spectrum - arrogance and insecurity. While in ego terms they may appear as opposites, in feeling terms their essence is identical, merely altering in form to suit any given circumstance or encounter. One challenge of earthly reality is to understand that matter follows consciousness and does not act independently or according to fixed ego logic. To drop the analysis is a wise decision since as you are aware, by the time you experience these attack thoughts in your mind, it is too late to recognise their source. The feelings manifest in such an array of different circumstances that they appear different and their essence is clouded by your fixation on this physical manifestation. The ego has learned to manipulate your stance to enable you to project onto others what you don't want to feel, as well as validate any feelings that support its learned self image, particularly where it is negative. You have experienced firsthand the manner in which our inner world manifests through the layers in ways that we then categorise and judge and so miss their true message. You have now begun a journey that can potentially free your mind from itself.

You have attached yourself, so to speak, to these teachings and the ego wants to make an ally of them, for it understands how important spiritual growth is to you and that you will not give it up easily. To keep pace, the ego must redefine the lessons in its own terms for it has no other point of reference at present. We will change this though. But for now, the only way ego can interpret this reality is through the notion of logic and polarities. In your case, if your new knowledge is superior (in its terms), then all others must be inferior. Internally, this 'logical' conclusion draws angst forward, since you believe yourself to be less than the knowledge itself and that you could not possibly be an equal part in this process. It is the same essence, but different manifestation, depending on whether your focus is internalised or externalised.

Although the ego does recognise the flow of information delivered via my words, it does not identify with the innate truth of the message. You will come to know that within the physical words there exists recognition at a feeling level of the truth or essence of the teachings. Not because they ring true, but because it is what you are now experiencing at a feeling level in your daily life. It is not as though this is new knowledge to you, far from it. Instead, it is a process of removing the barriers that have prevented you from seeing what is already your reality.

The ego wisely takes a back seat during the channelling process, not because it is conniving, but because it too feels a sense of belonging, or safety if you like, in the feelings generated in our higher state of consciousness. It is only once this sense of higher self diminishes, when you move out into the physically orientated world, that the ego again feels alone. Lacking the insight necessary to reconnect the two worlds, it then pursues the only valid avenue it perceives, which is its unique physical domain. Ego establishes rules and responses to abide by and alters behaviour to suit, which it layers a cause and effect expectation. Left alone to judge profound spiritual knowledge against a physical reality, which it consistently experiences as painful and unloving, ego is simply unable to generate that same sense of well being that is experienced when bathing in the light of higher self. It unconsciously seeks to compensate for a lack of power by drawing the energy of others, in making its own position superior, when this is not necessary.

My mind chatter can be just overwhelming sometimes, Virgil.

The mind chatter has always been there and serves the purpose of letting you know that your focus needs to alter away from mind analysis and toward feeling. Understand that focus is merely a choice. Incessant mind chatter is not something that you need to overcome or conquer, for it is not an enemy, but instead something you need to recognise and act upon. It reveals that you are touching on an important aspect of your belief system, but that the solution lies within the feeling body and not in the intellect. In your case Susie, you have been able to surrender and let it go and in doing so, you cease energising the chatter so that it can dissipate. This will quieten you sufficiently to enable moments of revelation to emerge through the feeling body, at which time the chapter lessons will have more meaning for you.

If you notice that you are judging others, understand that without a doubt, it is revealing far more about yourself than the subject of your attention. Judgment rises out of a bed of flawed internal beliefs that are unrecognised and trying to get your attention. In your case, much of your judgement stems from a belief around the notion that the proverbial 'Promised Land' will never be; you will never succeed in creation on this Earth plane. Experiencing and working with this fear will get you to a point of completion in the now moment of your life. To some extent, the whole cycle renews, but with deeper awareness. You must understand that following the grounding of this course, your next cycle of evolution will reflect that deepening connection to your own self. I am concerned that you may think that upon completion you will be a finished work. On the contrary, I instead intend for you to be so well attuned that your evolution will continue on at a more rapid, deeper and profound rate. You are constantly exploring the depths of your power and your oneness with source and this will not change. The journey through the feeling body is one of freedom and relief. It is one where your foundations cannot be shaken in the same way that your ego foundations can be shaken. It is the beginning of a new road, a new paradigm and you will not want to, or be able to, go back to the old.

Interestingly Virgil, I was actually well aware of that fear. Its symptoms are all through my journaling. For example, I had written that I was worried you might find someone better able to assist with the book, so thank you for your support. After I'd determined to just drop all the mind chatter, I did make an attempt to engage feeling. It was the morning after the birth of a friend's daughter which I was excited about. Soon though, my focus went to my own son's difficult birth and I could see how seemingly joyful events can work as a catalyst to take us to unresolved pain. I started breathing deeply and linked easily with the feelings of his birth, particularly the confusion, fear and exhaustion. It felt more genuine than previous attempts and I realised I was experiencing it all from the point of feeling instead of judgement.

As I allowed these feelings, I began to notice the ways my ego protects me from hurt in situations with friends, and tears began to form. I started sending these feelings love, which I imagined as a pink energy, and I could feel something change in my torso. It was as though the feeling body was aligned perfectly to my visualisation. I began to ask what lay behind the feelings, but I kept slipping back into my headspace which was calling them fear or lack of self worth. I knew these explanations came from my head, so I asked for your assistance. Immediately, I felt a weight on my arms as though the air itself was heavy. I then got the word 'weak' coupled with an image of myself crawling in the desert. I was exhausted, in a very barren land, and I was on my last legs. I wasn't sure what this image meant and asked for more information. A man came and jumped on my back until I was lying flat on the ground helpless. I didn't know how it related to my son's or my friend's birth experience. I then saw a white light in the shape of a person up ahead and started to move towards it. I was unable to reach it so I asked it to come to me. It merged into me, on the ground, and we just lay there. At that point, in real life, my son arrived home, so I ended the experience there. Could you comment on this for me?

This is an amazing lesson for you. What did you learn from this experience?

What I learnt from it was that I feel spiritually weak. That was the word I got in the desert and it felt overwhelming.

(Virgil smiles intently and the channelling connection seems to grow stronger.) This was an exceptional message directly from the being of light that you are, and yet because you had rationalised it through the ego, it became another message to judge. One thing that you need to understand is that the Soul will not send you judgements. In fact it will not send you messages that are anything less than uplifting and that expose the true nature of who you are, which is a magnificent being. This is a clear and classic example of how much you are operating in the ego space.

The image of self that was on its last legs in pain and the accompanying word 'weak,' is a representation of the ego. Again, it is not my intention to denigrate the ego. And I need to explain that in perpetuating the separation of the Soul self from the ego, this is literally what you are doing – throwing an aspect of yourself away and leaving it to fend for itself. The barren unsupportive landscape should show you precisely how you perceive this reality. The being that stamped you into the ground, so to speak, represents your ego's view of other egos it encounters. It ascribes to the belief that a natural outcome of your ego meeting another ego is an immediate fearful response of attack and defence. It also shows that your ego has exhausted much of its energy in trying to make a happy life for itself following its own rules and is ready to surrender control. There, quietly and calmly, is the Soul self calling to you and wondering why you had to be on your last legs before you would recognise it. This is because the ego had equated merging with the Soul self as a death, even though the truth of who it is lies within its love. The Soul has had to wait for you to call on it. A true union cannot be coerced but must be undertaken willingly. This image shows that you are now willing to seek wholeness.

Having said that, your interpretation was markedly different in that you assumed you were spiritually weak. The reality of this opposing interpretation is precisely what I was trying to explain in relation to how the ego, when left alone, misinterprets profound knowledge. In your vision, connection to your feeling body has led you to an experience of your true self outside of normal ego comprehension. The attack thoughts you constantly project inward are absolutely crucifying your ego and it is showing you the way to safety in its terms. The ego interpreted the vision quite quickly from its own vantage point only and thereby turned it against you by judging you spiritually weak. It sees the Soul as separate; a representation of the polarity of ego and it will not recognise itself as weak. It projects the feelings onto its perceived opposing force - the Soul self. Yet it is the ego that is weak – not in an inferior, negative sense, but as it operates from a weakened position, as it is disconnected from source.

The ego sees itself as dying of thirst. It perceives this pain because it senses that it lacks its life force. Of course the great paradox is that its life force is the Soul self and the ego at once both craves and repels it. It fears what it cannot understand and categorises in terms of time and space. How can it know eternity when it is so finely attuned to time that it does not even question its existence? Compound this further when you consider that reflected all around is convincing proof of the existence of same. Intellectually you understand that such proof is contrived only because the entire planet is ensconced in the same mass dream. Yet how do you know this? The ego will turn away from the one thing that can save it and dress your revelations in its own beliefs and language.

The only way that the ego can be nurtured into union with the Soul is through the feeling body. Your vision was a powerful and important revelation to assist you to move forward. Feel pleased that you were able to keep the headspace occupied for long enough to receive it. The process unravelled only when you sought to interpret it, categorise it and draw conclusions from it. The analysis was done through the eyes of the ego. If you had the opportunity to feel the feelings generating by the merging with the light being (the feeling body) and refrained from automatically seeking the ego 'expertise', then the true essence of the message may have come through. The message was that the ego is spiritually weak or abandoned, as it is without its connection to source and that all healing lays in the union you are seeking.

That is a wonderful interpretation Virgil and will give me much food for thought, as I contemplate it. Has my ego kicked in more since beginning this course?

No, Susie. Its actions and behaviours are just becoming more obvious to you. It is not exerting a greater influence, it is just that before it was allowed freer reign – now it needs to be more creative.

What do you mean by more creative?

The ego needs to assimilate the new information. In order to use this information, it must redefine or reinterpret it to fit within the constructs of its own reality. It is quite astute at doing this as it has been trained to interpret the physical by its own standards alone. So broadly speaking, in absorbing new information the ego must still rationalise it to fit the reality it knows. It will allow its reality to expand, but only within the limiting concepts that it cannot question, such as polarities.

Until the ego can experience a connection to source, through the feeling body, it will always perceive the Soul self as a separate entity. Its deepest fear is that the Soul directs the physical vehicle and discards both the ego and the vehicle at death. It perceives in this way because the ego feels more comfortable in the physical and is aligned more closely to the mortal body than the eternal Soul. It is intimately attuned to physical reality and the concepts of birth and death, beginning and end, etc. It knows these concepts as 'facts', and they are 'facts' of this mass dream, but this dream is not its entire reality. While assessing only the **physical** it cannot comprehend that it is part of a multidimensional being. When the ego turns its focus inward in balance, it will gain insight of this additional aspect. In other words, as the Soul self influences daily activities more, the ego will acknowledge this presence as part of its larger reality.

So Virgil, I have no way of directing the soul and the ego to act in unison at this stage. For example, can I go into a visualisation or meditation where the soul merges with the ego?

No, this will amount to merely serving the ego's purposes; it would be another mind game. The ego may reach a level of empowerment as a result of 'merging' with what it imagines through its intellectual training as a beautiful being of light, full of strength and grace. In reality however, because the ego directs mind visualisation at a conscious level, the outcome would be an imagined or contrived connection – not a genuine experience of Soul consciousness. The effect would be for the ego to continue to be in control, but in its own perceptions, with the added strength and knowledge of the Soul's power at its disposal. **Give a faulty ego the power of God and we may have acts without conscience.**

In regards to your recent experience, it was your intention to experience the feeling body that gave rise to the revelations you received via the vision in the desert. So you weren't consciously manufacturing a connection with the feeling body, you were experiencing it at a feeling level and attempting to understand it via words and images. You eventually became more conscious of the visualisation rather than the feelings and consequently actually gained an incorrect insight due to this change in focus. Therefore, at this stage of your development, visualisation is fraught with limitation.

The effect we are seeking is not so much the Soul merging with the ego, but it being more present in the conscious activities of daily life. We are looking for the Soul to penetrate the egos' defences, not for the ego to usurp the strength of the Soul. When the two align it would not make you feel more powerful and greater in an ego sense; rather it would generate feelings of humbleness and gratitude. It will most definitely change the way you view the world. You will be viewing it through the eyes of the Soul, but with the aid of the ego's expertise and ability to manipulate in this reality.

So is that why it's been necessary for us to study so many spiritual books and participate in so many courses? Is it so the ego can interpret the spiritual concepts?

No, your previous learning was necessary for your own purposes and life path. It suited your needs at that given moment. When I refer to the ego's ability to manipulate in this reality I am talking about its primary function. As foreign a concept as eternity is to the ego, time and space are as foreign to the Soul. That is why one cannot operate in this reality without the other. For the Soul to be incarnate in this reality, it is absolutely mandatory for the veils of illusion to be pulled firmly down. Time and space are root assumptions of this reality and cannot be avoided. These root assumptions are very convincing and completely foreign to your natural state, which is why many lose their way. They are so convincing because you have created an element of yourself, the ego, which is finely tuned to specifically understand and operate within these root assumptions. What frequently happens is the ego takes its place at the helm, so to speak, when it was only meant to be the lens by which physical data was interpreted, or converted.

The Soul as you are aware, perceives this physical dimension in vastly different terms. I see this physical dimension as a grand interplay of energy, for I do not have an ego lens that I can use to interpret it within the context of time and space. The only reason I have any concept of this reality at all is because I have, in your terms, a myriad of lifetime memories that I call upon to influence the messages I wish to convey, coupled with access to The Channel's consciousness. The ego is an absolute necessity to function in this reality – accept that – but it is now time to restore the ego to its rightful place. The ego is a valuable aspect of yourself which you have created in your own image to rise forth from the greater entity that you are. However much of the data coming through can be severely impeded if the ego refuses to turn inward and only looks outward.

So my ego's normal Virgil?

(Laughs) There is no such thing as normal. I don't understand, Susie.

Well, sometimes I feel like such an evil person, even though I know I'm not, and I guess I'm just bothered that I entertain such negative ideas of self.

The course focus and discussions will give rise to a level of compassion for the ego rather than judgement – compassion that will help you understand the difficulty it faces. It is the same as giving a child a task, not providing direction, and then berating them because they make some mistakes along the way. If you can understand the confusion and difficulty of this scenario, then you can have a measure of compassion for who you are. Understand that you're acting out from a group of assumptions that are real to the ego self. The physical data it experiences on a day to day basis generally supports the premise of being alone, abandoned and ill equipped to deal with an unpredictable reality. How can it believe differently except to ignore all that it is here to observe, thereby suppressing its most basic natural function? The ego has to now understand that if it would but acknowledge this guidance that there is a whole wealth of information within that will straighten out its perception. Following this guidance would enable the reality of the Soul to be reflected within the confines of the physical data.

Okay, let me summarise to see if I've got this right. I can recognise what a feeling feels like, that's a pretty major step for me. I can also recognise where my ego will kick in and direct conversation away from things that hurt me. I need some clarification – do I go into my feeling body every time I feel a feeling and explore it? Wouldn't I then be sitting around all day, constantly accessing my feelings and reactions to hurts and having to process them all?

No Susie, definitely not. Many of those surface hurts are merely at a level where an ego is hurting another ego. Generally, these are manifestations of minor slights and the ego uses them to embellish the illusion of enlightenment. The outcome of any preoccupation with the surface reality is the opposite however, that is, the inability to look beyond it for higher guidance. The lens tries to provide you with what it **thinks** you require in becoming the enlightened person that you want to be. It would have you remain focused on the outcome rather than the source of your pain. It is to understand that much of your attention is drawn to analysing ego pain. You will learn as we go forward to discern the real essence from which the pain stems upward through the layers. To focus merely on surface slights just creates distraction from feeling and keeps you in the limited stance of ego. Do not waste your life seeking an 'enlightened ego' for it will learn these concepts and run away with them to suit its own ends. If you get to that point where you can name the hurt in the ego's terms, then it is too late.

Right...so back to my mind chatter frustrations of the week. I assume at some level I recognised that exact concept, since I knew when it was time to go within and ended up with the vision from being in my feeling body. Is that what you are talking about? That it is at those times that you go within?

Indeed that is a timely example.

Right. So we don't have to process every fear we have.

No. The process that I had you undergo, although seemingly regimented, was to facilitate a turnaround in your perceptions. It was to bring to your awareness what is occurring within your own universe, and that's all. Before you can move forward, you need to understand where you currently are. I will help you to find that reference point by routinely observing and working with the thoughts and feelings. First of all, the mind chatter was recognised. Next, you moved into experiencing the feeling generating the mind chatter, to open your perception. As the mind chatter persists it hopefully gives you an indication of how the ego attempts to be your master. This is not through anything sinister; it is just because it has new information about its physical environment which must be assimilated. You have introduced a new concept to it so it must modify its interpretation of reality accordingly. It is a perfectly natural function of the ego to interpret reality through its belief structure. If you add to those beliefs, its perceptions will change accordingly. It does, however, get stuck in its own limited concepts. Your interpretation of the vision last week, illustrated that beautifully.

Now to the new lesson for this week. It will be to embrace all your surface ego hurts as important messages from Soul, and to understand that such pain is an outcome of feelings sourced in Soul, which you have failed to recognise. So when you are wounded at an ego level, seek a deeper message, knowing that the feeling is the key – not the physical trigger.

To explain the task further, let us stay with the example of the birth of your child. Do you agree that the circumstances of his birth still potentially generate emotion in you, Susie? You had a difficult birth physically and emotionally. It was the physical manifestation of the direct polarity, or opposite, of the situation you were trying to create. Instead of a birthing centre, soft music, essential oils, and relative calmness you found yourself in theatre; scared and relying on others to bring your baby into the world. Your ego has judged you as a failure and weak because you were unable to manifest your ideal birth experience. In feeling essence however, it is far less about the nature of birth and much more about the nature of manifesting your desires. Thus the visualisation in the desert came through when you tried to get behind the issue via the feelings, although at the time you could not assimilate the two. Through the mind chatter you convince yourself that the circumstance of the birth doesn't really matter, as long as you are both fine. You deal with this emotion by converting it to ego chatter and acquire a certain degree of closure, even have a cry about it, but ultimately feel glad that your son is perfect. This is how most would deal with their physical surface issues.

Suddenly, someone may say something judgemental about caesarean births, for example, which would 'push your buttons' and trigger emotion. If you processed this feeling at that level, i.e. 'I am reacting to my difficult birth experience', you are remaining in the realm of ego. This is an example of the notion that if you can name the emotion then it's too late. The underlying emotion of this entire episode is much greater and profound. It would continue to manifest in physical ways that you probably wouldn't recognise as being in anyway related to that 'original' event. The underlying emotion giving rise to all the ego judgement and self abuse has nothing to do with your ability to physically birth a child – the Soul makes no judgement on the physical form of anything. What was expressing itself here was the belief and fear that you are actually spiritually incapable of producing your ideal experience. It was this deeper feeling of inadequacy that was not faced. As I have said, our fears not faced must manifest. It is not as though you had not considered that things can go wrong in birthing either – for you had. This was not the fear to be faced and this perspective of trying to justify the circumstance in hindsight is still contemplating it at an ego level.

The ego wants to believe it creates its own reality, but rather than take responsibility for creations it cannot understand, it projects the power of manifesting on to an all knowing Universe that somehow knows what's best for it. No wonder it feels such a victim in this reality when the Universe is supposed to be all loving, yet seems to measure growth with pain. Again, the essence of the emotion that drove that manifestation is that you feel you will never be successful in creating your own reality. That emotion had come up, but it got stuck at the ego level. The ego found it difficult to reconcile in any way other than to work at not judging it (as it has been taught) and just allowed the emotion to pass through. This form of processing feels real but is essentially superficial. You never allowed it to take you to the root cause - "If I'm so spiritually aware and capable, why am I unable to create my own reality, despite the fact that I spent many hours pouring energy into creating my ideal birth experience?" It is this element that you did not face as you remained firmly in the ego realm, dealing with ego self doubt, ego justifications and rationalisations. All of this becomes a time consuming protracted exercise, as the deeper feelings just don't go away. They resurface again in different forms. The ego continues to label and rationalise these feelings, thereby keeping you from truly experiencing the deeper truth. All of this consumes much energy and is unnecessary.

You desire to have certain things. You can create whatever you want – but not when you are only working at one side of it, that is the physical manifestation rather than the essence. You were trying desperately to create the perfect birth experience because you were fearful of not being able to do so. Not because you were scared of the physical alternative, but because it was a direct test of all you believed about your spiritual life. Achieving it would show you and your friends that good things happen to spiritual people; that you can create your own ideal reality according to the love and energy you put into it. When it didn't happen like the theory espoused, despite your considerable efforts energetically and physically, your ego was left in great self doubt indeed. It had performed exactly as it had been taught and thus the birth should have manifested perfectly as you had imagined – so why didn't it? You felt more abandoned than ever. All your efforts to create seemed worthless. Never experiencing the fear of being unable to create your reality, and then moving through it to the other side, meant that it had to manifest to get your attention. It was the driving emotion surrounding the event and it had to be shown the light and healed. Your ego turned in on itself blaming you as spiritually weak for being incapable of manifesting your heart's desire.

Thanks for that Virgil. So, to this week's task. You asked us to discern the source of our ego pain as being from Soul. Following on from your explanation just given, would that mean to seek the true feelings, rather than agonise over the physical trigger that caused the pain. Is this correct?

Indeed. This will facilitate awareness that surface ego hurts are important and should not be judged as immaterial – we don't want to separate the ego further from this process. We need to treat the ego as a child. If the ego is feeling hurt then you can take the time to reassure whatever aspect is feeling unloved or unworthy. Where you may ordinarily dismiss many ego slights as not worth worrying about, I want you to stop and reconsider. Understand that the ego is a critically important aspect of who you are right now. To ignore or suppress its needs will have consequences. Take the time to commune with the ego and learn its reality. What we are facilitating is a growing understanding that the needs of our Soul self and our ego self are different, yet both need to be met. The only change is that we are operating from a level where we are now making choices through the wisdom of our Soul, rather than through the judgement of our ego. This will provide a marked difference in terms of who is controlling the ship, so to speak. Please do not allow the ego to now turn upon itself and attack. This will be its next obvious conclusion, as it follows directly from its belief in opposites and polarities. That is, if the Soul is so wonderful, I must be inferior, weak or worthless. If this is the focus, many slight hurts will be called forward as witness to this perception. Avoid this by allowing and pandering to those emerging needs, for it will encourage the ego to understand that there is a safety net within this new learning. It will gradually learn that the Soul can provide a home of love and truth. I want you to then journal those experiences where you are affirming back to your hurt ego, its inherent safety. Be aware of judgements - we will discuss them as they come up next week.

Remember, unrecognised or suppressed feelings emerging from the Soul will manifest as ego hurts. You need to attempt to enter into the experience via the feeling body and journal the outcomes. One word, such as 'weak', correctly interpreted via feeling, can give you a major insight far superior to a myriad of visualisations that may encompass specific physical events. I would like you to continue to try to interpret your own visions and messages so that I can gauge again where the interpretation is coming from.

Would this be like when I told you about the experience in the desert?

Yes, Susie.

Thank you very much Virgil, it's been a pleasure as always.

And I thank you all for your patience this evening. I look forward to our next meeting.

Be blessed.

Lesson Four

Discern ego pain as unrecognised feelings from Soul.

CHAPTER 5
Your Soul And Ego

In response to last week's lesson, we were again expecting some grand experience, where we would tap into a Soul hurt and everything would make sense. Despite trying to maintain a feeling focus, we seemed to get bogged down in the theory. In other words, we were seeking a formula that our intellects could follow, which would somehow make sense of our lives' challenges. Feeling awareness was new to Susie and I and we were beginning to show the strain of believing we 'weren't getting it' – this was especially evident in Susie. Normally a very upbeat, open and fun person, Susie noticeably started to contribute less to the discussions, and when she did contribute her frustrations were thinly veiled.

Virgil has always been an advocate of co-creation and his role as facilitator was going to be no exception. His philosophy is that if you are not ready to ask the question, then he, in his integrity, cannot simply bestow the answer. The lessons were designed to enable us to uncover our own insights which he could then expand on, yet we continued to hope that he would just tell us the way forward. To make Susie's frustration worse, I had fleeting moments of insight in coming to terms with feeling motivation. This would have been generating difficult feelings in Susie, but she was too 'nice' to be jealous of another's success, so these feelings were unrecognised or unspoken.

Susie was extremely committed to her spiritual development and desperately wanted to succeed. You will note her first comment at the beginning of this channel: "I don't feel as though I have that much to discuss this week". To compensate, her ego substituted experience with mind play. She talks about recognising ego games and getting annoyed at others' egos, etc. Virgil does his best to undo the tangent that her ego is taking her on by correcting her surface perceptions, but she quickly moved on to more intellectual questions that were actually irrelevant to this process. These questions were food for the intellect; how the ego is formed in childhood, why the perfect Soul seeks an existence immersed in seeming imperfection, and the difference between higher self and Soul, etc. Virgil entertained us by responding to every question and we enjoyed his insights – in hindsight though, I can now see it was all just feeding our intellects.

As the book progresses you will see that Susie's focus should have been on the feelings emerging because she wasn't getting anything profound from her weekly exercises, and the fact that she was witnessing the lack of struggle in others. This highlights how we can experience very obvious feelings and therefore potential insights into hidden fears, yet because it doesn't fit our expectations, or because we are so used to feeling that way (in Susie's case spiritually inferior or weak), that we don't even recognise them. It also shows how the ego will try to compensate your reality - matching your expectation in relation to the new information, by creating little issues to focus on and keep you occupied.

Take a moment to become aware of your ego chatter over the past week and in particular how it was connected to your feelings. It is timely to take the first steps in embracing your issues as something to be healed, rather than something to be avoided or perpetuated. In past courses, it is around this time that many became more deeply aware of the feelings connected to their 'issues', as opposed to merely contemplating them at an intellectual level. Strong feelings often emerge that, on one level, are probably familiar, yet also have been long ignored or pushed aside. Some began to waiver at the thought of fully confronting their 'demons' now that they had an inkling of them. It was clear that we had started a process that we had to finish. It was all making less sense intellectually, but there was a glimmer of light emerging from within.

Most participants were immersed in this phase. There were one or two who still managed to dismiss their ego ravings as inappropriate or not real, and so manifested unusual or challenging physical circumstances to trigger feeling and lead them to deeper insight. For example, one participant, had been working hard to 'release' her negative feelings. In truth, she didn't want to face them at all, just eliminate them completely. While cooking she burnt her eye badly with hot oil, which, of course triggered strong feelings in her. To her credit, this time she allowed them to emerge fully. She vented openly, but struggled with the concept that the event was created from within herself. At times we all want to eliminate things from our lives, to avoid the pain. However, this story shows that where we deny or suppress feeling, we do attract incidents or 'lessons' that trigger feeling so strong that they can bypass our ego guard and rush into conscious awareness. Her denial stemmed from the fact she could not 'see' the source of her ego troubles as within. She had been trying to release her so-called 'bad' feelings and consequently she had not yet embraced them, as was the purpose of the previous lesson. She instead drew on techniques learned in other courses that advocated the release of 'bad' feelings as a way to eliminate the pain. This technique however kept her occupied at a surface level and therefore allowed her to avoid immersion in feeling; the technique itself is a cleverly disguised form of suppression.

This chapter is a combination of about three weeks of our initial group procrastinating and struggling to actually 'feel the feelings'. Virgil just allowed it all to unfold, not giving anything away and we were becoming annoyed. Even to the point where some were being passive aggressive during the channelling sessions. He continued to steer our focus to the deeper feelings underlying all our surface angst. Each week he would listen to our egos' points of view, discuss these from his higher perspective, and then return them to us altered. He was learning from this process too as it was from our ego struggles that he determined the lessons for the next week. Sometimes I could sense his frustration in trying to undo the knots we'd tied ourselves in. It seemed the vision from the higher realms and the vision of ego were so different, that at times he had as much difficulty in understanding us, as we did him. He spent weeks channelling about essentially identical issues, but addressed them differently, until we finally felt something move. While that was our experience as the first participants, subsequent courses proved less difficult as Susie & I were more in tune with our feeling bodies and thus able to assist the process in others. Those seemingly endless weeks have been condensed here into one chapter, lest you become as bogged down as we did.

Sally...

Good evening my friends and welcome to Lesson Five. Thank you for your assistance with The Channel – it can be difficult to overcome the mind chatter.

Hi Virgil. I'm not sure where to begin. I'm worried because I don't feel as though I've come in with much this week. Last week you asked me to discern that unrecognised feelings from Soul will manifest as ego pain. I tried to start the day with looking in the mirror and using some sort of positive affirmation. I still have problems looking in the mirror due to the rashes I endure and I see my self image as an ego fear. I think I recognise that beneath that surface fear is a real Soul fear. I suppose that there was, some sort of recognition between those two. As I read over my journal from last week, most of my issues are about control and the fact that I feel like I'm under the control of my own ego, and that of others. I could recognise ego in other people, the games they play and the way people hide behind their egos and it annoyed me. Did you want to comment?

Susie, the work that you undertook last week was to provide you with a focus of viewing situations in different ways so that you can become consciously aware of your learned response, and then change it given your new knowledge. It was also an exercise in being kinder to yourself, in particular the ego, and therefore to be kinder to others. All your hurts are valid and if you immerse yourself more fully in the ego's painful talk you will quickly learn that there is a wealth of true feeling threaded throughout it. The only way I could get you to fully embrace the ego hurt was for you to recognise that hidden within it is the key to Soul, and that they are inseparable, not distinct. Much of the cause of your confusion was your expectation that you would be able to categorise your hurt in two neat little piles. The task for the task's sake was to learn of their interconnection and to identify their different forms of expression. That is, the Soul through feeling and the ego through its chatter, attack, projection, or suppression. Then you could cease spending time pouring through the ego's expression and learn to proceed directly to the point of feeling in any circumstance.

The fact that you have taken the last week's task so literally is normal and was expected as a natural outcome due to the way it was delivered, coupled with your current ego focus. Cease the intellectual analysis now and concentrate on the feelings that this task has brought forward – they are the keys at this point. Your confusion and frustration are genuine feelings of pain that need to be embraced and healed. You are at the perfect point in this journey inward. You have said that you were able to recognise others' egos. Again, this is a distraction from feeling – if you had truly recognised the ego in the way we discussed last week, you would have felt compassion or at least empathy for others, knowing that they are masking their Soul's need to express its love. You would have recognised that the ego was smothering the feelings and distorting them through processing, so that it could draw energy from others by game playing. So had you recognised the ego in its true identity you would have gladly given the ego the energy it was so desperately seeking. To know it, or recognise it at that level, your ego too, would have been immersed in the feeling body where all such high insights birth.

What you have done in this instance is once again met them ego to ego. You have judged them as inferior because you possess some sort of knowledge that they don't. So this has been a powerful experience in as much as you have interpreted a situation one way and can now identify an alternative view and move forward in the coming weeks with a different approach. Knowledge of itself is not strength; it is experience that we are seeking and your experiences this week have been valid. Don't invalidate the process by berating yourself with negative talk concerning a perceived inability to ground the information. We learn by experience, not through lecture. Does this make sense to you?

Yes Virgil. To expand on those egos I noticed this week, it was usually with males as well. For example, when someone comes across as being very arrogant and full of themself and loudly discusses acquiring large amounts of money as their main focus, that annoys me because I think that's not what life's about – okay, I suppose that's my arrogance.

Indeed Susie.

Yes, I understand that, yet it still annoys me on the surface. So how do I be kind to my ego and get to the inner feelings in times like that?

There are a number of ways that you can recognise what lies beneath ego. Firstly, to have an awareness of when you are involved in ego meeting ego, by using all the observations that were provided previously. In the example of the loud boastful male, such recognition would have revealed that where he has exhibited arrogance, you have returned arrogance to him. The other ego has built itself up on the basis that it can earn a great deal of money and derive a comfortable lifestyle, whereas you have built up your status and position in life on the basis of superior spiritual knowledge and the ability to see through certain situations. The form is different but the essence is exactly the same – arrogance derived from the perception of superiority. One is more obvious only because of all the ego dramas surrounding money.

To connect with the essence of the exchange, the Soul communication, and hear the true message within the ego language is to simply choose to be in your feeling body. By choosing to perceive the situation from your feeling body is to potentially take the ego control out of that situation. It may not be instantaneous – remember sometimes the ego needs to be heard – but follow the processes you have been given. At some stage you should get a sense of the insecurity that lies behind that ego. Essentially this is common to all, given the nature of its perceived physical reality, as discussed last week. So it is a matter for you to choose a different interpretation.

There is not a magical formula whereby I can say to you, to say this or think that and all will automatically change. It is a process of becoming and it requires practice. You have experienced an exchange from one level of consciousness which has now been expanded upon. This process allows another veil of illusion to be lifted so that your next focus will be stronger. We will continue to build on this process as other veils are revealed. With commitment, there will come a time when you are instantly recognising the Soul speaking within the ego language.

Yes Virgil. I've often felt a resistance in not wanting to look behind another layer of ego, because I enjoyed my own superiority in thinking that 'they' just didn't get it.

Agreed, Susie. Like that example, it is a way for you to ignore your own feelings of insecurity by projecting them on to others. You reason, "Well you can make one hundred thousand dollars per year, but I am going to ascend!" In your mind this is the ultimate trump. You have an insecurity that perhaps at some level you should be out there trying to earn large sums of money and maybe he's got it right and you've got it wrong. To justify your ego position, you have attacked his priorities by making his pursuits more ego driven than your own. This is the way that you affirm your own ego stance. These energy exchanges occur every day and while you continue to focus from ego, it will continue to exert the greatest influence in your reality. The Soul is focusing on a remarkably different level.

When you sense yourself entering into those sorts of judgements, understand that it is only the surface manifestation that has come to the ego attention. Therefore you've missed feeling in the moment and that is okay. However, go on to affirm that you'd like to be in touch with the essence of what triggered that judgement, or ego response. Very frequently you will experience your own insecurity or frailty which is a reflection of all that you have just encountered. You can only see reflected back at you, what is in you, at a feeling level. It is to look at every interaction with another Soul, as a potential opportunity to help you evolve your life.

When you operate at that level and actually maintain that expectation, (rather than automatically picking it apart to create a superior stance) then the outcome is altered effortlessly. It will stem from feeling body consciousness **which is your natural state.** The attitude you exude is different, and the initial perception will be slightly different. It's not a huge change in thinking because thinking cannot generate a higher perception. It is a change in focus and only a slight one. We are restoring the natural ego function to turn inward, not coercing it into a desired foreign behaviour. What we need to do is restore the ego's vision to enable it to see clearly into the heart of another. Then you will find that there is no training involved, moreover that the feeling just permeates your defences as a natural process. As you experience future exchange, from the wisdom of Soul, you can easily return (or reflect back) to another what they need. By contrast, the ego will withhold validation that is counter to its own stance. It is not as though you are forcing or manipulating your new response, as you may have done in the past, by sending love and light thoughts contrived by the mind. It is just an automatic exchange that occurs which is natural and beyond conscious control. That is why there can be no magic formula.

Oh that's good. So if there's an ego that I clash with constantly, there's a beautiful lesson to be learnt, isn't there?

There's an opportunity to learn more about your own self, yes. Your ego knows that truth only because it has been trained in spiritual concepts, but the key lies in actually enabling it to pursue the lesson inherent within the encounter for yourself.

Yes, but I've not been able to get to the lesson and I'm frustrated about it because it's something that comes up regularly.

Then Susie, you need to go back to the tools already given. To refine your ego expectation and focus, try affirming that you will encounter an experience at a Soul level. The next minor conflict that comes forward, the next ego annoyance, you can use as training or practice. When you sense the judgement, choose to experience it at a Soul level. Choose to be in the feeling body and tune into the person at that level. Journal again the response and become familiar with it. When you next encounter a situation, you will be somewhat ready to stay in your feeling body due to your familiar focus. This will help you overcome meeting them blindly and immediately using ego judgement to assess the situation, which would then have to be reversed. Prepare yourself, move forward and greet them at that higher level and see what evolves from that.

Virgil, if in an exchange I manage to come from my feeling body and truly express my Soul, will people recognise that?

It depends on what their reason is for entering into the encounter. How they perceive you is not important, this will just be another distraction, another aspect to analyse.

Why have I felt this week as if I've been controlled by other people?

There is an element to you Susie that believes a consequence of surrendering the ego self is that you, more or less, will be without personality and will move through life without conflict; this is not the case. It does not mean that you must mirror the existence of a monk, for example, who is in a perfect place of stillness, virtually egoless and without anger. Yet, this is one of your imagined concepts of how you will or should behave and respond if your life is influenced in a major way by the Soul self. This expectation is not very attractive to the ego, who considers it will be smothered by Soul (which would render it without purpose). Therefore, the ego is creating this focus around control because it sees a lack of control as a necessary outcome of surrender. It is of course another faulty perception or conclusion of the lessons to date and one than can be explored at a deeper level.

There will be occasions when coming from a Soul state of consciousness – from the feeling body – where you understand the situation so divinely, that you must respond to it at a level that would appear on the surface to be ego-based. For it may be that at a deeper level you recognise that perhaps the highest way to deal with the situation is to confront the ego and perhaps unravel some of the illusions therein. It is to disassociate yourself from any pre-conceived notions of what a spiritual being is and how they move through the world. If you feel that someone is seeking to control you, then go within and seek guidance as to why you are a co-creator of this experience.

I sense that you are thinking that you can deal with any situation that comes forward if you just feel it. This is part of a process, not an end in itself. You are still incarnate in flesh with all its challenges, including operating in the world of ego consciousness. In the future we will add to these lessons and teach you that it is also appropriate to take action. However, because of this groundwork, this action will not be a knee-jerk response. There will be occasions when it is necessary to even be aggressive.

Yes. The situation I was talking about was someone who likes to tell me how to lead my life, what to do, what to think, what to say – and it annoys me. It's very controlling and suffocating and what you've just said makes perfect sense. I'm very capable of making these decisions myself.

Indeed, that's right. It is to stand forward and project your inner self, your inner strength, in a way that is assertive, without putting the other person down.

Even to thank them?

It is not even necessary for this. If you do not feel gratitude then do not manufacture it via the ego. If however, you have learnt something from the situation, then generally you appreciate the learning. So thank yourself as well. It is to speak with the utmost integrity. **Spiritual integrity lies in responding to feeling and not in manufacturing the 'right' ego response.**

Now let's move on to your task for the week. In the first week I briefly touched on the concept of a feeling tone. Your feeling tone is what distinguishes you as unique in the realm of spirit, just as your ego personality distinguishes you as unique in the realm of matter. Therefore the concepts seem as polarities. From our new vantage point we understand that essentially there is no separation and they are part of the same whole. Do not question the existence of your feeling tone, trust that it is there. Do not box it into definitions or categories. As the ego speaks to you in words via the mental body, the feeling tone speaks to you in feelings, via the feeling body. Discerning your unique feeling tone, will assist you greatly in recognising the true messages of your Soul and will facilitate feeling body consciousness.

The Soul is infinitely capable of communication, but its messages become less when filtered through the limited concepts and language of the ego. Again, this is not because the ego is inferior, but because it is aligned to the mental body. Do not project limitation such as language on your Soul self or your experience will remain limited. We are seeking to open the channel of Soul communication by discerning your feeling tone. Feeling is the language of the Soul.

Infused within your feeling tone is all the wisdom of the Soul relevant to your highest potential in this life frame. It is not the Soul in its entirety, for it could not be contained within even the grandest earthly potential. This plane is limited in terms of the reality of Soul – which is limitless. You have heard references to your life's blue-print, paradigm or highest potential – well it is accessible here. Do not expect that your feeling tone is anything less than uplifting and wonderful or else you will not be focusing within the right vibration.

In seeking to discern your feeling tone a meditative state will assist. It is literally to still the self and feel. It is not about visualisation, which is limited. It is about sensing, discerning and experiencing. It is your own unique self so I cannot provide you with a tool to know it. It is the aspect of your greater self that I most frequently exchange with, as it is attuned specifically to this life frame and therefore relevant to the now you are experiencing. If you are undertaking this course then it is seeking communion and you are ready to use its wisdom wisely and not against yourself. Go forward with clear intention and allow it to come forward in a way that is uniquely your own.

Thank you very much Virgil.

Indeed it is my pleasure and I feel very excited for you in reaching this phase.

Be blessed.

Lesson Five

Discern your Feeling Tone.

CHAPTER 6
Discerning Your Feeling Tone

We approached this week's task of discerning our feeling tone with a degree of excitement. This time our positivity was not linked to expectation, but instead freedom and allowance. Individual experience of this truly personal aspect of self was, of course, unique and we were finally beginning to accept that there truly were no 'right' answers. Threaded through our contrasting experiences was a common essence, or sense of a greater, calmer and more profound aspect of self that was just below the surface. For a few, this feeling was pervasive. For others it was only an inkling, but we all had nurtured a sense of acceptance of feeling as a genuine reality. Significantly, we did not idealise the feeling tone via a judgement or expectation of inferiority versus superiority as we may have done previously, when comparing ego and Soul. Instead it was more of an acknowledgement and acceptance that all of us contained a great deal more than we were currently aware. The illusion of separation versus the notion of union became a tangible concept as we glimpsed the duality of both influences upon our present. Grounding the higher aspect of feeling into our daily lives seemed a distant goal, yet within those fleeting moments of discerning the feeling tone, we sensed so much possibility. It was an exciting time, but it was happening very gently and many of us still hoped for that powerful religious experience to obliterate any self doubt.

This chapter has limited theory so as to avoid enchanting the intellect any further at this point. We need to support our feeling awareness and concentrate on the task of bringing the feeling tone into our everyday lives. These new lessons continue to build on the old and it is important to remember this sense of ongoing growth and revealing. Do not discard the lessons (or tools, as Virgil often refers to them) that you have already been given. You must draw upon any, or all of them, to help clarify your inner - and therefore your outer - life. Remember to continue diligently with the journaling, for this will help clear the chatter and enable you to identify the source of any difficulties more efficiently than any amount of inner debating or sleepless nights.

To qualify the opening comment in this evening's channel, I should add that before commencing Susie and I were involved in lively discussions on spirituality in general. In particular, how this course was changing many of our long held assumptions and beliefs. We recounted much of the past theory and it showed us that we had really taken the new information on board and were working with it. We were still manifesting some resistance, but within that, excitement was building as we were starting to glimpse our lives moving ahead. Certainly we considered spirit was more present than before, so we concluded with some joy, that our focus seemed to be moving into higher awareness. As we now begin this new week, embrace all that you have learned about yourself so far, for you are amazing!

Sally...

(Virgil smiles broadly before speaking; it appears a particularly strong, high connection)

Good evening my friends.

Good evening Virgil.

It is a pleasure to be in this space with you all. The energy is much lighter despite the fact that there is a great deal occurring and massive energy movement at this time. Your preceding discussions have automatically moved the group vibration to a higher level and this enables us to connect much more easily. So I thank you.

No doubt you were listening to our discussions this evening, Virgil. Did you have any comments you wanted to make?

I do not wish to diminish in any way the nature of the discussions that occurred tonight, however I would at least like you to be aware of the level at which the discussions took place and then use this awareness to your advantage. It is grand that you have grounded the information via the ego intellect. The process in itself though will not take you to a place of feeling, which is our ultimate aim. Accept now that you have a level of completion in your ego thoughts and then let it all go. Do not, throughout the coming week, entertain your ego by playing in its realm, for you will not come closer to feeling from that vantage point. Continue to affirm that you choose to be in your feeling body. If you find you are confused by events that manifest in your lives, avoid trying to work them through the intellect in terms of applying the right or wrong answers. Allow that type of analysis to move on. Know other opportunities will come forward to facilitate the experience of feeling the essence of the situation. You are to refrain from recounting what could be construed as an opportunity missed, for there is no such thing.

Thank you, Virgil. I hear what you say but I noticed this week, that I had a whole lot of experiences occur that I kept missing the essence of what they meant in the moment. I felt sure I would have to write them down and then process them all at some later stage. I could only identify triggers and ego dramas in hindsight, so I felt like I kept missing all my opportunities for growth. Do all of these surface experiences lead to the same place within?

Indeed Susie.

So there are no missed opportunities.

No. Allow this learning to unfold in due course. Follow the natural and normal rhythm of evolution; do not try to control your process of becoming. Now, what has arisen as a result of the lesson given last week?

This week Virgil you had asked us to try to discern our own feeling tone. I ended up getting only words and essentially they were that - "I am spirit". It is as though I know on some level that this higher aspect is me, but I can't say that I always feel it. It was a particularly difficult exercise for me to keep out of my mind.

At this point, it is important only that you have a conscious awareness that your feeling tone exists. As you retrain your focus more, this aspect of self will become easier to recognise. Do not now use this outcome as a weapon against yourself to judge your seeming inability to connect with it. You are already connected. It is a matter now of recognition. Always remember that you are undertaking a **process** of returning your focus to its natural state. Accept that last week was your first step toward discerning the feeling tone and build upon that. Exercise your new skill in allowing thoughts to pass without judgement, but retain the awareness of same. When you feel drawn to participate, take some quiet time and continue to try to commune with the feeling tone. I assure you it will come when you are focusing in the right vibration.

Do not let the concept of discerning the feeling tone carry you away. You cannot **enforce** recognition; it is something that you will **allow** when the conditions are aligned. Accept that it is there and know that you are working towards communion. If you see this process as a destination in itself, then you will be working from ego and in order to participate it will try to make a connection through visualisation or mind control. Remove your expectation and do not be concerned, for you will know when you have established an exchange.

(Susie asks on behalf of Sally) Virgil, when I made attempts to discern my feeling tone, I found that I was in and out of a feeling state. I knew as I wavered between feeling and ego, that there was definitely something occurring. At the time I likened it to communion with a familiar - but at the same time ignored - aspect of self. It was difficult to abate the mind chatter.

You and Susie now have awareness, even if it is only intellectually, that the feeling tone is not foreign, but rather vaguely familiar. You can go forward in your attempts to connect with greater clarity, resolve, and a degree of comfort. You now have some common ground established – a foundation so start to build on that. Facilitate this by deliberately focusing more on that feeling of union rather than the feeling of separation you have been perpetuating. Focus on the Soul's reality of oneness, not by mind manipulation but by experiencing the true feeling generated by that union. You will gradually open to more insight. This insight, via feeling, will amount to an even stronger and more conscious recognition of your greater self.

So Virgil, when we feel that sense of a greater self, we just focus our attention there and allow the feeling to develop?

Indeed and accept whatever comes forward without judgement.

Okay, I look forward to being in that feeling space again.

Indeed. Now on to this week and of course we will bring in another layer of awareness. Intellectually you understand the concept of creating your own reality. You have been taught that no event or object exists that has not had its origin in Soul. I want you to now own this concept fully. **There is no physical event that occurs just for the sake of it or because of coincidence – there is always an underlying Soul purpose.** I want you to now move through the coming weeks with this awareness. Measure the events of your life as reflecting your self love or your lack of self love? Moreover, to ultimately take responsibility for what you are seeing reflected around you. This will take you further into creating the conditions necessary to allow discernment of the feeling tone.

Let me recap. We now understand that there is ultimately no difference between an ego hurt and a Soul hurt, but you are now able to readily identify their different forms of expression. You are capable of nurturing the ego and speaking to it with kindness and love. You may not choose to speak to it kindly on a daily basis, but you are certainly capable of it, so the choice is your own. It is time to take responsibility for those choices. You have analysed and critiqued the ego then made judgements about yourself for many years. It is time to put all that aside and treat yourself with kindness as an active choice. Following on from this internal perspective, we then expand this awareness to view all the physical reflections in our lives, knowing that they come directly from our source.

As you encounter the reality you are creating each day, do so now with a greater awareness. Treat your creations as direct messages from your source self. Are you reflecting love or fear in your creations? We will choose to be kind to ourselves and now start to take responsibility for those times where we choose otherwise. While you are comforting your ego through any difficult circumstances, you will ask for higher messages on how that situation can be healed. You do this not by entertaining mind chatter but by continuing to discern the feeling tone, thus allowing it to be grounded into your daily reality. Feel the messages coming forward; do not try to hear them. Please journal whatever comes to the surface without judgement in readiness for next week.

Sounds like this could be a big week Virgil!

Indeed my friends. It is an important week. It is time to introduce the concept of taking responsibility, which will be expanded on in subsequent lessons and is an absolute major step in this process. In taking responsibility one removes convenient, yet fatal errors contained in the intellectual rationalising and justifying of life's challenges. It delivers a real acceptance and knowing, that only you have control over your own reality. Responsibility for consciousness is a key to facilitating the state of grace necessary to experience the higher, lighter, and more loving aspect of your own spiritual environment. The only way to manifest the qualities of your higher self, is to be able to recognise it and others in any physical guise. You will facilitate recognition of your higher self in first acknowledging total responsibility for what you experience and to eventually choose only love. You will then have aligned your physical energy with that of your feeling tone and can create with grace. So this is the first phase in choosing to experience that higher reality which is overlaid upon your current experience at any rate. Which one will you choose? This week's focus of identifying whether your creations reflect love or fear is critical to moving forward. Look at your reflections carefully this week. As always, this process is experiential, so anything that comes forward is valid and is to be accepted without judgement. Feeling as ever is the key.

Be blessed.

Thank you Virgil.

Lesson Six

Are your reflections showing you love or fear?

CHAPTER 7

Your Reflections As Messages From Soul - Love or Fear?

Our enthusiasm of the previous week had waned as we progressed through the new lesson of closely looking at our reflections. All of us had managed to manifest significant problems in our physical environments or lives, and it was disappointing. Susie and others in later courses were physically sick; some so bad they were unable to attend the class. Some had to deal with sick children, or their own existing conditions became worse. Some were comfort eating, consuming more junk food than usual and feeling the worse for it. All of us were showing signs of stress in one or more areas of our lives and we were all finding it very uncomfortable.

Despite the fact that Virgil had instructed us to look at our physical creations only as reflections of our feeling choices, we overlayed this focus with a consuming attention to the events themselves. We saw this dual focus as contradictory, which inevitably gave rise to much confusion and therefore we didn't know what aspects of our week we should discuss with Virgil. Susie in particular was almost too embarrassed to begin the session, (her confusion is evident in her first question). She feared that if she related her week in terms of the physical environment she had manifested, instead of feeling, then she would be failing Virgil. We all agreed that our difficult circumstances were our own fault entirely and concluded that we just weren't capable of grounding the information in a meaningful way. In actual fact, it was the feelings behind these ego thoughts that were the key to accessing the source of our problems, yet we were simply unable to 'see the forest for the trees' during this phase.

In attempting to remain sourced in feeling, we didn't heed the messages manifesting all around us. Ignoring the ego's irrational stirrings ensured we could not possibly acknowledge the truth that was underneath them, seeking our attention, seeking healing. For example, our feelings of failure, of being unworthy to receive assistance, of not belonging, or of not being able to create a supportive reality; any of these could have taken us inward if we had just allowed it. Instead we considered that the very issues we should have been embracing were at best insignificant and at worst living proof of our ineptitude. Our response in identifying ourselves so completely as failures, also demonstrated that none of us had yet learned to be kind to our ego selves, as we turned our attack thoughts inward. No wonder we were manifesting trying circumstances!

In truth we were observing the outcomes of our inner resistance to the new beliefs Virgil had been gradually introducing into our awareness. It revealed again that we don't create with our surface conscious beliefs, for all of us had been so positive and yet had manifested difficulties. It was clear that we were still not aligned in feeling and were not engaging the ego and our creations as allies. Our ego self had learned well the new lessons of peace, yet we were seemingly creating from a source of chaos. We had again fallen into the trap of assuming our lack of success in manifesting positive reflections, was the source of our feelings of hopelessness, failure, and the like. In actual fact, these feelings were the source of our reflections. With our feelings of failure and unworthiness manifesting so brilliantly, we at least knew we were really good at creating our own realities.

Within all the trying physical circumstances however, there were genuine moments of inspiration that came from observing our reflections closely and owning them. There were many stories, mostly surrounding our most intimate relationships. Some participants recognised for the first time how they had actually set up and accommodated the perfect conditions to enable themselves to be hurt by their loved ones. They then observed how they immediately blamed others and their behaviour for their hurt feelings. Some noted how they enjoyed the attention of being a 'victim' and wondered why they were fond of being so self-absorbed. At times, some genuinely felt that they were outside of the events, almost like an observer. Others noted that what they consistently nagged their partners about were indeed their own shortcomings, traits that they had never before considered to be part of their own character at all. These were all small steps in the grand scheme of things, but they were the beginnings of our change in focus. We all noted feeling vulnerable in not being able to blame others for the way we were feeling, as we were so used to this behaviour. Sometimes looking in the 'spiritual mirror' can be difficult, but it is an essential aspect in this process of becoming. We must recognise and acknowledge who we are at this point in time, if we are ever going to allow our true self expression in this lifetime.

And so to Virgil's lesson for this week...

Sally...

(Even though The Channel had spent sufficient time in centering herself and clearing her mind chatter, Virgil came through in a more subdued way in keeping with our sombre mood. It was not long before we felt his love and grace touch us. As the lower energy lifted to make way for Virgil's presence, we were all grateful to be back once again within his wonderful vibration.)

Good evening my friends, and welcome to Lesson Seven.

Before we start Virgil, I'd like to raise something with you. Every week I'm having a bit of performance anxiety. I've been speaking to you for years about seemingly trivial things, which I know at the time were important, I feel like now we should be moving beyond that surface stuff. I come in each week and I don't know what experiences to bring up. I don't want to go back into that old space where I looked at every little thing and mulled it over for a meaning, because that's not what I want to focus on. I never know quite what to ask you.

Susie, you just need to discern the difference between an intellectual question, as it is exercise for the mind, versus a discussion that will help you get beneath a feeling, or inkling. One will help you to uncover something that is rising forth, seeking expression, clarification, even confirmation. The other will actually distract you further from true feeling. Discern for yourself what is truly important in your spiritual growth and what are ego distractions. You must learn to take care of your own ego; that is why we have spent so much energy learning its reality.

The sessions of the past that you speak of, were part of the process of coming to this now. Whilst you focus on them and look backwards in a negative or judgemental way, you are more or less creating the same in the future. You need to understand that all of this, including the past, is part of our grander evolution. To judge one aspect of this process as inferior is to say, for example, that the person who invented the candle was a simpleton because someone else was able to invent the light bulb – of course this is not the case. Focus less on what occurred in the past and more on what is occurring at the feeling level in the now and this will by its very nature guide you in the most appropriate direction.

Virgil, there's a part of me that feels a little bit self-indulgent if I come in and talk about myself.

It is this feeling that will deliver you should you follow it through. It is coming forward because you do not consider yourself worthy of my attention. It is an opportunity to work through the feelings and assert your worthiness. It is time for you to take responsibility for this tendency. It is a tool that the ego uses to hide the true nature of who you are; it is another game, not a real feeling, if this makes sense to you. Although it is convenient for you to hide behind this self depreciating persona, it is nothing more than an ego contrived barrier. This process has facilitated an unavoidable recognition of this faulty belief. Remember, you are now learning how to deal with these beliefs from a higher level, via the feeling tone. It should not surprise you that they have surfaced.

Thanks for that Virgil. I will ask you to comment on a dream I had this week then. Amid all the surface confusion, I had a strong feeling that it was a direct and positive message from my higher self. I was in my home, but there was a new section in it – a giant built-in closet with an annexe attached. It was impressive, yet as I looked around the shelves I noticed only a small section was for my use. The majority of space was taken up with my partner's clothes, baby clothes and clutter – it reminded me of an opportunity shop. I was unperturbed though and decided I was going to use most of the wardrobe for my things. I noticed a huge shelf filled with shoes and there was a beautiful white pair that I knew I hadn't worn yet because they were too big for me. I was going to just look at them, but eventually I tried them on and discovered that if I put the silver strap across the top then they fit perfectly. I was absolutely delighted. Would you like to comment?

Indeed. The dream was quite literal not in the physical symbols (although those that have seen your shoe collection might argue otherwise), but in the feelings that gave them life. You are discovering and exploring a part of yourself that is very precious, an aspect of consciousness that you know is there, but have to date been unable to connect with in a meaningful (conscious) way. You have a long held desire to be a truly spiritual example, yet you have simultaneously avoided actualising this desire into the physical due to intellectualising and judging circumstances, then ruling out specific outcomes. For example, in your dream you were initially not even going to try on the shoes as you knew they wouldn't fit. This is reflecting your tendency to predetermine outcomes based on your surface thoughts of not being good enough, or of being unsupported by the 'Universe'. As the process of embracing this precious aspect of self unfolds and you allow it into your life, then you will be in a position to wear the 'spiritual shoes', to fill the shoes you have always dreamt of. Of course, the shoes were not only already there, albeit 'tucked away in the closet' and hidden by 'op' shop clutter, but they actually 'fit' perfectly all along. The 'strap', which enables the perfect fit, is in fact the process of this course. Followed through, it will clear the ego clutter and be the means by which you make the connection to your feeling self and fulfil your spiritual dreams. No wonder you were delighted when they fit perfectly.

Thank you Virgil, it's been interesting how our life events and visions have been so closely aligned to the weekly lessons. You asked us to look at our mirrors this week which I found very enlightening. There is a significant person in my life that is, in my view, reluctant to change. With our new focus, instead of attacking this person as I usually do, I chose not to. I then realised that there is an aspect of me that really doesn't want to change and it really bothered me. It seems this aspect may be blocking my progress in this course.

There is certainly an aspect of you that you are unwilling to embrace that would create and delight in change. Your unwillingness to embrace this aspect stems from a belief that you are incapable of success in this reality. You therefore have a fear of moving forward and rather than face the fear where it is manifested physically, you conveniently project it on to others, so this is a valuable insight for you. When you chose not to attack, in other words not to project, you didn't 'off-load' the feeling on to someone else and were therefore left to sit with that emotion and own it. In doing so, it gave rise to the revelation regarding self and then offered the opportunity to transmute feeling to the other side of the coin. Within that other side, is someone who embraces change because they understand that this is the nature of the Soul. The person you are seeking to 'become' is not something that you are required to learn in the sense that you needed to learn to become a school teacher by training the mind in concepts and theories. All you need do is discover, accept, and integrate who you already are. This revelation has the potential to have an immediate and profound impact.

So what do I do when I am reflected back such revelations?

What you have learned this week is that you have choices. This is an example of where your source self is presenting, in a seemingly minor way, the denied aspects of self in the physical so you can take notice. Within any feeling there is choice. You can feel fear and lack, or with a clear focus of intent, you can feel the love and abundance of the other side of the universal coin, so to speak. When you experience pain and negativity, feel the feeling, but further, follow it through to the other side of the coin, to the ever present love. As you become further immersed in this process, it will become your natural approach to life. You will become increasingly receptive to love which will attract more and more of the same. Eventually, it will be your normal state to perceive the love around you and to perpetuate fear will result in an obvious reduction in vibration. In essence, love will become the feeling tone from which you meet this world of matter.

Now, I caution you again not to allow the ego to run away with this as an intellectual concept. This is the first phase of allowing a more intuitive focus and therefore being more in tune with the messages manifesting from the source self. You are to allow the feelings to emerge rather than rationalising them away using your faulty belief structures as the tool. At the same time, when you feel the 'other side of the coin', acknowledge the feeling and allow it to pass through you. In time it will pass through more quickly as you become better observers of your own reality and more easily identify and transmute your faulty perceptions.

So Virgil, I don't necessarily work towards feeling the love in that moment?

No. You need not name the emotion or work at anything. Choose to be in your feeling body without judgement and allow the feeling to expand. So if you are feeling fearful, don't allow the conscious mind to move it on to a state of love, for you will be manipulating from the realm of ego. Understand that feeling is the key; only your judgement makes the distinction between good and bad, fear and love. I am not saying that the mind does not have a role in this process, in fact its skills are especially valuable when used in conjunction with this process, particularly when you journal your experiences.

In the past, many have labelled what I refer to as the source self or feeling tone, as the higher self. I do not use this higher self term freely because of the now entrenched notions this holds for you. Many have sought to commune with their higher self conversationally, assuming there are verbal messages to be heard. This leads to confusion and an utter lack of knowing as to which of the many voices communicating in words is the one of love. An ego, intimately trained in the 'rules' of spirituality can easily manipulate any situation so that a course of action could appear at once both loving and fearful, depending on your perspective and justifications. The ego's belief system is coloured and framed in fear, but it has learned and rehearsed the language of love. Trying to access the higher self, or feeling tone, through language and precepts of the conscious mind and ego, will eventually become very confusing, as they are simply not compatible.

We need to first change these precepts to align with the feeling tone so both are coming from the same reference point of love. Then, your ability to bring heaven on Earth will be boundless. The higher self, or what I will refer to hereon as the feeling tone, is a subtle body and is simply incapable of wielding punishment or understanding 'logic' that is based in fear. **It is you – and communicates in feelings via the feeling body.** It gently caresses you if you are receptive to it. If you are not open, then at its most forceful, it will gently nudge you into wakefulness. Just as I am able to access this reality more effectively through an open channel, the same applies to the feeling tone. If there is an open willingness to accept and experience life and reality for what it is, irrespective of how the ego judges it, then you will move through life with love, for you are open to receive this higher vibration. This is the key to experiencing more of your feeling tone.

It sounds wonderful, but I've not gone beyond the level of frustration.

You've not gone beyond this level at this point because you are still intellectualising the feelings, even though at some level you do not think this is the case. You are very excellent at observing your conscious mind. It has been a necessary aspect of this process for all the reasons we have discussed in the previous weeks. However, you are now standing at that reference point of ego self-awareness and you need to accept the feelings as they arise – without judgement – which is a characteristic of ego. Life is about flux and change and what we are experiencing in this now, is all we are able to offer ourselves. Accept that, but keep moving forward.

You must learn to hold your light in this reality. To do that one must experience whatever comes forward without judgement. You will then begin to understand that many of your subtle decisions, judged by the ego as insignificant or fearful, are in fact still messages from your feeling tone, but communicated at a level that you would accept. Embrace the concept of 'is-ness', i.e. what you are experiencing, just 'is'. Know that every experience in the now can drive you forward, rather than judging every experience in hindsight. Embrace life with open arms and an open heart and you will find the feeling tone will contribute at a much higher vibration and it will therefore be the level at which you meet the world. Alternatively, you can choose to continue to judge and categorise your life and remain closed, which will necessitate the feeling tone communicating at a very low level, which when intellectualised, will be judged as negative.

I've noticed this week that I'm so tired of thinking. I don't know anything anymore. The way in which I've always processed and dealt with experiences no longer works for me.

Susie, this is an excellent sign for you. One of The Channel's favourite lines from a book she once read was that, 'not knowing is the key to knowing'. Congratulations on being in that state of unknowing, that reference point we were aiming for. The past has been undone. Now to restore the natural balance. When you get to the point where you don't understand, the ego self is acknowledging that it is trying to do too much.

In the past you have been able to intellectualise your experiences and arrive at a logical explanation that seems convincing from the highly trained ego. However, the principles that you draw on from your past spiritual learnings, are rudimentary and correct in only a very general sense, as the individual expression of Soul is vastly different. For example, money may not be an issue for me in this lifetime, but it does not follow that I have necessarily mastered abundance. I may have profound barriers to creating abundance in love or whatever the case is. The physical manifestation of issues can be vastly different, yet reflect the same underlying emotional cause. Furthermore, our own ego lens will cloud the picture further, so we are really interpreting the physical in terms of our own ego reality, which is fraught with limitation and judgement.

Each of life's experiences needs to be interpreted from the higher perspective of Soul consciousness in conjunction with the frame of reference of this reality that one has manifested since childhood. Very rarely in knowing someone's surface personality self, can you honestly purport to know their Soul. It is good that you are faced with an unknowing. This ability you have fostered, which allows you to interpret yours and others issues, has been a badge of honour in the past, which you don't necessarily want to surrender. You have to allow that to pass into the past in order to make way for your truer talents to emerge. This is one of the ego's principal reasons for resisting the change you have spoken of, so you need to placate its concerns kindly. For example, you have asked in the past whether your willingness to assist others by using your skill was a way to build up your ego. I have said to you, and now reiterate, that this was not the case. At that time and in that phase it was done with the utmost integrity. You were often in a higher state of consciousness during those times and were able bring together the physical and elements of the spiritual. Do not now judge your past in terms of the now. We are at another phase whereby it is not appropriate to intellectualise your own or others' processes and your ego is protesting. Your challenge at this point, is whether you believe and can feel there is a larger aspect that is much wiser than the ego.

I believe it Virgil. So if people continue to ask me for assistance in interpreting their experiences, your advice to me would be to tell them to go within and ask themselves?

My advice would be to link with your feeling body, go within and ask yourself. You have the ability to assist others in reaching their own conclusions by helping them access their own higher guidance, just as I am able to assist you in this way. Understand that their issues are not going to be yours. It will be relatively easy for you to reconcile the old with the new and make the transition.

What you have done in the past - learned through books and study groups - is adapted a vast amount of information and applied it to different circumstances. You then naturally provide solutions based on this learning, when you are merely reiterating another teacher's or author's words. That was perfect at that time as its truest purpose was to share information, which is a great service in the higher plan. Now, however, we are moving through another transitional phase. We are seeking direct contact with the source self via the feeling body, which can deliver a unique experience for each person. Also understand that as people come to you with problems, your immediate reaction is often a gift from them to you. It is almost as though they would come to you humbly and offer you a gift if you can help them sort this out. So, for example, if your immediate reaction was judgemental, then there is a reflection there for you to look at as well.

So to ask what it is mirroring in me?

Indeed, insofar as the feeling is concerned, not their physical dilemma. There is always a fair exchange, so in offering your skill there will be a gem in there for you too, and it may appear quite insignificant in ego terms. For example, it may only confirm that you are beyond that level of questioning, so it may attest your own growth. I provide a positive example because I do not want you to intellectualise this advice and turn it against yourself by always seeking a negative reflection. Conversely, if your initial feeling was say, one of attack, then there will be something there for you to look at, for as we know, unrecognised feelings would be at the source of any such attack.

Can you provide an insight as to why I was physically ill this week?

Last week everything was very exciting as we moved further into discerning the feeling tone and sought to view our creations as direct messages from the source self. Now you can see that this positive, nurturing focus has actually manifested resistance in the physical environment. This occurs because the new mental affirmation or focus is opposing your current, accepted and mostly unconscious inner beliefs. This is inevitable. You were able to ascertain that the resistance prevailed at a more subtle level, even so physical illness developed. You have previously moved through this reality with the adage of mind over matter, yet it is now time to refine our focus to **spirit over matter.** Until now, the self received all recognition and validation based on its ability to control matter or the environment. Now its role appears weakened.

Recognise that there are two perceptions of reality co-existing within the one physical being. It cannot continue – a clear defined choice has to be made. We either agree that we are magnificent creators of our own reality one hundred per cent of the time and take responsibility for everything that occurs in our life, or we believe we are bodies and things happen to us. A foot in each camp will ensure difficulties arise as evidence of your fluctuating focus. If we want to move through life with love, and you have affirmed this, then the debris has to be cleared. This was manifested in the purging illness. Such illness keeps you quiet physically and exposes your vulnerability, which is a favourable condition to facilitate the clearing of the debris of past beliefs.

I would say to continue to affirm your preference for love, but to add that I allow myself to be guided, and then open up to this wisdom. This will keep the focus and attention where it should be, as opposed to the illness in the body. Then ask to be taken on a visual journey to communicate the essence of what is occurring, so it can be framed in a way that is uniquely your own and can be understood at an ego level. I have spoken before of the limitations of visualisation as a tool to commune with the Soul. However, the objective of this visualisation is to speak gently to and nurture the ego, therefore this visualisation can be very effective. The ego is in fear for it doesn't want to lose its control. Feeling, derived directly from the feeling tone, converted to visualisation, is an effective way in which the ego can understand messages from within, while also maintaining an important purpose in the process. The ability to nurture oneself at this level has to be flawless if we are going to bring the ego into the fold, so to speak.

Thank you, Virgil. Would you like to give us our focus for this week?

Indeed. It is to understand that feeling is just feeling. I haven't had to tell anybody to expand and allow joyful feelings because this is judged as a preferred or natural state of being. In fact feeling – period – is your natural state of being, so that includes allowing the so-called 'negative' feelings to come forward as well. It is the suppression of feeling that is unnatural, and negativity has its basis only in judgement. Now we are looking to embrace this reality with more openness and to affirm to feel whatever comes forward, without judgement.

Understand that we now need to coach ourselves into fully experiencing the love energy as well. To recognise when it comes forward and allow yourself to expand and grow and absolutely glow with that energy. Affirm to experience your feeling tone at the highest vibration. Avoid listening for a voice or a message, but just sit in the glow of the love energy that you are feeling. Once you have experienced the expansion of your own energy, you will be more readily able to discern the purpose of events and objects that influence your life, regardless of their physical guises. The impact of such awareness will be significant.

Often I find the messages come through later when I reflect on my experiences.

This is usually the way one experiences the feeling tone in these early stages. Experience the feeling as fully as possible, without judgement, then when the event has passed you can look at that situation and take action according to a higher perspective. This is how you learn to grow through love rather than pain. Once it gets to the point where you are begging your inner self for messages, then you are in a state that is hardly conducive to experiencing the subtle energy of feeling body awareness. It will seek you out in order to provide you with these messages at a time when you are most receptive to feel them. The problem is, because we have not consciously chosen to pay any attention to love energy we do not use this as a yardstick, or a tool to move forward. Instead what we have done is measured our spiritual growth by the pain and suffering we felt. It is in those times we turn to spirit. We want to change that pattern and seek spirit communion in the loving times as well. With practice, you will experience the feeling in the moment and readily understand the message being conveyed, which enables you to respond in a higher manner. It will then be unnecessary for the feeling tone to communicate via the ego through the lower vibration of fear and discomfort.

That's very exciting.

Indeed. Once the feeling tone becomes more integrated your vibration rises and you become more attuned to the messages coming forward. It is through this process that you will eventually understand and directly experience the true nature of your Soul. This is something that we can do with purpose and intention, when we choose to allow it. Your feeling tone can communicate with you at any time and at any level in this physical environment. It will do so subtly through the feeling body, or obviously in the physical via the ego. Its communication encompasses a full polarity of vibration and with all its potential physical manifestations. Despite this, whatever the physical cloak, it will always be sourced from love.

I have so enjoyed speaking with you Virgil.

As I have enjoyed speaking with you as usual. I'm very pleased with the progress each of you is making. You need to understand that all of your experience is valid and part of the process of unravelling and rediscovering your true loving self.

Thank you. I look forward to speaking with you next week.

I look forward with great anticipation to our next meeting.

Be blessed.

Lesson Seven

Feeling is just feeling – your natural state.

CHAPTER 8
Red Wolf: An Enlightening Chapter

By this stage of the course we were beginning to tire of looking at our lives, since most of the time we were manifesting difficulties. Our previous lesson had been to experience the totality of our feelings without judgement, to glow in the light of love, and to allow the expression of fear, as the unique feelings emerged. Despite our conscious efforts in non-judgement, it became clear that we still held a preference for the joyful feelings and tried to manifest these as a priority. Significantly, for the most part, we endured another week of manifesting the opposite of our preference and intention.

While the physical circumstances that manifested for each person were varied, all were following a familiar individual pattern. For instance, Susie's despised rash maintained a constant burning presence under the surface of her skin, and threatened to become full blown at any minute. My relationship, which had been showing signs of strain for sometime, became increasingly distant. Everyone continued to show signs of stress – both physically and emotionally. It seemed nothing had really changed despite all that we had learned over the previous weeks. What was a feeling of frustration, festered into a genuine fear that we were forever destined to struggle with our issues, as they painfully manifested to dominate our physical lives.

In the hours before tonight's session, Susie and I half-heartedly played with our oracles; drawing cards and runes, trying in a vain effort to determine our immediate future. It was all approached unenthusiastically, for deep down, we both knew that only we could make our destiny. We continued hoping that somehow everything would just work out for the best. Devoid of any responsibility and feeling let down by the course and therefore Spirit, we were ready to demand answers to our problems from Virgil. We were therefore completely taken aback when he did not connect with us. Instead one of my other guides, who I usually channelled alone through automatic writing and not in a group discussion, unexpectedly came though. The guide is known as Red Wolf.

Red Wolf is a wonderfully peaceful and calm energy. As his name suggests, he takes the form of a Native American Indian following his one and only Earth existence. He lived in a time that was pre-European contact and has a unique view of life on this planet that encompasses a deep and unassailable connection to Earth and all things upon her. Many times, during the channel, he could not understand our questions because to do so would require a concept of separation from nature, which is something he hasn't ever experienced and could not relate to. I have always loved to channel Red Wolf because of this aspect alone. While I was one with him as we channelled, I could feel his confusion at our state of Earth separation and his love and deep respect for this wonderful planet that has become his speciality in spirit.

I have left the text of the channel largely unedited in an effort to allow the essence of the guide to come through, despite the apparent awkwardness in his style. Remembering that as a conscious channel my voice remains the same, yet we knew from the outset that this was not Virgil. Not only were his usual confidence and trademark greetings absent, but the aura and energy in the room was clearly different. Red Wolf is somewhat reserved and I could feel Virgil helping us connect and get started which for me, during that period, was the most difficult time in channelling. Obviously Virgil needed to touch us at another level and drew on the support of other guides to assist.

This chapter of the book is what you might refer to as an interval or rest period. It is an ideal time to just be in your life and simply allow all that you have learned so far to settle and ground. Be kind to yourself and indulge in positive behaviours that bring you peace or contentment. Readers are urged to continue to work this week with the previous lesson of embracing all feeling without judgement, but do so in conjunction with Red Wolf's instruction. Enjoy this change of pace and take a well earned break to allow everything to date become even more integrated with the help of Red Wolf's wisdom.

The channel begins... (The connection was obviously difficult this evening).

My posture, facial expressions and general confidence were clearly different. My concentration was broken several times and I would have given up for the night except for the encouragement of Susie. The energy was gentle and seemed as though it was waiting for an invitation to join the group. Throughout all initial attempts, it was too gentle to enable me to connect with any measure of confidence and recognition of it being 'real' – it was very frustrating. Intuitively, Susie knew that there was a definite energy present and having sat in Virgil's space for many years she was quite sure it wasn't him. She also sensed that I was unable to get started and knew it only came down to a lack of confidence. This could be a major barrier for me in taking control of the channelling process. Rightly so, Susie thought that perhaps I was experiencing difficulty in recognising the energy. With this in mind and knowing that I needed to be assisted in bringing in new guides, Susie broke the stalemate by initiating conversation. Many years of holding the space for me, under many varied and sometimes trying circumstances, has shown her that I will generally answer any direct questions. This will move energy, which then allows the guide to enter more so that I can experience the presence with greater clarity. Susie had an image in her mind of a man with a beard, and in an effort to get the energy moving used that to break the ice.

Sally...

Hello and welcome. My name is Susie. Are you a bearded energy?

No. Red Wolf is with you.

Thank you for joining us tonight Red Wolf. It is a lovely surprise. We have been drawing oracles this evening, so could we start off by getting some insight into the coming times and what might be in store for us?

While I am not able to assist on a personal level in the way that your oracles have, I will provide an insight into the energy that is coming forward that will have a unique effect for every individual on this planet. The main focus, from where my speciality lies, is in the awakening of the Earth's spirit and the reconnection of this through the human beings. The interconnection of all things upon this planet and the awakening and realisation of same (are stirring). This is one of the facets that will herald the new age, whereby for some this is a requirement of the new. The energies will become more pronounced and more obvious as the nature spirits awaken. They presently sit just beyond this dimension and as your energy vibration rises en masse, there will be a greater ability to communicate with them. Therefore, the living soul nature of this planet will come more to the fore.

Red Wolf, are you talking about the divas?

Yes... the divas of all kingdoms that are presently overlayed upon this reality and the keepers of the nature spirits. These things will become more noticeable via feeling them. I am not saying that people will see fairies in the garden, rather there will be a soul connection. Recognised and honoured, this connection will positively manifest physically, with many people becoming more concerned with their natural environment. The essence of this energy is touching every living thing, including the souls of human beings. Know that this is the current natural energy touching the Earth. To abuse the environment is to go against the natural rhythm of this age. If you take action that contradicts this energy, and therefore block it, then it will manifest the opposite polarity into the physical, as is the nature of this reality.

Red Wolf, one of the cards I drew tonight was the Goddess of Crystals, which was representative of Gaia. Was this my hint to commune with Earth at a greater level?

You require a connection with the Earth Mother to help awaken your feeling body so that your cycle is in tune with hers, since all creation is part of the greater whole. You also need this awareness to help ground your feeling body into the physical so that it is not a foreign aspect, but one that is truly walking with you on your life's pathway. So yes, to be more in tune with Earth is a natural phase of this process. This is why I have been permitted to practise my channelling skills and come through at this time – to share my speciality and express my expertise; which is the awakening of the Earth's feeling body, and to help ground it in some way.

Are you saying that all of us should just be present in nature?

I suggest you act as a catalyst to assist in taking our understanding of nature beyond its current level. We are seeking to ground a feeling of respectfulness where one would treat nature in all its manifestations as one would treat another beloved human soul. To learn via feeling, rather than intellect, that

Earth and nature represent part of the greater soul of all humanity in this unique reality. To further incorporate via feeling, recognition that all is one energy, as opposed to the current hierarchical separation of different kingdoms and creeds. This is a challenge, for the human race that is yet to master the global thought form of one humanity. As you would understand there are many that will be incapable of this step forward, fortunately many will be capable. At any rate, inclusion of all things is necessary in order to progress to a higher dimensional view of the world – to know via feeling that all things are part of the greater soul that is the God self – if you can understand this.

Yes.

It is to commune at a deeper level, rather than at a respectful distance, or seeing nature as a living element that is quite separate to oneself. It is to understand that the energy of you and that of nature does not just cease at the boundaries of your respective physical vehicles. To approach your time in nature from the level of energy exchange, which could include the sharing of knowledge, healing or any other exchange that is agreed to. In communicating at this level we facilitate the intellect taking a lesser role, which of course assists your own individual goals at this time. In other words, nature will help you connect at a greater level to your own feeling body as this is the only way in which you will communicate with the Earth and the nature beings.

In the past you have had some experience with energy exchange in nature, where you may have experienced a certain level of give and take and therefore fulfilment within the process. We are looking now to communicate at a deeper level. This can be transmuted into genuine knowledge in the larger Earth Soul in this life frame, as opposed to a mere energy exchange. It is to now communicate at a deeper level, via linking the feeling bodies. This will be a part of the process of experiencing your feeling tone. It is through this process of experiencing the nature divas that will assist you on the road to your own Soul self. This focuses and refines the pathway to the feeling body, for feeling is your common ground or 'language' with nature. Once the pathway to the feeling body is very well worn and obvious, then you will be experiencing the world of matter in a vastly different manner. The guide, Virgil, has allowed me through in the hope that this will offer some of you an alternative focus to help you access your own feeling body. It is a task that should remove the emphasis away from the intellect.

Wow. I don't know what to ask. I want to keep discussing the topic but the level of connection you speak of is so foreign to me. I have no idea how to connect with nature other than with the intention.

(Quite clearly the connection began to strengthen here. The Channel's relaxed posture became erect and she became more animated in both facial gestures and hand movements. A familiar and very powerful energy was now present and it was obvious that Virgil was influencing, to a large extent, what was said from here. It began at the end of the previous paragraph and is evident when the text is re-read given the different styles of speech. The Channel reported a definitive switch in focus, and although she still felt sure she was sitting in the energy of Red Wolf, she noticed for the first time that Virgil was present (and had been all along). She likened the sensation to Virgil stepping out from behind a curtain. He was assisting both parties, but as always was ever ready to add his opinion when necessary. Red Wolf integrated Virgil's advice into the material easily and effortlessly (while all the while maintaining his own integrity, identity, and unique perspective).

Your intention is critical to the process and you are put on notice that you should now commence a daily connection with some form of natural energy. By 'natural' I mean the Earth Mother – a plant or a rock, for example. Whatever nature you select, it must have a grounding in the Earth Mother, for it will emit energy that contains an instinctual knowledge of the flows, the flux, and change of the seasons; the Earth's feeling body. Leave the domesticated pets for the time being from this exercise, as many are far more in tune with your human rhythms rather than that of the Earth's. Just practise the connection with a view to experiencing the energy at feeling level and ensure recognition of nature becomes part of a daily habitual routine.

It is important that the **intellectual** self is well and truly removed from this process. Can you see what the guide Virgil is trying to achieve here? You now have a task for the next week which is quite different from the lessons he has given in the past. Your intention should be to commune in your utmost integrity and focus on the desire of being a clear channel for the Earth Spirits. This provides an incentive outside of yourself to remove the intellect from the equation, and gives you a break from your constant self-analysis. Done with diligence, this exercise has the potential to blaze a trail through to the feeling body - to enable you to more readily distinguish its presence in your daily lives.

In time, people will come to know that the only way to self-realisation is through the respect and honouring of all that they are, which is so much more than their physical vehicle and personality self. If they understand that all they perceive both physically and psychologically is a reflection of the inner self, then eventually they must treat these reflections with love. Respect and inclusion will therefore replace abuse and separation. The planet may learn to evolve in a gentle, loving way. Although this may sound very basic, the road to evolution is only hard for the limited ego. It was never meant to be difficult. The key is in recognising all that you are and - via feeling - accepting and honouring every aspect.

That sounds so beautiful and I look forward to beginning my communion. It's funny: I feel like in the past year or so I've really lost touch with Mother Earth. I used to be much more relaxed and enjoy her but the stresses of daily life have gotten on top of me. As you speak now I've realised how much I want to get back into just being at peace – it sounds so wonderful. How did we lose our connection with nature?

In my life time I experienced oneness with this planet. I therefore have no concept of the separation from nature that you experience. Consequently, I am unable to heal separation in others; I have no reference point or common ground. That is why I am a...'guest speaker', and not the author of this course in self-awareness, you are undertaking. My love and energy is with you all however.

Thank you.

I have further information that is being relayed directly from the guide Virgil for you. The oracles that you have played with tonight have been viewed by your grand teacher as almost a recess or a playtime for you both and were meant to enable you to talk and experience lightness. However, they have no larger bearing on your immediate future other than conveying that growth is imminent. This is what you would have understood at any rate. It is not to pre-empt the course outcomes. It is not to create the future before it occurs. It is an important part of your development that if you choose to use oracles then you do so with play and with abandonment. Do not focus on using them as signposts, that seem to urge you in a particular direction. The essence of this course is to facilitate your ability to create in the moment, to avoid creating the future before it arrives, and to cease to repeat the past by constantly energising it. Understand that your power is in this present and misusing oracles will only cause you to speculate about future events and to perhaps predetermine them, or perhaps ignore present opportunities that seemingly don't fit. In time, through feeling, you will know the essence of the challenges that are manifesting and recognise them in the moment, regardless of their form. You must simply choose to be in your feeling body in the moment and that is where your focus will be.

Thank you. What a relief. I've just decided I'm not going to photocopy any of the oracles' messages as I had planned, which is a good thing, as they were all negative anyway.

This is good to hear. You can say that you had a 'break from the course' which is a much improved pastime, compared to some of your activities of the past. (The room laughs heartedly). If this is what you do for some light pleasure, then this is fine. However understand that this does not serve your growth if you choose to study, respond and tackle the oracles. Observe your feelings each day and respond to those. Affirm your willingness to grow and your willingness to be in your feeling body – and you will grow.

Thank you. That's excellent advice.

I am most grateful for the opportunity that I have had this evening to bring through my forte, if you like. I thank you for your patience in the time that it took us to connect for I had difficulty in identifying myself through the layers, especially when the expectation was for the guide, Virgil. I wish you well and I hope that we will speak in the near future.

Likewise. Thank you very much Red Wolf.

Lesson Seven

Feeling is just feeling – your natural state.

In conjunction with...

Lesson Eight

An ongoing commitment to daily connection with nature.

CHAPTER 9
Feeling Is Just Feeling

We all enjoyed the change of pace that the Red Wolf channel provided, especially the sense of respite from the constant self-analysis. Everyone had spent some time in nature. For many it was a joy, and for others it was a chore. Some found it difficult to find the time, generally it was those people who expected instant results. For those able to undertake the exercise without expectation, it was just a pleasure to be outdoors experiencing the natural environment.

The importance of Red Wolf's message should not be underestimated going forward. The Earth and all the natural beings that dwell upon her are an essential reflection of our own natural humanity. We must always remember that we are, of course, sourced from spirit; in this now we are consciously and willingly incarnate in flesh. This human body is part of a vast physical manifestation of beings that also have their source in spirit. They are therefore co-creators of this mass dream and we must honour and respect their role and identity within it. This course is designed to bring you back to full awareness of your own uniqueness, which extends far beyond the flesh we call 'me'. The daily contact and connection with nature will facilitate this knowing of self that exists beyond the body and is consequently something that will greatly assist you.

In the first course following Red Wolf's channel, I did not appreciate the significance of his message. My time in nature was sporadic at best and was usually done in times of deep confusion during the course, my life and my relationship. During these periods, I found being in nature brought to the fore my deepest feelings in a way that could not be denied. This was especially helpful for a person in deep denial of feeling, yet having no conscious recognition of my state. Nature gave me a chance to 'be' and allow my true inner messages to emerge. I didn't receive any great insights of a rational or religious nature as I was hoping. At the time I was disappointed. More than anything, this expectation unrealised, was the reason I was not diligent in connecting daily.

Despite my lack of tangible success in nature, I would somehow find the resolve to keep moving forward, as it facilitated the acknowledgement of my deep faith in Virgil as a guide and teacher. This in turn inspired me to keep trying to ground his wisdom in my life. In hindsight, I can now appreciate how much more valuable this feeling of resolve is when compared to what I was seeking - a message or spiritual intervention urging me to take some form of 'right' action. On my own, I didn't have a clue where to turn next. I was still seeking the answer to myself by looking outside for explanation.

I encourage you to continue a daily communion with the natural environment. Notwithstanding the simple pleasure in being outdoors, immersion in nature during times of ego confusion is a fantastic way to release the pressure valve and allow some peace to enter. A walk in the park, sitting by the beach or a lake, swimming in the ocean, simply leaning on an old tree, or placing my palms on the earth have all helped me shake off my destructive thoughts. Always remember to exchange energy with love. If you have been able to discard some negative chatter, remember to do so within a frame work of gratitude coupled with the intention that it will transmute via nature into positive energy. As your connection grows you may find, as I and others have, that you automatically try to walk lightly upon the Earth as an active choice. Some of us have looked at what pollutants we use in our homes and sought benign alternatives. We have considered what we buy and how we dispose of our waste. As your connection with the Earth strengthens, do not be afraid to show it – at this time she needs all the help she can get.

To the channel. Virgil joins us again this week. It is as if there has been no break at all. We moved directly into debriefing the lesson from Chapter Seven, that 'feeling is just feeling'. It's fair to say that none of us understood the importance of that lesson initially, but in the time after, its influence became significant as our inner awareness expanded.

During this early phase, we were still very engrossed in our preference for positive feelings, entrenched by our belief that if we were truly spiritual people, then only positive circumstances would manifest. Therefore again this week, we all felt for the most part as though we had missed the point and failed. Susie unwittingly managed to overcome a direct test of feeling consciousness, via manifesting a long held fear during a significant fire event. Others felt more acutely their negative feelings and in all cases failed to pass them through as just feeling, but rather judged and intellectualised the surface manifestations that triggered them. This was not surprising, to coin a cliché - old habits die hard.

As in previous weeks, there was no best outcome for the lesson, merely an opportunity to work with and ground a new notion, that over time will be added to. It should be obvious to you by now that although we thought we were failing each week, in actual fact there was no measure of success or failure outside of our own inner judgements and turmoil. If you feel a measure of helplessness, or perhaps believe that not much is moving, or that you are failing – please keep going. All will be revealed in good time, and the 'wow' factor will definitely emerge. Good luck and now over to Virgil...

Sally...

Good evening my friends and welcome to Lesson Nine.

Thank you for coming through this evening, Virgil. It's great to have you back.

(Grins broadly) It is my pleasure as always.

Virgil, my task over the past two weeks was to acknowledge that feeling is just feeling, as our natural state. Basically I have no idea what you mean other than when things 'happen' in my life they make me 'feel' a certain way. Is that what you are talking about?

I am pleased in one way that you 'have no idea' what is meant by feeling is just feeling, for it is not a state that can be explained, as it is a state that must be known – or experienced. We are trying to remove the notion of feeling in your life, as something to be judged and critiqued by the ego as positive or negative. It is this tendency that leads you to cower from or avoid certain aspects of feeling, thus requiring them to manifest physically as objects and events to get your attention. I required you to allow feeling – no matter what – to allow your true self expression. You only need to allow connection to source, not create it. Feeling is the manner in which the Soul self communicates with you, it is therefore the basis of your very foundation and must be acknowledged as such. Feeling your true self via the physical and emotional bodies is how you come to know your divinity in flesh, how the notion of Soul becomes reality. Feeling is just feeling, Soul is just Soul, eternity is just eternity. These things cannot be explained via the limited concepts of ego and must therefore be experienced in the moment and acknowledged by you. You currently ignore or suppress feelings (Soul communication) that your ego regards as unsavoury, too difficult, or not real. You are therefore perpetuating an unreal, unnatural environment from which your reality must spring. The exercise was an attempt at removing judgement from the manner in which your Soul communicates – i.e. in feeling.

Now understand that events do not 'happen' and make you 'feel' a certain way. You feel a certain way, are incapable of acknowledging or accepting it and therefore create an event or object to trigger the feeling, not as gentle Soul communication, but instead as ego emotion. Nonetheless, the block of feeling is temporarily cleared, and if you have grounded the episode as your own creation, then perhaps you have identified where you are not reflecting your highest potential, or Soul's blueprint, and can then take necessary steps to rectify. **When you consider the lesson 'feeling is just feeling', know that you are being called to experience the feelings associated with any moment as the priority, while relegating the physical situation as merely the outcome.**

To some degree, all of you held preference for 'happy' feelings and moreover assumed that this would be a natural outcome of working with the lesson. When negativity arose, it was used as another opportunity to affirm your inability to assimilate the new lessons - as opposed to an opportunity to commune with the natural guidance of the inner self. That is fine, however, for on more than one occasion I have indicated that this course is a process of becoming. **'Feeling is just feeling' will be something you will need to hold in your mind forever more.** Should you forget, the ego will automatically try to categorise your existence in terms of its basis of polarity.

Our friend Red Wolf was brought into the course to provide you with a way in which to aid the process of feeling your life. When things get too much for you, where you find yourself creating situations that you know are a result of an avoidance of feeling in the first instance. Where, despite your best efforts, you remain immersed in the physical dramas, the judgement of right and wrong, good and bad, valour and cowardice, virtue and sin. In these moments, restore some sanity by venturing into nature. The Earth is undergoing these exact paradigm shifts and her energy will align with your own if you seek it, potentially giving you an impetus to push on through the seemingly insurmountable ego assertions and help you to feel clearly. This is an important phase of your journey. If you ask - 'How do I know when I am in feeling?', then you are really asking, 'How do I know I am a Soul?' Feeling is your natural state; it is not an outcome of ego existence. How do you know you are a Soul? **Soul is just Soul, it is who you are.**

Wow. Yes, I can see that now Virgil. When I considered the lesson each day, I did so with the expectation and intention for positive things to happen. Immediately following our session with Red Wolf the feelings were very light and fluffy and it was really lovely to experience that. Then I managed to manifest one of my biggest fears, which is fire. My ego plays a lot of games to do with fire; whenever I leave the house I'm plagued with concerns that I've left appliances on that will lead to the house burning down. My work place, which happens to be my brother's office, caught fire and a huge amount of fear rose up. It was after hours, so I knew my colleagues would be safe. I just sat there breathing through the fear. I had to sit for probably half an hour. The outcome was fine; it was quite a miracle in fact as the office survived with only water damage, though the building upstairs was burnt to the shell. When I was a child I was in a house fire where part of our house burnt down, so you could say that this fear has been prevalent in me for many years. It seemed very timely for such fears to be triggered given our focus of feeling is just feeling. I wonder whether you could comment on that.

Indeed this has been a great opportunity to use your new skills in relation to, holding your light while all around you is chaos. We would reframe that statement to read – learning to experience and respond to your Soul communication, amidst the chaos of ego consciousness. You were given the opportunity to meet a real, surface, ego fear head on and in that moment had to decide how you were going to deal with the situation. You could have easily pushed all that you have learned aside and reverted to ego panic. Instead you chose to practise your new skills and rather than focus on the physical events, felt the emotions that were emerging. You will never create a situation that is outside your abilities to handle – you do however have choices in how you respond in the moment.

It was a substantial test, in your terms, of all that you have been working on and your response was a measure of your success. If you had allowed the ego to run amok it would have immediately associated the 'now' fire events to those of your past, and automatically degenerated the situation, into one of complete tragedy. This was shown to you in your father's reaction of total panic, during the recent fire, and was why you were able to show him empathy. This reaction of relating past fire dramas to the present, which in feeling actually recreates it, would have been yours, if you had ignored your new insights. Understand that I am not asserting that your response influenced today's positive physical outcome. What I am saying, is that your ego would have felt the intense panic and dread associated with the past, in the present, until it was proven wrong. So you are to be congratulated in the way that you left the past in the past, breathed through and allowed the feelings to rise up rather than suppress them. You have successfully allowed one of your surface fears to move through in the most appropriate way.

Thank you. Virgil, I've noticed this week in trying to experience feeling that nearly every day I have created for myself incredible, little annoying distractions. For example, I've forgotten things and missed deadlines. I've continued to do this all week and it's been driving me crazy. Why have I manifested these things?

When you experience moments of annoying distractions and inconveniences, your energy seems scattered because it appears as though the ego is less in control. It is a phase that often accompanies a period of transition, because you are so focused on the inner and not so much on the outer, that at times things get by you. If you pour too much energy in analysing these surface difficulties, you will in fact be distracted from experiencing true feeling. You must keep these minor, unwelcome events in perspective. Day to day physical challenges are in the area of ego expertise, so draw on its skills to manage you through these times. Such events serve as a reminder of ego's true value and purpose. You need to acknowledge and appreciate its strength and skill as it is immersed in the challenges that characterise your current physical environment. For a time, the flow of mundane daily life can seem thwarted as you attempt to align the balance between ego and feeling consciousness. It can be tempting to revert to old habits of over analysing these distractions. From feeling, you would automatically appreciate and acknowledge the ego's ability to deal with the physical challenges and not be so concerned. You need to value all that you contain.

It's interesting because it coincides with a notable shift in my perceptions this week. In situations that cropped up, I felt a slight shift when I would go within. Instead of my consciousness being in my head as it always has been, last week I felt distinctly that I was in my heart, that I was coming from feeling. There was something there that was a little more in tune.

Indeed. Susie, the work you have undertaken has directed your focus to this area and you are sensing the shift as a movement in energy from the head space to align with the feeling self. You are in the midst of a transitional period where you are learning to adapt and respond within the new paradigm. With time and practice you will strengthen your feeling connection which will ensure a new higher perspective around all of your life's circumstances.

There will be a sense of the timeliness, or order to events, since you will recognise their link to the feelings coming through the inner realms. Such awareness generates acceptance which is the first step in working with your life in a positive fashion. Presently the ego damns itself for being stupid or weak, whereas the feeling body will generate a greater sense of acceptance that will permeate that negative chatter.

In the recent past, you have sought an acceptance of physical circumstances via attempts to justify the events in hindsight, using the ego to provide logical reasons as to why it was 'meant to be'. Now you will be able to understand that it is indeed your creation and therefore be ready and able to deal with it from the source in the moment. As the ego becomes more aligned to the feeling body, it is less likely to berate itself and instead more likely to accept feeling as a genuine guide to understanding its immediate reality. In time, it will extend its faith and expertise in looking inward to recognise its greater reality. It will know the true meaning of gentle growth, which is the direct opposite of its current beliefs of trials and tribulations. Does this make sense to you?

Yes, it does.

(Smiling) It is a sane way of viewing the world and is the difference between a guided ego and an ego experiencing the world alone.

I've noticed a pattern in my life that has come to the fore since we started this work. About once a week I have this day of melancholy. It feels like quite a thick overlay. It's usually triggered by some fear I have that I won't create a wonderful future, or when I'm bored or having to do housework. The triggers are minor, but the feeling of it is quite genuine and it's something I find really hard to slip out of. The next day I'm usually fine, I just snap out of it. It happened on Sunday and I was sitting in the space of experiencing it, yet trying to get behind it. I know the goal is to experience the other side, the polarity of feeling, but I'm still unable to have any experience of the flip side of the coin.

This is an important phase for you to undertake because it is the missing link, the element of yourself that you have yet to acknowledge – **the shadow self.** This is not something that I can hand to you in words, as it is uniquely your own and therefore it is important that you are the one to uncover it. Up until now, you have failed to embrace the feelings because you have remained focused on the physical events that trigger them. For many years, despite your spiritual beliefs, you have looked at these menial, so-called trivial events as just that and have not considered the feelings in any way as a reflection of the inner. You have not looked beyond the surface, because the events seem meaningless – almost as a necessary evil. You need to explore that. Just as you dislike housework, there is somebody else who is fastidious about it to obsession. Although you would be more than happy to assist that person in delving into their issues, you're so used to the way you feel about it, that you don't perceive it as an issue, let alone a choice.

Yes, but that's just one of the many triggers.

Indeed. So you need to look at what is behind those, in terms of feeling, now. I mention the housework because it is always there and is something that you can explore with a fair amount of light-heartedness, because of the fun and jokes that you've had over the years with that issue. But the underlying feeling is far more significant and pervading, so much so, that it appears out of balance when compared to the benign trigger. This is because the feeling encompasses an aspect of self, that has also had expression in past lives, of being unable to totally commit to the present. A way that you perpetuate this trait is to project negatively into the future or entertain perceived fears about the future. Although you are yet to experience the significance of the feeling that lies below these seemingly minor triggers, you can appreciate how very important this process is, as it directs your attention away from the physical, toward feeling. To this end, because you are focused in feeling, you will not need to create upheaval in your physical life to get your attention, if this makes sense to you.

At this point you will merely journal the physical experience that has triggered your melancholy and then explore why you **feel** the way you do about it – just allow whatever emerges. Ensure you allow the ego to speak freely, without fear of judgement and responsibility. Once you have done that, you should uncover an impression of the essence of your experience - the thread of feeling that runs within. Follow this thread and allow it to take you deeper, which will promote a more intimate encounter. Keep going until it merges with the other side of the experience, so to speak.

Okay that sounds good... I hadn't realised until Sunday just how common this pattern is in my life.

It has to do with the previous life frames where you continually decided you'd had enough and where on some occasions you decided to suicide.

Really? I assume that's something I've never really quite gotten over in this life. (Virgil smiles and nods.) I shall explore that. There was another thing that really annoyed me this week. For the past few months I've continually had sore eyes and really itchy scaly skin and I'm just constantly tired. The rash is coming up again, big time, and I hate it. Are these symptoms associated with the layers of self-worth that keep coming up?

Until such time as you are fully in your feeling body you are still in need of trigger points, yard sticks, the physical familiarity, that you can measure your progress by. You will probably not wake up in the morning full-blown red and itchy as was required in the past. These issues are yours and yours alone and highlight that change is afoot. Things are happening. You are struggling in certain areas and you need to pay attention to your life, while continuing to move forward and maintain your focus on feeling. As problems and situations arise, remain in your integrity and affirm your preference for communion with the inner and avoid being drawn into ego struggles. All things that occur are a reflection of your spiritual journey and your inner world; you are growing, evolving, and developing. When you are immersed in negative ego chatter, be it in connection with the rash or indeed with other people, remember that there is an alternative way that is seeking expression.

It's just that when you have something physically wrong, it's very hard to put your attention anywhere else.

There is no doubt that the physical is extremely compelling. However, you need to understand that while you put your attention mainly on the physical subject, then you ignore the cure. You fail to recognise the opportunity to, at any time, ascertain exactly what the disease or problem is showing you. It is showing that you need to clear this aspect from feeling, and then the physical will align. Know that you will be given the scope to do so and the choice is yours. Growth, should you seize it, is imminent. The ground is being shaken once again. As you feel the pressure of this shake, you need to be aware of what is reflected to you so you can grasp the opportunity to move forward and beyond it.

To reassure you: You have no need to create the rash symptoms with the same vehemence as in the past to get your attention. You are far more in tune with your body and your life as it manifests around you, and such awareness will continue to expand should you allow it. You can use these situations as tools or oracles to measure your prevailing focus and commitment. At this point you are still required to keep your focus on feeling. The ego has been alone and in charge for most of your life and your new focus is exposing your inner fractured reality. This is again part of the transition phase where we see little reminders of what is truly seeking expression from within. An acknowledgement of this truth will assist you to remove yourself from any ego games and illusion and not waste energy in them. Once you have learnt to react and commit, even where there are only subtle changes to the physical body, then you will be ready to act on instinct and from feeling. Following on from this you will have no need for physical symptoms to manifest to get your attention.

Good. I look forward to that day.

What you need to understand is that you underestimate the changes that are occurring in you. When you remove control from the ego in this way, confusion can result for a time, which impacts on the physical body. This is a sign to you that there is too much struggle occurring here and it is not necessary. Your requirement is to pay attention, to go with the flow, not to second-guess options and choices, because to do this, is through a trained ego that has learnt the practices of spirit. This type of analysis will get you to a certain point only. It is to understand that you will go with the way you feel and accept the consequences of those decisions, knowing that your own self will reflect back to you and provide guidance along the way. Understand that every reflection will be the result of whether you chose love or fear; the ego's urgings or that of your feeling tone. Continue to affirm that you choose to be in your feeling body.

Virgil, I've noticed that following the lesson or focus of each week, I manifest situations which basically reflect all the blocks or fears associated with the lesson itself. For example, in focusing on the feeling experience over the last weeks, I had one lovely day and then it was days of feeling unworthy and a great deal of self-deprecating mind chatter. With all those fears coming up, are they released if we genuinely notice them? Is it normal in trying to manifest experiences of love and joy that we first have to shift the layers that stop us from experiencing them?

Indeed. (Virgil nods approvingly) This is as simple as it comes. The affirmation that you introduce each week gives rise to an inkling of what is beneath the surface. It is through direct focus then attention to what is coming forward via situations, events, or people that can generate those feelings forward so that we can release. We can look at these people with a different mind frame once we understand that they are bringing us major learning opportunities. We do not need to agree with their tactics, or understand their motives. **The fact that you can perceive a situation and grow from it is what makes you a person that is within the feeling body.** It is only when you meet these reflections at an ego level that there is a polarisation of energy and the learning is stifled.

You will be given an opportunity from these people, events, or situations that enable you to shift the blocks – sometimes major, sometimes minor shifts, in physical terms – but all important nonetheless. If you have not accepted that these feelings of love and acceptance are your birth right then you must, by its very definition, have a mind set or a belief about reality that is in direct contrast to that. **You cannot change a belief system by changing an opinion at an ego level.** It is impossible for contradictions to live side-by-side within the one Soul. If you affirm to choose love and then in your actions you choose fear, you will create much stress and strain in your life, which can translate to much physical exertion on the body. When these situations come up it is your responsibility, if you seek to become fully conscious, to choose to move through them with love and to recognise when you are choosing fear. These choices can be very deceptive, which is why you need to know the feeling body, because the ego can turn any fear situation into a love situation by manipulating spiritual wisdom.

Yes I agree. That is the space we have sat in for many years, isn't it?

Indeed. Indeed.

We will always be given another opportunity to choose love when we fail to do so?

Indeed. The way that it works is simple. All of you have encountered many situations and events in your lives where you have been confronted with seemingly difficult choices. You have known intellectually for some time now that the basic premise of all choices is between love and fear. You would analyse the situation and not know whether you were choosing love for this reason, or fear for this reason. In other words, both concepts could be rationalised within the same choice. For example, one of our friends here is faced with a new job offer. As she dislikes her current rude and disrespectful boss and hates her job, she has rationalised that to leave and free herself from this negative environment is choosing love. However, our dear friend has frequently identified her problems with commitment, with working things through when it is easier to just 'bail out' and abandon a difficult situation. Maybe in choosing the new position and again failing to commit fully to the present, she is in fact avoiding facing her problems. If this were the case she would be in fact choosing to leave not in love but in fear – fear of her ability to influence her environment and she would therefore miss an opportunity to experience her true power in the present. In looking at the two opposing perspectives of this basic dilemma, you can see that it is truly impossible to work a spiritual miracle from the ego mind that is logically arguing a case – both are seemingly valid. Therefore this demonstrates that the feeling body is a better way, but there needs to be motivation to venture into the uncharted feeling self.

The gift of the journey is to uncover all that is within you, which at this point you do not believe is your birth right. Unless your life is perfect, you must have contradictory, perhaps unrecognised beliefs about who you are, which are being actualised in this reality. Mental affirmation alone will not sort through all of these beliefs, but will merely add more layers. For example, each time you choose to affirm your worthiness, automatically opportunities will be created to allow this affirmation to be reflected back to you in the physical environment. Yet competing with these positives images are many thoughts of an opposing nature, some obvious, some not. Each thought has to balance with an opportunity to birth, so it appears it is a never-ending cycle of negative and positive images. This cyclic nature of thought gives you an indication of how slow the process is, if you were seeking to access and ground your positive self-worth through mental affirmation alone. Waiting constantly for thought to birth into the physical in order to gauge the health or otherwise of your inner self, leaves you as an observer rather than an active creator of your own life – quite unacceptable. Furthermore, many external events can seemingly be a reflection of lack of self-worth; all the events are then layered on top of the other and slowly processed individually. To bypass this arduous process, one must access and experience the root cause of all the negative chatter – that which drives it up and out into the world of matter. If that were known and dealt with, then all would make sense.

The feeling body by-passes all the ego creations - all the ego interpretations that have smothered the issues - and goes straight to the core issues. Therefore, if you remove the foundation of all your perceived negative feelings, then all their manifestations must crumble and fall. **You are in the midst of getting to your own unique core belief so that you can heal it.** As you go through these processes things start to shake and crumble. Some of the hurt feelings you perceive at a deep level are actually your protection, because you are scared of who you truly are. It is as though the ego self fears being totally overrun by the Soul self, if this makes sense to you.

It makes sense, Virgil, but it's hardly tangible.

This is the key, though. It is a feeling. The root cause of all these so-called negative manifestations needs to be experienced so that it can be followed through to the other side of the coin. The only way that you can truly love self and feel safe is to experience who you really are. Once you experience this, you can do nothing but love because that is all there is. You know this intellectually, but you have yet to experience it. In times past you have experienced periods of self-loathing and tried to overlay them with thoughts of self-love. These efforts do not eliminate the negative expression so we end up living a complete contradiction and wonder why our lives are so confusing. It seemingly depends on where our focus aligns as to what we project out. Therefore, what we are, we create as a result.

Understand that self-love is not to be attained or acquired, it is what we already are – in experiencing that love, everything else will fall away. This is the key for all of you. Cease to worry about it on an intellectual level. If you remember from one of our previous channelling sessions, I had spoken that the feeling tone communicates with you through fear when you are vibrating at that level and therefore offering yourself no alternative way to communicate. Continue in experiencing moments of joy - for example, interacting with your child or loved one, which gives rise to that heart expansion. You need to do this at every occasion where you actually feel genuine expansion. Expansion of the heart is the ultimate goal. However, in this interim transitory period it must be a conscious effort that you not imagine the feelings, not remember the feelings, but you actually experience them in that moment. You will know the difference when it comes. It is a similar experience to what The Channel has when I come in; it is a definitive physical experience of expansion, and it feels physical. Once you are more in tune with this, it will provide you with a thread in which to link further into the feeling body.

What I am asking of you seems difficult as you immerse yourself in your daily life only because your mind finds the theory fascinating. It plays with it in a myriad of ways creating distractions. My advice to you is to acknowledge this becoming as a process and continue with the tools provided to you in lessons of the past. When I say journal the trigger, I am referring to allowing the ego to speak freely as identified in Lesson One. Allow it to express its judgements without fear or failure, for what is has to say is valid. If the ego is ranting, it is wounded. This means it could provide the way inward, via the feeling body, to the real source of your problems, being the core belief. So speak to the ego gently.

So we should just journal the trigger?

Exactly. Allow the ego freedom of expression. Understand that the ego is the surface layer, so in any situation you encounter it holds the key to knowing the true essence. This is why we journaled its processes in the beginning, so that we could understand it – for it is the doorway.

Thank you, Virgil. Would you like to move on to our lesson for this week?

Indeed. In previous chapters we have touched briefly on the notion of taking responsibility and it is now timely to ground this fully into your lives. To some degree you accept that you create your own reality, but for no reason other than you have been told by great teachers, either through books or in classes. Therefore you are aligned with this notion only at the very surface ego level of self and this lack of real belief is reflected in the chaos of your daily lives. In short – you entertain the thought that you create your own reality, but you don't really believe or own it. If you really knew the power of manifesting at your disposal you would not require this course, for example, for to know your own power of creation is to know your true self.

There can be no degrees of taking responsibility. It is a contradiction, for example, to blame a childhood event for a perceived 'issue' in this day and age and then in the same breath espouse that you are a conscious creator of your own destiny. All you have done in identifying past hurts is pinpointed the physical circumstances that birthed what you already contained into the present, which cannot heal you. Childhood events especially appear out of your control because the ego has not yet asserted its dominance and the child is still in touch with its feeling core. Early childhood is almost completely devoted to stifling this feeling and developing the ego, both as a way to view the world physically and psychologically, but also in learning to manipulate within it. Events of childhood are manifested unconsciously; a result of the choice of parents, circumstances, siblings, etc. that facilitates the development of an ego that is aligned with an inner core belief that needs to be healed. **The fact is that, specific circumstances manifested in childhood are not a reflection of parenting styles, but a reflection of your own ability to manifest what you most need to heal. If this were not true then identical circumstances would produce identical reactions in all individuals, which is clearly not the case.** A nasty word can cause some to run and hide, while in others, regular childhood beatings give rise to a great will to overcome and take on the world. Identifying how certain events shaped your ego is critical to this process as we have consistently stated, but it is only a step toward full knowing. Taking responsibility for all that you are and see reflected around you, will lead you to this full knowing.

The lesson of this week is simple. You will observe your life with the same diligence as you have in previous weeks. Pay attention to the ego chatter, continue to affirm to be in your feeling body, spend time connecting with nature – in short do not discard what we have already begun. However, now within everything you observe, you will take full responsibility for it. If you encounter a joy then bask in the glow and feel the feeling back to its source within. If you encounter fear then sit within that feeling and by taking ownership, see where that takes you. Even those things that are seemingly 'outside of yourself' we have learned are not, therefore you must take responsibility for your part in them. Of all the lessons to date I cannot stress the importance of this one enough. Although the grounding of taking responsibility may bring up some uncomfortable feelings initially, in time it must and will, set you free. I wish you well in your efforts and look forward with great anticipation to next week, and hearing your outcomes. I wish you all a very happy week.

Be blessed.

Thank you, Virgil.

Lesson Nine

I take full responsibility for everything I observe.

A Time For Reflection

Congratulations on completing the foundation part of the course which has been designed to facilitate a journey into your ego realm. You might not yet sense just how far you have come in terms of expanding your consciousness, but you are in fact on the precipice of new and exciting learning. From here, the journey quickens and what was before a seemingly arduous project now begins to move and flow in greater alignment with your inner self. Virgil will introduce a new focus; one that if followed through to conclusion, will provide you with an opportunity to ground feeling as the way in which you meet the world. However, before attempting this new phase, it is necessary to take some time to reflect on your outcomes to date.

It will be beneficial if you are able to tackle the remaining course with a clear idea of the way in which your ego meets the physical world. This self knowing is described in subsequent chapters by Virgil, as the reference point of ego awareness. You can facilitate this state by considering your ego outcomes to date and summarising them. To assist you in this process, Susie and I have devised a list of questions that provide food for thought and, when answered honestly, should allow this summary, guided by self reflection, to emerge effortlessly. The aim is to bring to your conscious awareness the way in which your ego meets the world, its defences, its form of attack, its strengths, and weaknesses. A conscious and consistent awareness of the ego self as you go forward, will assist you in reaching the highest potentials of this course. You will recognise when you are indulging the ego's whims, by creating unnecessary drama, as opposed to a preference of actually feeling the essence underlying any event.

Our initial participants were not given these questions and as a result, most found the final stage of this process tough going. In later courses, where such introspective reflection was encouraged, the lessons delving into the ego consciousness seemed more grounded, making way for a smoother transition into feeling body consciousness and Soul communication. Time and effort invested now, will bear fruit during the lessons that follow; so please take some time to reflect. There is no firm time frame for this exercise; be guided by your own knowing and be mindful that this is not a stand alone lesson, but rather a tool to assist you in clarifying your ego state. The questions are a guide only; if you can think of anything else to journal by all means do so.

Consider the following and record in your journal:

** From incidences journaled in the past weeks: highlight examples in which your ego naturally responds in this world when confronted with pain/stress, both from other egos and as a result of specific situations.*

** In reflecting on the above examples, are you able to identify a dominant thread or pattern emerging? For example, do you usually become aggressive/emotional/withdrawn?*

** Often, in situations that 'press our buttons' we find ourselves responding in our usual manner identified above. Can you recall when you recognised your pattern response and knew you were acting from ego? Furthermore, were there times when despite this awareness, you actually preferred to remain in the ego focus? If so, why do you think you prefer the ego's vantage during these times?*

** What do you currently believe about yourself?*

** What time and effort have you made to connect with your feeling tone? What does this tell you about yourself or your real beliefs?*

** Amidst the ego drama, have you had an awareness of feeling in the moment? Try to initiate this awareness this week. Do not look for an outcome, merely recognition.*

** How diligent have you been in focusing on the lessons each week? Consider your focus in your daily events and your reflection at the end of each day/week.*

As mentioned, in the coming weeks we will be changing our primary awareness toward the feeling body, while maintaining and nurturing the greater understanding we now have of the ego's reality. It has taken many years to form your ego self that takes on the world today and your automatic response in the short term will naturally align with its current perception. If, in going forward, you find yourself immersed in ego dramas, it is paramount that you recognise the situation as your own pattern and have the courage to step beyond its apparent safety and into feeling. A useful tool to facilitate an opening for the transition of perception to occur was more recently given to us by Virgil and is known as the 'I Technique'. Essentially the 'I Technique' is useful during those times when you are seemingly a victim of circumstances, especially where it seems you have no control or influence. Those times when all would be well, if this or that hadn't happened, or if a certain person would only treat you better....and on and on it goes.

If you find yourself immersed in a sense of helplessness or feel at the mercy of circumstances or other people, simply allow the ego to vent all of its frustration, or misery, or anger, or whatever the case is. Then review your journaling and simply reframe all the ego's ravings preceded not by he/she/it etc., but by 'I'. For example, the ego's language could read: 'He doesn't love me enough'. This would be reframed using the 'I' technique to: 'I feel unloved'. Again in ego terms: 'My job is awful, my boss is a pig and he never compliments me on a job well done. How can I change him? He's the one that needs to alter his behaviour'. This reframed could read: 'I really hate my job, I feel inferior around my boss and peers, I never feel valued there...I am worthless...etc.'

Such reframing gives you an insight into the real feelings such situations are trying to get you to recognise and heal. While you remain distracted by the physical – i.e. the events or people - then you miss the true feelings and therefore they must continue to manifest in other areas of our lives. This was a powerful tool for all of us. Actual physical events, more often than not, prove our ego beliefs to be correct. For example, I'm sure we have all worked with a difficult boss at some time, and that their poor attitude has negatively infected the entire staff. You could argue that clearly the terrible boss is the cause of your problems and given that everyone else feels the same way, it cannot be your own perceptions. However, you create your own reality – you are participating in these unpleasant circumstances for a reason. The moment you recognise, feel, and own the situation at a deeper level instead of remaining focused on his unpleasant behaviour. You may just get that better job that appears to come from nowhere. Alternatively, you may reach an understanding of mutual respect, (maybe to the surprise of co-workers) where you find the negativity has simply transcended your relationship and begins to foster acceptance. Changes in your environment occur because: in acknowledging the source of the physical and responding to that, you no longer need to draw in physical dramas to trigger feeling. In communication from Soul you automatically choose harmony, and thus you are able to reflect it all around you.

Good luck with your reflections and the final phase of this remarkable journey into the self. No matter what occurs in your life as you proceed, please ensure you ask for help and support and allow it to enter your reality – in whatever form. Affirm your intention to grow and know without a doubt that what you are manifesting is presenting a unique opportunity to clear all that has been holding you back to date. Feeling is your natural state, not a tool to be utilised when all other means have failed, so choose it first. Delve into the feeling tone of your life and your awareness will expand. We reiterate once again that this is not a stand alone lesson; however it must be completed before moving onto Chapter Ten.

Sally and Susie

CHAPTER 10

Your Responsibility For Consciousness

The lesson of taking responsibility proved to be one of the most challenging so far. The concept was simple enough to understand, yet when connected to highly emotional events in our lives, was difficult to live by. We approached the week with a clear intention to look at our experiences with a new awareness of responsibility. Consequently, everything that we had failed to accept as our own increasingly came into the fore. My personal relationship was still strained, with each of us polarised into inaction, while Susie's rash made its presence increasingly obvious in her itchy eyes and skin. We were beginning to entertain doubts whether there was actually any spiritual teaching that could lead us to heal our lives and wondered whether we should just give it all up.

For many years we had clung to the positive theory of spirituality like a life boat, and so were aware that to surrender it would break our hearts and leave us feeling abandoned, but still we could not ignore how entirely let down we felt. If our connection to Virgil had not been so concrete, I seriously doubt whether we would have pursued his teachings further. In our hearts though, we knew the integrity of the connection and felt his love and hope for us. We also knew that in embracing our feelings of victimhood and hopelessness we were coming in direct contact with our shadow selves and we were aware that this was critical to the process, no matter how uncomfortable we felt. In allowing these feelings, we were hoping to be led to the healing of separation, although at the time, we could see no peace in sight.

One of my most dominating patterns in the past was to suppress feeling by moving on and away from any situation that was 'pushing my buttons', especially matters directly involving spiritual growth in groups and relationships. After days of ego 'to-ing' and 'fro-ing', I was very adept at justifying my departure as being in my highest growth, even so far as believing that I was being urged in another direction by spirit. I have reams of past diary writings where I have neatly categorised and justified all my decisions to run as being in my greatest good, and have even congratulated myself for my fine insights.

I can see that I was avoiding feeling and removing myself from any responsibility and placing it firmly at the feet of an 'all knowing Universe'. Through the ego observation of the past weeks, via journaling, I had at least admitted and grounded that aspect of myself. I knew a well worn pattern was emerging in my relationship with my partner. I was determined to not act on the impulse to run, but instead try to follow the feeling through to the source. I also knew enough spiritual theory to understand that every event, no matter what, had a myriad of probabilities which could be manifested into the physical. What actualised physically depended on what you believed in this reality – in other words, your life matches your beliefs. I felt, via my feeling body, that somewhere amid the confusion lay our greatest potential for happiness together. An inkling began to emerge that we were somehow capable of birthing this higher vision into the physical at any moment we chose. My partner, who was also undertaking the course, also felt this basic truth. Despite our love for each other it seemed we were incapable of making it materialise. On one hand our own egos were telling us that it was all too hard and not fun anymore, while on the other hand, through communion with our feeling bodies, we were being gently nudged into the potential of our relationship. We knew we both wanted that potential. There we sat, within the apparent contradiction of ego versus feeling; neither of us taking decisive action in the physical, hoping that the haze would clear.

Susie, who had been haunted for a decade by a rash that disfigured her otherwise attractive appearance, was again faced with its presence. It had really heralded her move into the spiritual life as the medical profession, naturopaths or homeopaths had been unable to diagnose it, let alone suggest to her a realistic cure. She had eventually turned to spiritual healers for help and while they had no success specifically with the rash, the healers had enriched her life in other ways. Having said that, her quest to heal this physical nemesis coloured all her searching and every new spiritual course afforded her hope that finally she may be able to rid herself of it once and for all. When the teachings of her most beloved and trusted guide/teacher in Virgil had caused the rash not only to return but more severely, you can appreciate her confusion and despair. In fact I would say that she was equally desperate in facing this aspect as I was in dealing with my relationship. Both situations provided another example confirming that we must avoid analysis of the physical manifestation of our 'issues' and instead focus on the feelings they generate. This will ensure we do not fall into the trap of categorising one manifestation as being more important than the other.

Both Susie's and my examples in this chapter illustrate beautifully how easily we avoid taking responsibility because it is seemingly justified. I avoided it because in my view, my partner was always the cause of my angst. I was clever not to blame him specifically, but rather fall back into believing we just weren't meant to be together, as though there was some force above me which had already determined we weren't compatible. I drew on the old 'not meant to be' and other spiritual clichés, such as, 'if there is struggle then you are not in the flow with spirit'. While this is true, it doesn't necessarily follow that running from the pain would put me in the flow, as my ego would like to think.

Susie's example is included because she was manifesting something physical which the ego self believed it really couldn't control. It is very hard to take responsibility for something physical that seemingly 'happens' to you, especially in her case where you have put ten years into conscientiously trying to face it and conquer it. In this chapter, Susie first asks questions of Virgil on my behalf and then adds her own questions directly underneath.

You will see that Virgil does not need to distinguish between our different problems to answer our concerns. The physical manifestations themselves are not the issue, our inability to take responsibility for them is. Any issues arising for you at this time can be lumped together from one source - the inability to take responsibility for consciousness. One thing is for certain – this must be grounded if we are to move forward. There are no exceptions to this requirement and no 'issue' that is outside its realm. If you are manifesting difficult circumstances, remember that it is merely your resistance in taking responsibility. Try to view it from that perspective and avoid immersing yourself too much in the detail. At the time, most of us found this period extremely difficult and time with nature helped. In hindsight it was the beginning of real and unassailable growth for each one of us, that even today still continues to bear fruit. If I am ever immersed in negative feelings I find that by taking responsibility I automatically begin to see everything from a higher perspective and can therefore glimpse a way forward. Virgil is in fine form as usual, and despite the group's shared difficulties and seemingly low vibration, he comes through strongly and with great empathy.

Sally...

(The Channel smiles broadly and her posture improves markedly) Good evening my friends, it is a pleasure to reconnect at this time. We will move directly to debrief last week's lesson so I await your insights.

(Susie on behalf of Sally) Thank you for joining us, Virgil. This week's lesson has been the most difficult for me so far. Problems arose where the essence appeared connected to people or events outside of myself and over which I had no control. At the time, despite really trying to own the circumstances it was just impossible for me to take responsibility when it was always another person that led me into that conflict and pain. It felt like the only way I could get past the feelings would be if the other person modified or changed their behaviour in some way (which I don't see happening). I didn't want to project my bad feelings onto the other person. I then began to entertain thoughts of leaving the relationship, as my only way forward. With everything we've learned I know this is avoiding my issue and if I don't face it I will just keep manifesting more of the same. I believed the only alternative was to just sit with feelings, which felt terrible. I felt a failure and very trapped and couldn't pass the feelings through. I really want these issues in my relationship to be evolved, but it seems too hard. Would you like to comment on this?

(Susie) Virgil, I simply can't cope anymore. My rash is out of control and I have thought all along, I was taking responsibility for it, simply by trying to

heal it. Now I see this is not necessarily the case and I am so frustrated. Why is this inflicted on me?

Indeed. As always you must remember that we are undertaking a process here and the outcomes of your efforts last week are exactly what we were trying to achieve. Taking responsibility is not a new concept in spiritual theories; however we are endeavouring to evolve this notion to a new level of awareness.

Previously you have taken responsibility for certain aspects of your reality, but have drawn the line at those situations or events that 'appear' to be outside of your sphere of influence; especially within your primary relationships. You have been able to take responsibility on the surface insofar as the way in which you respond to certain triggers or events in your lives. For the most part, your response has been trained from years of spiritual rhetoric on how a spiritually evolved individual would react when their buttons are pushed. Such responses are therefore generally manufactured from the stance of a spiritually trained ego. Responsibility for the actual manifestation of such events is left firmly at the feet of the Universe for the purpose of providing you with spiritual lessons for your own good.

You do not recognise the source of the manifestations as being within the self, but instead see them as something imposed upon you. Their real essence or meaning remains shrouded in a myriad of possibilities. To try to make sense of these events you invariably end up spending hours and maybe weeks, in endless mind analysis of the situation trying to ascertain the message that the Universe had for you and the inherent growth within. Often this gives rise to confusion surrounding issues such as 'love versus fear', which 'voice' to listen to, and which direction serves the highest purpose. In short, it leaves you guessing. This is hardly an empowering approach to spiritual evolution. Therefore you have a foot in two camps. One that asserts you create your own reality. The other that believes that overlaying this, there exists a 'Universal' influence that will deliver to you lessons in the form of situations which you bear no responsibility for, other than to learn from them and somehow move on.

This basic belief contradicts much of what has been brought through about universal law. Notions such as universal support and love appear untrue when you are in pain and confusion; also the concept of free will must be questionable if circumstances can be imposed upon you, 'for your greatest growth'. Despite these obvious inconsistencies in theory versus your reality, you have managed to sustain simultaneously beliefs in a supportive and unsupportive Universe, determined by your interpretation of your physical lives. Belief in a universal force acting independently of your own will is so prevalent that it is gaining momentum through mass thought forms. We are intent here on undoing this untruth. **There is no force outside of yourself that can exert its will upon you.**

The truth of universal law lies in the opposite of this notion. Universal will is loving and supportive, but above all else it is constant. Your will is seated within this truth, yet is capable of total freedom of expression. So, where your life is showing you great joy or contentment, for example, you are indeed creating in alignment with the universal will. Where it is showing you pain or confusion, then you are creating from a collective pool of manufactured beliefs and notions about this reality. This lesson is a step to facilitate experience of this inconsistency and thereby allow you to know it and consequently realign your beliefs.

(Susie on behalf of Sally) Virgil, it seems much harder in practice. I sat in nature trying to pass the issues through and I kept coming back to being unable to separate the feelings from the situations I faced. I kept thinking that either the person would have to change or I would have to surrender the relationship. I considered these my only options. I couldn't understand how I could deal with my feelings and then his behaviour would improve.

(Susie) Similarly, I've worked on this rash for years and I just kept coming back to how much better my life would be without it – how it pervades every aspect of my life from ruining my biggest occasions to being present in my daily grind. It's just always there and I can't feel anything else but anger and frustration.

These reflections of your issues and the feelings they are bringing up are positive testimony to your progress. This inability to fully accept and work positively within the framework you have created, the desire to just eliminate it from your reality, represents the missing link in this process - a link that I could not provide for you, as it is something you had to discover for yourselves and is uniquely your own. It is an element of inner self that you have failed to acknowledge and therefore its essence materialises in physical form seeking your attention. Presently you tend to eliminate the manifestation of this aspect of self from your life using varying ego techniques, as we have discussed previously. These techniques are your defence against embracing this aspect and can take the form of projection on others or the 'Universe' or suppression or mental rationalisation. Your natural state is union and wholeness, so this aspect can only be temporarily removed from the ego world; it retreats then re-emerges in another form, seeking completion. This aspect of self and the nature of its communication is oftentimes referred to as the shadow self – that which contains all that will restore your wholeness, which is why it is frequently referred to as shadow wisdom. Although unique to each person, I can tell you both your shadow and your unwillingness to embrace it, relates back to many existences where you were unable to commit to the present.

If the shadow is an aspect of self and the self is perfect and negativity is of ego, why does the shadow manifest as negative? Why is it so dark? If it manifested in a positive way, wouldn't that get our attention just as well? It doesn't seem tangible.

It manifests in ways that you may perceive as negative but only because you are encountering the situation from the vantage of ego. You have not recognised or embraced all that you are, and all that you are is perfect. Soul is perfect in union not in separation. The shadow being separate is an aspect of self that is actually missing from the creation or manifesting equation; it is an aspect of self unfulfilled. You are therefore only partly present in this reality with the ego trying to compensate for the missing link – the shadow – by attempting to interpret and categorise your physical existence. Without the entire self present in conscious awareness, there are holes if you like, or a missing ingredient that undermines the entire structure.

It is the lack of guidance and influence from this aspect of self, not its meddling, that ensures your creations will be lacking, so to speak. They appear as negative because it is a reflection of your inability to deal with this reality, given an aspect has not been allowed expression. For example, you are constantly painting the living picture that is your reality. Imagine you were given a set of paints by your parents that you believed was complete but actually only contained one-third of the colours of reality. You could still paint an adequate picture that appeared complete given the confines of your colour reality and even be satisfied with it for a time. Your ego awareness would eventually look beyond its own picture and you would discover others with a far greater colour spectrum than yours and who, as a result, seem to be living far more impressive paintings. You could try to make more hues, spending many hours toiling, never being able to quite replicate, but at least adding to your picture. You may be satisfied with your progress. This is where I see you now in the expression or creation of your own painting. The key is not in manufacturing new colours from the example you witness in others. It is bringing forth your own unique perspective or hues and removing the limitation on just how many options you have available in painting your picture. It is not replicating the achievement of others through toil; it is birthing your own uniqueness and adding your own stamp of individuality to the canvas. This individuality is inherent in your feeling tone and an aspect of that self, the shadow, that has yet to be allowed expression. Without it your painting is less alive or incomplete. When you stop trying to make the colours happen and just remember those that are uniquely your own, your landscape will be breathtaking.

That is a wonderful analogy, Virgil, one that clarifies the concept beautifully. So how do we access the shadow and allow our creative potential? I'm sick and tired of manifesting the rash.

You must be prepared to use all the techniques we have practised in the past. These are tools to assist you from falling back into old behaviours that have allowed you to avoid dealing with the shadow – they are not ends in themselves. For instance, you need to allow the ego to speak freely of the way it perceives the triggers. That is, if your partner is the problem, let the ego get it out, clear the chatter and blame, use the breathing if that works for you, the "I" technique, etc. Pay attention to your life from the point of feeling. Be mindful that feeling is just feeling, ground it in nature and remember to take responsibility; only you can heal it, for only you created it.

Virgil, it's just that when you have something physically wrong like I do, it's very hard to put your attention anywhere else.

No, it is difficult only because this is your shadow manifesting and your resistance to embrace the feelings it brings up, gives rise to pain. It would be equally difficult for you to face no matter what its physical form. Understand that while you are narrowing your attention on the physical subject, then you are ignoring the cure. I have told you this before, yet you continue to resist grounding it into your life. If you focus on feeling it brings the shadow into your awareness and you would then have to take responsibility for your life.

The difficulties you experience afford an opportunity to embrace this aspect of self and the choice to do so or not, is always yours. You have had sufficient practice by now in learning the ways of ego to know in your heart when you are avoiding the issue by remaining in the ego premise of victimhood or helplessness. Do you have the courage to step outside of your 'issues' and challenge the ego's theories? Remaining in the ego space is immediately easier, but in the long-term, much more difficult. When triggers occur that give rise to a response of anxiety or stress, make time to immerse yourself in the moment. Taking responsibility in the truest sense can only be done in the moment, not in hindsight or in advance of feeling. **Link in with the feelings, not the physical event.** Own the feelings, knowing that they are seeking union and allow them to take you on a journey inward.

Now as previously grounded – feeling is just feeling. It is your ego interpretation of it that classifies it as negative or positive as it is charged with the emotion surrounding any given event. Remember, we espoused that emotion was merely a build-up of feeling not experienced in the moment. As you journey the feelings in the moment inward, detach from the ego analysis and seek the guidance of your feeling tone experience which should still be a regular exercise. Discard expectation as you focus only on feeling, which when not charged with ego judgement, is aligned with the Universe and is constant and rhythmic. Follow the feeling through to a point of stillness. Within that stillness, open to the clarity of self, the ever present meaning of being; the sanctity of Soul. When ready you will automatically engage the flip side of the feelings that have lead you to the point of stillness – in the seeming polarity of what was negative, the shadow wisdom that is yours to use. Do not force union; allow it to come into being. Experience as fully as possible the feelings at this time. Identify how closely aligned they are to the original hurt, yet so utterly different when experienced from the clarity of the feeling tone perception. Know that this is about feeling not visualisation. When the journey is complete, ensure you fully journal the experience to assist in grounding this new perception into the ego reality. Ask the ego to journal how this new experience can be used in its day–to-day existence to prepare the ground for an expanded, richer and more supportive reality. This is your task for this week.

Thank you, Virgil. It sounds very exciting.

Through our weeks of lessons designed to facilitate ego observation, we are now moving forward with a greater awareness of our patterns and self-imposed limitations. This next phase, as discussed, is to facilitate reconnection with our Soul self, without the limiting confines of ego, and to ground this connection in time and space. The concept of 'flipping the coin', particularly within this reality of polarities, is an important aspect, another piece of the puzzle, something that takes a giant step toward union. I wish you well in your efforts and look forward to our next meeting.

Be blessed.

Thank you.

Lesson Ten

Journey to the point of stillness and engage the flip side of shadow feelings.

CHAPTER 11
Your Shadow Wisdom – Flipping The Coin

The course is coming to a definitive crossroad at this point. The process of becoming more conscious of the manner in which our inner feeling vibration affects our outer reality brings with it many challenges. It can be an intensely difficult time, peppered with moments of great clarity and power. Be true to your own self now, and know that you are standing at the threshold of serious and potentially life changing growth. The foundations of long held limitation are being shaken so that it can all fall away from your life. In the short term, this limitation will continue to manifest, but know that now it is coming forward to allow you to release it.

Without fail there are two distinct outcomes arising from last week's lesson of 'flipping the coin'. Firstly, there are those that naturally hold a predisposition for moving though their spiritual lives at a feeling level. These people were able to experience their feelings fully and even identify the many guises it wore and the way it coloured their life experiences. Despite such clarity however, upon reaching the point of stillness they felt stuck and unable to move through to the flip side to reveal the gifts that lay beneath. For example, one participant felt the pain of always feeling a failure and was deeply upset. She recognised how this sense of failure shadowed a large part of her life from relationships to career. She concluded, with some determination, that she did not want to spend the rest of her days grappling with this sense. She saw her inability to 'flip the coin' as further evidence of her failure and concluded that she was powerless to change it – instead declaring it as an undeniable fact. In reality, she had achieved a critical aspect of this process in the recognition of her limitation. It was however, not an end in itself, but instead a beginning to build upon in the following lesson.

The second outcome for this week came via those that naturally lean toward intellectual rational analysis. As their experience of feeling intensified, these individuals tended to automatically assert their perception solely back to the intellect. They strived to manufacture flipping the coin via a cause and effect type premise and sometimes a meditative style visualisation. As our example of failure, these people unconsciously reverted to an intellectual approach as to why they are failures in order to sever the experience of the pain itself. They might intellectually identify childhood trauma as the 'cause' and then apply affirmation to talk themselves through it. This smothers the true experience and makes it impossible to follow the feeling through to the gift awaiting them on the flip side. Again, the recognition via feeling is critical, but it is not an end in itself. Reverting back to the intellect to rationalise your current circumstances is fraught with limitation - for all the reasons already covered in the first half of this course.

Prior to proceeding further in the course, you need to identify which camp you are in – feeling or intellect – and take responsibility for your own outcomes. Our experience has shown that those with a feeling focus, albeit superficial, tend to fear meeting their shadow expecting a negative experience. Conversely, those immersed in intellectual analysis tend to fear that experiencing their shadow will necessitate surrender – giving up an aspect of control and allowing vulnerability. All people, regardless of their approach, use their preferred stance for the same purpose - to avoid the experience of painful feelings. If you have been diligent with your journaling, you should have an inkling of the way your resistance manifests physically – take note so you will not be drawn back to ego confusion. Struggle is struggle, no matter how we dress it up in our physical lives. Fortunately, it doesn't matter whether you are predisposed toward feeling or intellect as the lessons designed to cease the struggle are the same. You just need to identify which is your preferred focus, so you can easily identify your resistance.

I preferred an intellectual approach and it took me a long time to trust my feelings long enough to learn that they can serve me better than the mind analysis I was so attached to. Susie was also of intellectual persuasion and played with the theories for a long time because she really didn't know any other way existed. For both of us and many others, this 'feeling stuff' was just theory, but eventually it became our experience. Those who preferred feeling, really just needed to trust and open to the experience, rather than collapse into the intensity of it. Persistence and practise are the keys.

Our communication with Virgil again became difficult around this time. For many of us it was a totally new phase in our spiritual journey and we were confused by it. Virgil, on the other hand, had never before tested his course. Depending on our outcomes each week he was making adjustments to his lessons as we went along. As always he was patient, yet within his calm approach there now seemed an aspect of frustration creeping in – just under the surface. It was not directed at us particularly, but seemed to be with the communication process as a whole – frustration at just how he was going to get through to us. Somehow though, we managed to leave his presence each week with renewed hope and enthusiasm for the next challenge.

Sally...

Good evening my friends. Welcome to Lesson Eleven. This is an undeniably important phase; one that will require commitment and, to an extent, faith that a process is unravelling here. We will proceed to debrief last week's lesson as I await your questions.

Hi, Virgil. I tried flipping the coin which was quite an eye opener for me in many ways. I managed to stay with the feelings to a point, but experiencing the flip side eluded me. I'm still putting my focus on what I'm thinking, especially all the self pity 'poor me' attitudes, and I noticed that my intellect doesn't serve me in the way that it used to. I had never really grounded that before and it helped me to make new choices about the way I'll deal with experiences in the future. The problem is, I have recognised the limitations of intellect, but have yet to master the feeling body consciousness and that leaves me in a very uneasy place. I feel spiritually weak, like it's all too hard for me. Intellectually I know that's not true, but it feels true.

This is good news for you because that feeling is exactly what will lead you to experience the flip side. Your intellect is overlaying these feelings of spiritual weakness with rational judgements and asserting that they are false. It is easier to accept the ego's familiar stance. This is why you have been unable to engage the flip side of the feelings, because you follow them to a point then rationalise them out of existence. You do not have a weakness of spirit, but you definitely feel that you do and it is from this paradigm that your reflections spring. At this point it is your familiar stance and only in experiencing the reality of the other side can you then ground it as your new paradigm. You have a very highly trained and attuned ego self that is slowly relinquishing control, so to speak, which is why you are feeling uneasy. This should only be a temporary experience.

Over the past weeks in actualising the lessons provided, you have spent time in dual focus. One focus is of the intellect, where you feel comfortable; you believe it is your natural state. Overlaying this is a strong desire to actualise feeling body consciousness, desire converted to action via the lessons. You have been able to follow this new desire through to a point. When the feeling became too intense to bear or to understand, the ego has come to your rescue - it has intellectualised then projected, internally or externally, these 'foreign' feelings. Please give me a specific event and I will reframe it for you.

I experienced one particularly disturbing situation. I was attending a friend's party and took my young son along. It seems I was not supposed to take him despite the fact that I wasn't told so and there were other children who also weren't meant to be there. I felt really hurt that he should be singled out for exclusion, but tried to breathe the feelings through. As the night progressed the host was treating my son badly which cut me deeply. Despite the fact that this raised strong emotions in me, I remained mindful of all of our lessons and didn't project and make an issue. The next day, I was trying to take responsibility via owning the feelings and flipping the coin but it was too emotionally intense. I realised at some level that it went much deeper. It really upset me that there could be an aspect of myself that could feel this way about my son to attract it into my life and I just couldn't deal with that. Then I spilt burning oil on my finger which I journaled as a signal that I was 'only touching the surface of the problem, look for another way beneath the singe'. So really I'm back to square one, although I know I don't like what was reflected at me.

Indeed Susie. Take careful note of my explanation because this is a manifestation of your own resistance and one that you can learn from for the future. You have analysed a situation and immediately tried to reconcile it into something within you that is negative and dark. Is this the paradigm from which you view your shadow? If so, it is no wonder you create such resistance to experience it. You were unable to follow the feelings through largely due to the expectation that what lies beneath is negative or destructive. You were therefore left with the counsel of the familiar ego. The outcome of its interpretation has left you appalled by the so-called fact that you could be witness to this obvious attack on your child. You recall the premise that all things are reflections for which you must take responsibility and consequently conclude that somewhere within you, lurks similar negative feelings toward your son. This notion of course is more than a loving mother can bear. It is more than you can bear, because it is utterly untrue.

Your whole processing of this event was done via the ego that thinks it is experiencing genuine feeling. Your feeling self however, could not frame this situation in such literal terms of cause and effect. You have again come from the space where you have taken your spiritual knowledge and applied it at an ego surface level, which is only half-seeing. Understand that, yes, these events come forward to offer you gifts in the form of a way to access your internal world. Yes, they are reflections of your internal environment – but not as literally as you have interpreted this situation. The host's dislike for little boys and the feelings this brought up in you, does not mean that you harbour the same dislike.

Understand that when I say to you that all experience is a reflection of your inner reality, that this is indeed the truth – the most important rule of this reality is that you create it absolutely. But if you remain only in the physical interpretation, then your access to the inner will be limited. Had you stayed with the feelings in the moment, then you would have identified the pain as your own, relating not to your son, but to your own childhood experiences of being excluded both within the family and the outside world. In short the physical event triggered the feelings that if allowed expression, would have led you to the core of your own pain. Seeking any other interpretation of this event is merely feeding the ego. Remaining immersed in the feelings and then flipping the coin would have allowed you access to all the growth that the inability to recognise this pain is withholding from you. **It is your response – that is the feelings – triggered by physical events, that are the mirror, not the events themselves.** It is this basic premise that makes this course so necessary for spiritual growth. Without this understanding, one just keeps focusing outward onto the physical which is limited and confusing.

Know that this resistance is of your own making. You are not ready to feel, you are too scared to feel, so you remove the focus back to the ego which automatically directs its focus outward, thus keeping you occupied with the physical event, rather than the internal environment. In not being prepared to feel the experience that is your life, you can now identify the pain that accompanies this choice. The ego is quite markedly hurt by what has occurred, feeling evermore as a victim of other people or events. It is quite a paradox in fact. The ego is in its own terms, is protecting itself from integrating the shadow that it perceives as fearful, but in the act of so doing, ends up opening itself up to further pain and attack. No wonder you have experienced duality, frustration, and contradictions over this period.

You say that the intellect doesn't work for you in spiritual matters anymore. This is a positive recognition and proof that your awareness is expanding. The ability to step back from the physical chaos and simply surrender the need to grasp the cause and effect of your highly charged emotional events is a prerequisite to facilitating genuine feeling communication. To live and manage your life from this higher perspective is the essence of feeling body consciousness. The challenge is to voluntarily allow this feeling state, rather than choose it last, when all other control methods have been exhausted.

Virgil, I am so tired of all of this. I realised this week how much I was still relying upon all those old rules and methods that we were accustomed to in spirituality....the signs, the signals, reflections, oracles etc. My choice from now has to be one of feeling.

Indeed. Again, it is the feeling that is your mirror, not the event. No longer energise the notion that the Universe is a force outside of yourself that directs events or provides triggers as though it knows what is best for you. Instead understand that you are responsible for the essence of any event, the physical manifestation of which is supported by the Universe. The way in which you interpret it depends solely on the focus you are holding. From feeling, you will view the physical events as reflections of your active participation, in other words identify your hand in them. From ego you tend to view the physical as something that happens to you. To be truly active, free, and responsible for consciousness, one does not ponder an equation, ask for a sign from spirit, then proceed according to the dictates of that sign. You will instead proceed based on your inner knowing and recognise the benefits or otherwise of your decisions based on the reflections manifesting in your physical environment. Does this make sense to you?

Yes, it does. It seems so obvious that the feelings we feel in that moment, are our reflection, not the events. I'm sure you've told us that many times. I can't understand how I had, in this whole process, completely missed that point.

Susie, do not use this situation as a weapon against yourself to confirm failure. Your response does show me, however, that you do not consider feeling as your natural state, but rather assume it is something new to be learned. You were actually 'feeling' a great hurt, yet you were identifying it only as a result of the physical situation you witnessed. The ego was hurt, too, and you were only able to explore it from that level which is limited. Therefore you were taken on a tangent where the focus was on the event itself and the feeling was seen as a by-product, if you like. The original hurt is underneath, at Soul level where the source of creation exists. In the physical environment of this life frame, the hurt you felt in this instance, first manifested in your early childhood. You have pushed down those hurt feelings for so long that you cannot identify them with your past instantly, so you got stuck accessing them at the level at which you could relate to them, in the moment.

When you feel stuck in ego, always go back to focusing on your ego thoughts. No matter how self-absorbing or illogical they may seem, journal them, act them out if you must, but clear the ego's faulty perception. Certainly accept the consequences of that action, be also prepared that it may provide you with the opening you need to pursue your greater reality. Take the example with your son. Had you have acted out what your ego was truly feeling, it may have exposed an emotional overreaction on your part to another's odd behaviour. Then having to sit with that outcome, your focus may have shifted away from the physical event, toward examining why you felt so much emotional attachment in the moment. This may then have led to the source of the pain, as opposed to the manifestation of it. A shift in focus can enable the layers to unfold. As a footnote to what I have just said, remember we are not undertaking an inner child workshop. **I reiterate that your pain was first manifested physically in childhood, but your childhood is not the cause of this pain.** To progress, you merely need to be aware when the feelings are triggered and to have an understanding that you own them, they belong to you. No one imposed anything upon you; it is part of who you are. Once you experience feelings through to exposing the other side, then you no longer need to release them as you have been taught in the past. Instead they are restored to the self as artificial barriers causing separation and are exposed and obliterated.

(Susie on behalf of another.) For those of us who are sitting in feeling Virgil, why is it that we are so scared of our shadow. I don't feel the need to analyse anything. Frankly, it's all too much to get my head around. I just seem to accept my negative feelings as aspects of who I am, something I just can't change, which is why I think I couldn't flip the coin in the moment. I did manage to follow the feelings through to a point of stillness and it seems I could lay the blame for everything that's gone wrong in my life squarely at the feet of my shadow. I feel powerless, I guess, to change anything. Intellectually I know what I'm supposed to do, especially in terms of action I could take, but I'm too scared to move.

Now, this is another level of resistance, although taking on a different form compared to that of our friend, Susie. Not everyone fears their shadow self, many actually fear the integration of it and interpret this as resisting the shadow per se. The shadow contains all that you have withheld from yourself, and it takes on the role of 'caretaker', of this aspect of self that you will not embrace. Have you ever heard of the notion that it is not your darkness but actually your light that you fear? This is true for those of you who are already predisposed toward feeling. For those of a more analytical nature it seems somewhat of an incongruous statement that requires deep analysis.

There are a few hints contained within your original question. Firstly, you identify with the aspect of self that has failed you and perceive it (the shadow) more as an independent characteristic of self. It is real to you. Therefore, it is subject to intense projection and is energised emotionally. It represents the fall guy to you in a similar way that the ego intellect does for those relying on their mental processes. It is the keeper of your limitation; it keeps you now from delving into certain areas because you believe you are not capable. As you have said, so many of your past problems can be identified as sourced from shadow; it is in short the keeper of your issues.

Identifying and personifying your shadow allows you to project your failures, for example, outside of yourself – yourself being your normal ego awareness. You talk about your issues like they have a life of their own and therefore accept limiting ideas about yourself as an aspect of who you are. All you are doing is failing to take responsibility for consciousness. Why would you actively seek wholeness? You don't really believe you're capable, successful, and self-determining, because you are used to aligning with the limitations of the shadow. To expose these limitations brings forth great fear of losing them. Collectively they presently represent your one solid reason for not moving forward. What other excuse could you use to justify your stagnation if all the familiar self-deprecating tools are exposed as false? You would have no alternative but to embrace life anew, trusting yourself to succeed and blossom in every moment and this seriously scares you. Not without good reason.

The shadow has been built on a foundation of things gone wrong. Great hurts are filed there and only brought out when like feelings are triggered. This identification of current feelings to past events tends to deter you from action that may result in the risk of further discomfort. The framing and interpretation of your life's experiences into good/bad, shadow/higher self, have caused you to lump everything unsavoury at the feet of the shadow.

Remember, it is the lack of input from an aspect of self that gave rise to all the things gone wrong, not the meddling of the shadow self. Start to reframe your thinking. Look at journaling this notion to expose some of your beliefs about it. Begin to know that this aspect of self is a void that needs to be fulfilled, not a demon that needs to be exorcised. Above all, be conscious of whether you use the shadow and its issues as a way of avoiding taking responsibility for your life as it is manifesting in the now.

Some people actually prefer to identify with the shadow and again are scared of surrendering its power. It's a place of relative safety. Victimhood, be it of the Universe, the shadow, or childhood to name a few, is a convenient and popular way to avoid being challenged to action. To take responsibility for consciousness is my greatest desire for you all – while you personify the shadow, you will not achieve it. Prefer pain and that is what you will manifest. Step outside of your self-imposed limitations and change your preference now.

Thanks Virgil, I can identify with that. Shall we just continue with the focus of flipping the coin?

We will as usual add to this notion. Firstly, I want you to know that I did not expect you would achieve an experience of the other side of the coin. As always, we are undertaking a process and were, of course, preparing the ground for this week's lesson. It is critical to this process that I give you an opportunity to undertake a lesson that allows you to draw your own experience. If I provided too much detail last week then this would have created unnecessary expectation. Above all, own your experience.

The ultimate aim of the lesson is to consciously flip the coin in the moment from feeling and this is what we are building to. I will provide an example of flipping the coin that I hope will add on to your own experiences and help you to see its value in the 'real' physical world. This should then facilitate greater awareness as you undertake the subsequent lesson. I should note that this story has been taken from a real life experience that The Channel viewed on a television program. (keep in mind that there are no coincidences in your reality)

A young man was faced with the death of his father, whom he loved dearly. Their relationship was extremely close and the son viewed the loss of this great influence with tremendous sorrow. In their desire to honour their father's memory, all the children decided to construct the father's coffin and excavate the burial site. It was an especially difficult thing to do, and much emotion was released. Eventually their task was completed and the son lay in the hole that they had made and where the next day his father would be laid to rest. The range of emotion in that moment led him to some important realisations that show the value of 'flipping the coin'. As he lay in the ground, the son was nearly overcome with the grief of losing his father, but as he allowed the feelings freedom the focus soon become that of the enormous love he felt for his father. The intensity was the same and as he immersed more in the feelings, wavering between the two experiences of love and loss, he noticed that it was actually the same feeling. The only factor that determined his interpretation of whether the feeling was love or loss was where his focus was. He realised in an instant that he wouldn't be feeling this intensity of loss unless he had been able to experience the intensity of love. He then chose to ground the feeling with a focus of love. His way forward from this major event in his life was one of love and completion. He could just have easily perpetuated the sense of loss. The feeling is the same, the choice is yours.

This course is primarily about experiencing, recognising and consciously navigating those choices to higher outcomes. But as you are ensconced in the mass dream of polarity with the ego as your guide, thereby ignoring your true nature, it has up until now been necessary to experience both sides of the coin. As you allow your feeling self to guide your Earth journey, all ego polarities will be naturally balanced and made whole.

Above all else, do not try to exert pressure on this task as an outcome. Flipping the coin is not something that can be coerced; it is a natural process of experiencing all that you are. Polarities in any form are merely constructs of this world and do not exist in your greater reality, therefore if you actively seek the opposite feeling you will be definitely operating from ego. The essence here is that feelings are not opposite but identical and it is your ego resistance that determines them any other way. When the ego allows the feeling tone to embrace its perceptions with true knowing in the moment, it will clarify the true meaning of any situation in the same way that I can reframe your experiences, outside the cause and effect notions of ego.

Yes, I can see now that was a problem for me last week as I was definitely looking for a different feeling, something to obliterate the pain.

Indeed. It was necessary, however, for you to experience the task in that way in order to expose your current reality and we will continue to build upon this awareness, via a new focus. I would like you to challenge yourself to a direct experience of being in the feeling tone in the moment. You are to call forward a crossroads experience. A point at which you can take a leap of faith into the counsel of the feeling tone, or you can remain 'safe' in the ego's judgement or the shadow's limitation. I would like you to affirm immediately, then again tomorrow, that you are prepared to step into your feeling tone. Journal whatever comes up within the ego as a consequence of this affirmation. Set the intention that you will have a crossroads experience, then let it go. Do not think about it again. Within this whole experience will be an opportunity to flip the coin because of your allowance in the moment, coupled with the further explanation provided this week.

Remove the ego stress over right and wrong responses, which is only an attempt to control and seek a more gentle rhythmic approach to your week. Allow the flow of your life to reveal itself and accept responsibility for what comes forward. Let's take a step away from our daily rigours and problems and tap into the flow, so that when the crossroads experience manifests it will be obvious to you. I don't want you agonising over the superfluous, this will free you up to recognise your true crossroads, created with your own hand and intent.

I would like you to journal the crossroads, detailing the physical form as well as spiritual essence and be ready to share your experiences next week. You are ready to journey through these feelings – know this to be true. I wish you well in this journey to uncover more of your beauty.

Be blessed.

Thank you, Virgil.

Lesson Eleven

I call to myself a crossroads experience.

CHAPTER 12
Your Crossroads Experience

The experience of revisiting and editing Lesson Twelve was a challenging one for me for several reasons, mostly because it was simply a difficult phase of the course process. I remember feeling as though we were always falling short of our efforts - as we reached out, we would return empty handed. Our insecurities mounted as the foundations continued to shake. While the feelings were distinctly awful, being in them is what eventually delivered us. Stay with the feelings no matter what, for in them lies the answers you are seeking. Avoid attempting to manufacture an outcome, your own revelations will come in their own time – and believe it or not, the time is not yet upon you.

Despite our apparent difficulties, I recall a sense of completion looming around this time, as though we were on the precipice of genuine understanding. We were still expecting to be lead to a point of spiritual integration. This was only a vague expectation as we had no idea of what such a state would actually feel like. We waited for so-called divine intervention, anything that would eliminate our struggle and facilitate an opening to manifest all we desired in the physical. We continued to respond in feeling, and hoped that the haze would soon clear.

As a channel, I also remember feeling Virgil's frustration around this time - not that he was annoyed, it was just that he had given us all he could and the last steps had to be taken by us. He had to witness our struggle, and I could feel that sometimes he had difficulty in identifying why we were finding it so hard. We wanted answers from him and he wanted us to access our own. In previous chapter topics there were reams of channelled material to explore that supported the general theme of the weekly lesson, now he just reiterated much of what had already been covered, reframing our experiences, urging us to use the tools. One time he even told us all to go back to Lesson One and focus on our ego thoughts, such was our confusion. We immediately thought we were just too stupid to get it. Now it is clear that even this time was full of purpose.

The critical thing is that there is no magic formula, no highly evolved guide that can tell you who or what you are. There is nothing outside of yourself that can save you, no affirmation that will make everything fall into place and no course that can gift you with what you do not already contain within. We really believed that if we just did this course diligently then we and our lives would be transformed for the better. This was partly true. The course gave us the tools to experience our physical lives with a new focus and a greater awareness of the paradigm we were working with. But life still had to be faced each day, decisions had to be made, fears faced, and love embraced.

Before the course, Susie's and my surface focus had always been on evolving toward a higher level of spiritual being. We would have appeared less concerned with the physical, maybe even created the illusion that we were above it. In truth, our pursuit of spiritual enlightenment was motivated by the hope that, as a result, our day-to-day physical lives would magically improve. In working with the chapter lessons, our focus was slowly becoming tuned toward being physical and allowing our human imperfection, while simultaneously aligning spirit via feeling. This dual focus and legitimate allowance of each in learning to respond to our lives established the foundation template to allow us to consciously create our lives. The only way we could do this was to be conscious of both our apparent, yet unravelling, ego limitations together with our spiritual strength and allow the two to create in unison. This was a major shift in perception for me and although I could not see it at the time, it heralded a period of significant growth where I actually embraced my physical journey with a measure of commitment and grace. Before, I would unconsciously avoid the physical by retreating into the safety of spirit and the never-ending analysis of my 'issues', thereby observing my life instead of fully living it.

Despite the emerging awareness of both our ego and Soul needs, we were still manifesting difficulties during this time. Our resistance to owning our experience was kicking in, taking a range of guises that we just didn't question. Situations still appeared to 'happen' to us that we concluded were beyond our control and were an undeniable fact of our circumstance, rather than a reflection of our beliefs. Life doesn't just randomly happen to you; if you still think that it does, because you can't rationalise some of your co-creations, then this belief has to be overturned before you can proceed. Exposing your resistance is critical and this is where all the tools given previously come into play. This is why we kept getting held up by Virgil: sent back to re-do lessons we hadn't touched in months. He was actually giving us the grounding on how to make this course a way of life. To take it beyond a spiritual circle, a few hours each week, into where it really mattered – our daily lives. When it becomes the way in which you meet the world, we can assure you, nothing changes, yet absolutely everything changes. It is utterly amazing.

As a teacher, or editor, of Virgil's work I find this point in the book difficult also. I'm aware you want answers, yet neither I nor Virgil can give them to you as they must grow from your own experience. You must seek your own insights by continuing to observe the paradigm you've come in with, which is reflected all around you - once you choose to see. Take responsibility right now for whatever is occurring because your struggle is your resistance and absolutely your own creation. Avoid projecting any difficulties you may be having onto others, the course or against yourself. If you find you are projecting, failing, apathetic, angry, or confused, etc., remember that you've probably felt it before with other teachers, courses, or experiences. Do not let the opportunity pass to flip the coin and return to yourself that which you have kept hidden all this time.

On to debriefing the lesson for this week. We all expected our 'religious' experience to manifest with the calling in of the crossroads experience. We hoped that we would experience an epiphany that would make everything fall into place, demonstrate our enlightened natures, and render us spiritually successful. No-one had a religious experience. Generally this week's outcomes fell into two sections; those that came in with a loose identification of a crossroads challenge but were unable to do anything with it, and those that believed they didn't manifest anything at all. Some of these people tried to make situations fit into the moment, only to later understand that they had missed their true opportunity somewhere.

I fell into the former category. I knew my crossroads came in the form of my relationship. It was more an intellectual knowing because I had been working within that framework for some time. Consequently, I was unable to do anything but label it and sulk about it. I felt an even bigger failure for my inability to evolve the situation in the moment. Susie fell into the latter category. During the week she shared a dinner with a group of like-minded friends. Talk always focused on matters of spirit but this time instead of lecturing them all on her new found spiritual course knowledge, she let people be, and didn't contradict anyone else's point of view or beliefs. Susie felt very proud of her control and assumed that she had identified and passed her crossroads experience in the moment. Later Susie realised that she was really just clutching at straws in an effort to make something fit. Suffice to say, all of us get another opportunity. We will share our true crossroads with you in later chapters.

In the majority of cases people actually manifested quite obvious crossroads, yet due to their trained resistance, completely failed to identify them and therefore own them. For example, in a later course we asked the participants to share their crossroads experience. One participant said she didn't have one, that nothing of note had happened. However, in relating her week in a more conversational tone she couldn't wait to let us know that while she had been out and about with her new boyfriend, they had seen her ex-husband at a local cafe with another woman. The participant and her ex-husband had not parted on good terms, due to him having a secret other life that she only discovered a few years into their marriage, so she hadn't seen him in a fair while. She pointed the man out to her boyfriend with the following narrative quote...

'Oh my God, it's my ex-husband. Just take a look at that cross-dressing misogynist transsexual lover posing as a charming womaniser. You can see by the way he's sitting he'd rather be wearing a slinky satin number with high heels. It's obvious his eyelashes are tinted! My God what did I ever see in him? He never really wanted to marry me, just wear my wedding dress!'

Susie and I (after composing ourselves from laughing) expressed our opinion that seeing her ex-husband was her crossroads experience, not because of the physical event per se, but what it had brought up in the moment. She was unable to identify it as her crossroads because she was too busy resisting it, choosing to remain firmly in ego, and thereby allowing the surface judgements to manifest in the form of her tirade of abuse and projection. She had not owned these judgements at all. She believed it was his fault and therefore she was kept firmly from feeling or - in the ego's terms – felt safe. When we told her this she looked shocked. It hadn't even remotely occurred to her to look at it as a potential crossroads experience because she was convinced that she had 'dealt with her whole marriage issue long ago and moved on'. She very well may have reconciled her marriage, but remember, we are dealing in feeling here, not in events, and the feelings of that moment were most definitely lost in the ego ranting. She had to date, been grounding the course very successfully, but as we moved closer to the feeling centre, her resistance kicked in just like everyone else's.

Essentially you need to try to identify which category you fall into as a result of last week's outcomes. Generally, those who identify more with feeling tend to see their crossroads fairly easily, as it seems to be the same-old, same-old, but feel helpless to do anything with it in the moment. Those that tend to identify closer with the intellect and logic tend to manifest really obvious crossroads events that they completely fail to see, and then play with many surface issues to try to make them fit. Either way, most people feel that the week has not been a huge success. As mentioned earlier, most sense that the past lessons are coming to a point of confluence, yet this coming together seems to be eluding them personally. It is a meaningful time, you are learning to consciously recognise and work with your life in the moment, and therefore there are more opportunities in the present to master this aspect of the course. Good luck and be assured you will have an important experience in the week ahead.

Virgil, as ever, remained supportive and focused. As Susie tried to pull him further into explaining spiritual theory he just kept returning to feeling. I, The Channel, was in as much confusion as everyone else, so it took longer to establish a strong connection. Despite this, I still found it very refreshing to channel. I would sit for quite a while trying to connect and could literally feel Virgil's presence in my mind and body. Silly, often self-deprecating thoughts would emerge seemingly from nowhere and I would keep reminding myself to focus on spirit and the clarity within. I learned in time to relax and enjoy the process as I knew Virgil was helping me to clear the way for a strong connection with him. Finally Virgil, not my irrational thoughts, would dominate my mind and I would know it was time to utter the statement that let everyone know he was present.

Sally...

Good evening my friends and welcome to Lesson Twelve. Thank you for your patience. There was some energy work that was required on The Channel so we took the opportunity to bask in each other's energy, so to speak, and refine our connection somewhat. Given the episodes of the last few days there was some...debris is not quite the right word, but there was some cleaning of The Channel required. So I thank you for your patience and we will now move directly to debrief our crossroads experience.

(Susie asks on behalf of Sally.) Virgil, I know I had a crossroads this week and it centred on my relationship as usual. It was tough and I reached the point of utter helplessness, so I gave up. I just sat in that feeling and it

wouldn't move. I still feel the same days later. It all leads me to think I really should be moving on but I know I would just be playing out an old pattern. I know the rules, but I just can't seem to get out of that head space. I journaled during the week that you'd have to be Gandhi, to remain in feeling and out of ego. It's a very hard time at the moment.

I understand your frustration, but there can be no one rule book containing the definitive solution, for this would fly in the face of individuality and uniqueness. Each person will manifest their own triggers, reach their own depth or shallowness of experience, and each will have their own limits on how far they will follow feeling through. I cannot control this, nor can I even influence you in the moment. Taking responsibility for consciousness by very definition calls you to make your own choices in total freedom. The key is whether you are able to own your experience – and by this I mean the feelings triggered by these events. Your struggle is a direct measure of your resistance to meet and restore the shadow wisdom. Step one is to sit in that knowledge and cease blaming yourself, others or circumstances.

You have set a clear intention to heal your life. Your commitment to the course is supporting this intention in the physical. Therefore, opportunities abound to allow you to partake in direct experience with all that keeps you separated so you can heal it. As opportunities are presented, you fail to take ownership of the feelings but remain firmly focused on the events themselves, relegating the feelings to mere outcomes of your circumstances. The focus on the events, although misguided, still keeps your intention to ground the course essence strong, so you manifest opportunities again and again – only to project them outward again and again. You will get sick and tired of this cycle, and I will patiently await your choice to own your life via the feelings and be here applauding loudly when you do.

What will be required for you to get to the point where you actually choose ownership of feeling through positive choice, rather than through fear or other motivation, differs between individuals. It may be an experience of profound sadness, the threat of loss, desperate confusion, anger, to name a few. The question remains, whatever the feeling is – do you have the courage to own and move through it? Surrender of control, be it intellectual control or keeping feelings under control, opens the doorway for the true solution to be recognised from the feeling tone. The solution is already there; you need but only recognise it. Your past training is important here. You have an underlying faith in the integrity of spirit that will shine through. Know that if you seem unable to break out of your ego focus, it is merely because you are choosing to experience the event from that level. Not as an active choice as such, but due to resisting the way of feeling that is being offered. To immerse yourself in feeling is automatically choosing to own your experiences.

Thanks Virgil. I'm sure that helps Sally. I (Susie) thought I had identified my crossroads experience when I found myself in the middle of a discussion about spiritual theories. Much of what was being espoused as fact by the group, I no longer believe. Instead of spouting out my new knowledge (because perhaps in a way that would build up my ego as I may have in the past) I chose to remain apart from it and not attack their beliefs. I thought therefore that I had not only recognised my crossroads, but had also responded appropriately to it. Actually though, I now know that wasn't it at all and I must have missed it. Can you tell me what my crossroads experience was for the week?

I cannot provide that for you Susie, but know that the intention you set did bring forth a clear crossroads opportunity. The recognition of such cannot be imposed upon you. It is something with you in each moment, and can therefore be accessed in any point going forward – that is your hint. You are correct in that you have not experienced it at all at this point, but as always you will be given another opportunity as we go forward. So that brings me to the focus of next week.

You are to again call a crossroads experience into your life. Set the intention clearly and without judgement twice in the next twenty-four hours then allow it to go. Do not think about the task, do not expect it will come in a particular form or necessarily stem from great upheaval or pain. Given your experiences of the past week, coupled with the greater explanation already provided, I know you will be able to recognise your crossroads when it manifests. There is, however, a further level to this task that must be grounded in the next week. You must experience the situation in the moment and from the vantage of feeling. When you recognise your crossroads, sit in a space of allowance. As you do so, you will be encouraging the feeling to expand and envelope you. Do not entertain the ego's processes which will be seeking to manufacture a desired outcome that is of its own making and therefore not real. Care less about the physical circumstances and focus entirely on the feelings and in the process of expanding them. Trust that this is a natural process that you have temporarily forgotten, not a new concept to be learned.

What will make this week different from last? If I couldn't recognise the crossroads last week what can I do to ensure I will identify it this week?

Do not do anything Susie; merely allow it all to unfold. Clear and clarify your intention and resolve. Do not move forward carrying the baggage of last week's perceived failure, for we are involved in a process of becoming; it is not a destination, so there is no failure. Let it go and create anew with diligence and intent in the coming week. I wish you well in actualising your intention.

Be blessed.

Thank you, Virgil.

(We were all shocked by Virgil's seemingly abrupt departure. He clearly didn't want to entertain an involved discussion on crossroads at this point. Follow this pattern and don't overdo the reading of theory or think too much

about the process. Just affirm it twice in the next twenty-four hours as Virgil suggests then let it go. We wish you well.)

Lesson Twelve

Experience your crossroads in the moment of feeling.

CHAPTER 13
Your Experience In The Moment

Well, what a week this turned out to be. In the allowance (finally) of feeling, amidst all its seeming ugliness, came a turning point in perception that continues to grow and evolve to this day. To truly feel the crossroads in your life is the most reliable, efficient, yet at times difficult process to undertake. However, it is an essential facet to ensure you understand the purpose of your co-creations and where they can take you. I will expand on this in our final chapter. In the time being, let us move directly to the usual debrief of our experiences.

Both Susie and I managed to identify and experience the feelings associated with our respective crossroads, including a sense of its polarity (by flipping the proverbial coin). For the first time, in what seemed like quite a while, we felt like we were finally glimpsing the true value of the course. The greatest revelation we both gained from the week was that flipping the coin was not something that you tried to do, or tried to imagine, or even tried to feel. It was a natural process that emerged when we sat within feeling long enough and fully enough to really own it. Resisting the urge to rationalise, blame, project, or internalise the dramas that triggered the feelings, crystallised the sense of their source being within the self and so the answers could emerge - also from within the self. These answers came not in words, or actions to take, but in a feeling sense of self and the need to identify destructive internal patterns. When left alone and not judged by the mind, the feeling naturally became fluid, almost like it was seeking fulfilment in the moment and then transformed seemingly effortlessly. It is for this reason that we didn't really understand what had happened, because the process took place beyond the questioning mind. We were so happy to have some tangible and positive growth in our journey that it didn't matter to us that we could not understand the process.

You will recall that Susie missed her crossroads experience last week and that Virgil gave her only one hint, which was that it was present with her in every moment. The week before, after her dinner with friends where Susie had refrained from speaking out and had identified that moment as a crossroads only later to dismiss it, she went home and took a pregnancy test. The test was positive and she was overjoyed, it had happened in quick time following her last miscarriage and she felt very positive about it. She did not for a moment even remotely consider that there was any foundation of a crossroads experience in that event and kept looking for one as the week unfolded. You may recall that last week she turned up to the course with nothing to report. She had missed her opportunity so went forward into the next week with a new determination to identify and deal with her crossroads in the moment. She was pondering her life and what would emerge as her test when a few eerie signs began to emerge.

She was on her own for the weekend, as her husband was bushwalking and her son was having fun with grandparents. Then, just as she was about to go into the shower, she noticed an enormous, hairy spider and like most of us was too scared to try to remove it and therefore left it alone. She opted for a bath instead. She then confirmed with her brother her intention to book his beach house for the following weekend. Susie had in fact manifested identical circumstances immediately prior to her last miscarriage. Back then she was teaching an infant grade when an enormous hairy spider fell into her hair petrifying not only herself, but a class of screaming children. (She always felt in hindsight that this had been a bad sign). Her husband and son were also away for the weekend and she had booked the holiday house for the following weekend. As she hung up the phone after confirming her house booking this time around, she started to sense something building within her. Slowly, she began to notice the similarities in the other two events of the day and in a moment the connection was made – she was right back in the days just prior to her miscarriage.

Susie believed she had dealt with the pain surrounding her previous loss, having seen a healer and received all the clichés: 'It was meant to be; the babe will return; and it wasn't the right time'. She knew well enough though that the signs were glaringly obvious and not to be ignored. The realisation became more apparent that this must be her crossroads. She sat in the apparent joy of her new pregnancy and allowed the feelings free reign. The rest is told by Susie directly to Virgil, but it highlights a very critical point that not all surface thoughts that are masking inner pain or fear are going to be negative. Hopefully, it also demonstrates that we do manifest our intentions (in this case a crossroads experience), but it is up to us to recognise them in the moment.

Susie and I still have a chuckle about her choosing to notice a dinner party with friends as her crossroads experience, instead of the seemingly obvious event of this pregnancy following a miscarriage. As it turned out this new pregnancy was a perpetual crossroads from start to finish, with many opportunities for her to flip the coin and consciously create a wonderful experience within the paradigm she knew she was working with. It was an important journey in becoming a conscious creator for her.

I hope that you were able to recognise your own crossroads experience this week. If so, enjoy the sense of satisfaction this gives you and allow it to ground as a natural outcome of your human existence, not as a one-off exercise. If you were unsure of your crossroads, do not be concerned – provided you keep setting your intention, the opportunities will present again until you finally grasp them. We have learned to accept that our lives will never be that 'idealised perfect paradise' we always yearned for. We now understand that we will continue to manifest dramas that afford us an opportunity to heal our trained resistance in the moment. To this end, crossroads have become a natural process in engaging any challenging aspect of our lives - from the joy to the tumultuous. It has helped me heal my life more than any other single teaching. Only in self-identification of crossroads in the moment is true self-awareness grounded – so there is no other option here but perseverance. Continue to create with strong intention because then you can be assured that it is manifesting – you need to only recognise it. You can spend another week on the crossroads if you see fit. When you deem you are ready, move on to the next lesson. Trust in what your feelings are telling you and embrace your revelations.

I have again included my questions as asked to Virgil by Susie and her questions, one after the other. This is to illustrate that form is not nearly as relevant as essence and that despite our creations being physically different, their essence is drawn from the same source and Virgil can therefore answer them as one. Just how critical essence is over form will become more obvious as we progress.

Connecting with Virgil was easy and the difficulties of the past few weeks had seemingly vanished. I thought I could detect a sense of relief in Virgil, or maybe it was my own energy, either way we were truly as one while we channelled during this period. Now over to Virgil, smiling broadly of course and with an air of satisfaction...

Sally...

Good evening my friends and welcome to Lesson Thirteen. As the course is drawing to a close, I know that this week you are all excited by your responses to the last lesson, so we will immediately begin with debriefing your experiences.

(Susie relates this experience on behalf of Sally.) Virgil, I was already fairly sure that my crossroads experience would manifest once again in my relationship and it did. This time though I was able to sit and expand on the feeling and allow it to really envelop all the ego confusion. It preceded an amazing turn around in my perception and I don't understand why I had to create so much drama around it in the past. The feelings became as one as the ego chatter ceased and I reached that point of stillness, following on from which I fully realised how much I loved my partner and how I did have the desire and the strength to seek and create positive change between us. Whilst I held this feeling, I easily and effortlessly exposed my most vulnerable aspect to him and despite the difficulties we have had, I pledged my desire to love and be loved. Later, he approached me with the same level of vulnerability and love, and I know that somehow we have transcended our judgements around the relationship and each other and have now turned our focus inward. I know that that act alone has grounded our partnership more fully than ever. I don't understand it but I believe all the anxiety and doubt, while it might not be behind us, is an aspect we can work on from within, that will positively foster our mutual growth. Having said that, this

has lead me to see that there is something within me that is seeking healing. I know it is independent of the relationship, but I can't identify it exactly. It involves frustration at having to grow in pain, despite my conscious intention to grow with grace. I don't want to pursue growth in my relationship in this way again, I want us to continue to evolve 'hand-in-hand' in love, but I don't know whether I am capable of it.

(Susie) Now my turn, Virgil. This week I know I was able to identify my crossroads experience and I can hardly believe that I missed it last week. Of course it was in the fantastic news that I am pregnant again, particularly joyful because it happened so soon. I didn't consider it last week because I was so happy about it, and I was expecting my crossroads to be fearful. When I manifested all those amazingly similar signs, well I could hardly miss it. (Virgil smiles knowingly) I had really only felt joy and relief at the time I learned I was pregnant, yet I had decided to wait to announce it, to allow the feeling to emerge and embrace all the ego chatter. Yet quite quickly I felt an enormous amount of fear there, it just washed over me and was very powerful. The fear was obviously of having another miscarriage and losing this child that I am already in love with. I was fearful of being unable to create another healthy child. Of never realising a desire, that I find so fundamental to who I believe I am, which is to raise several children. So, as the fear expanded, it did embrace other aspects of my life and my inability to create what I want. It was not pleasant. Then I reached this point of stillness, where calmness prevailed. From there the same feeling washed over me, yet I wasn't fearful; I didn't really understand what happened.

Congratulations to both of you. It is indeed positive that neither of you understand what has occurred because understanding is not the desired goal – feeling is. In that moment you have linked the entire course process, bringing it together to work as a cohesive way of meeting your life's circumstances. The Channel has understood that in her vulnerability lies her strength because they are one and the same. Before, she has sought her strength via intellectual weighing up of events, of who's right and who's wrong, of drawing conclusions and taking action. Now she understands that the strength she has been seeking was contained within the vulnerability that she was too frightened to feel, therefore the answer to her prayers was always there, only just denied or suppressed.

You, Susie, on the other hand, held an expectation that your crossroads would be negative and dark. When you felt the joy of your ensuing pregnancy you simply focused your ego attention in that area only, yet another aspect was lurking, for why else would one keep such joyful news a secret but for fear of something? Although you felt nothing but joy you were actually suppressing a very real fear, simultaneously. You did this brilliantly because the conscious mind was not even slightly aware that there was anything else there except joy. For this reason and because your intention to identify the crossroads was so clear, you manifested remarkably obvious signs to get your attention. Finally, when that attention was allowed expansion into the totality of the feeling surrounding the event, you were shocked by the depth of fear that dwelled there unchecked.

You have had an experience similar to the story of the man who had to bury his father amidst sorrow, but found love. You have embraced the love of a child and found that therein lays great fear of never actualising that love, of losing the child and then having to somehow rationalise it as your greatest growth. That love and fear of loss are one and the same feeling, judged and differentiated by ego only. Within that moment Susie, the feeling tone pervaded the situation and the ego chatter. You were then able to glean a sense that the particular fear had been exposed and released, despite being unable to name it in that way. The point of stillness you refer to is not a destination either but the absence of ego influence, which then gave rise to the acknowledgement of the essence of the feeling. The feeling was the key, and had you been able to name it, perhaps that would have blocked that knowing from emerging.

Now, what you have done this week is culminated the entire course process in one moment of the myriad of crossroads you have, and will continue to have, in your lives. This, as you know, is no small feat and I applaud you resoundingly. You have identified a moment in time and space where your response will directly influence your future creations and therefore your very life itself. More consciously than ever before, you have made choices of a higher nature because you have allowed your self expression. This allowance of feeling consciousness has automatically led you to flip the coin, or in other words has made the ego polarity whole. You have experienced, via direct participation, the process of creating your reality and you should now deduce that it is not shrouded in mystery or jargon, but is a natural state of being, as much a part of your humanness as breathing. Throughout the process of this course you have inadvertently, yet consciously, used many of the tools already provided such as paying attention to and nurturing the ego, affirming feeling body consciousness, spending time in nature, removing the judgement associated with feeling, etc. So I am overjoyed that after so many weeks of your ego **interpreting you as a failure**, you have trumped its perceptions by achieving your greatest success. Bask in the joy of your success, but remember we are not seeking a destination. I now add the final phase to your journey, the last stand of ego drama and false beliefs now need to be addressed.

Many of you would agree that the road to this point has been a difficult one and at times excruciatingly frustrating. Having trained you so well in a new way of meeting and responding to your life, I now want to free you of it at the same time. This entire process has been about introducing you to your own self; that is, introducing you to both the spirit that is eternal and limitless and the ego that is finite and limited. Through direct contact with both, you will come to understand the paradigm that you are working with in this lifetime. I think you would agree that if you had to spend the rest of your lives identifying and processing every single crossroads experience as it manifested in the moment as we have done this week, then there will be little time for much else. Spiritual growth should be undertaken in confidence and freedom, not in grappling for seeming hidden meaning. The final task actualised will deliver these qualities to you in abundance. While crossroads will continue, for the most part, you will navigate them effortlessly from the wisdom of Soul for you will know their source.

Within all the dramas that you have manifested into the physical lay a common thread. Once this thread is identified by you, you can work on making it conscious in every moment going forward which will in turn positively change your lives. This common thread when followed via feeling will lead you to a direct experience with the paradigm you came in with – what I refer to as your core belief. This core belief colours to varying degrees everything you create, both on the surface and from the depths of self. It is suppressed because it is not even noticed or questioned; it is considered a fact or aspect of this reality rather than a belief about it. It is so intimately connected to who you are that it acts as a distorted window to view your world. You are not even aware that your vision is impaired because the window is a familiar part of you. However, there will be no doubt when you have shed light on your core belief, because it will restore sense to all your past dramas. The core belief is already there, very obviously influencing your life so it will not be a surprise. The only reason you don't recognise it is that you have never questioned it before as something that is pliable rather than fact.

This week you are to use whatever methods already provided which work for you to determine and experience your core belief. It will not come in words, it will come via feeling which, when expanded, has the potential to be translated into words. This translation is possible because, as I have said, it operates both at the surface ego and inner Soul level, so the ego too is already familiar with its essence. I am deeply satisfied with your diligence and progress to date. I am with you, applauding, as you face the centre of your being in this life frame.

Be blessed.

(Again, Virgil left somewhat abruptly this week. Clearly, this is a time for feeling focus. There is nothing else we can add to help you this week. It is essential that the recognition of your core belief comes through feeling not through an intellectual analysis. The reason for this will become clear, yet we cannot expand further at this time as we will be revealing too much too soon. Just go with the flow...)

Lesson Thirteen

I choose to experience and know my core belief.

CHAPTER 14
Conclusion

Susie and I had left the group last week walking on air. We felt like we had actually achieved great success. We were bubbly and chatty to complete strangers, even our postures and gaits exuded confidence. We were enjoying this state of grace so much that we didn't focus too much on the core belief task assigned to us. Virgil had made it clear that we were to identify it without his help, so we took a break from our regular channelling sessions and waited for the revelation to emerge. We were feeling a sense of contentment so complete that we thought we had healed our lives in that one moment of flipping the coin, whilst immersed in a crossroads experience. Although we didn't articulate our feelings, we both assumed we had passed a test and that as a consequence the struggle would cease while we sat back and began to manifest only positive things in our lives.

Once again we were tackling the course as a destination, not as a way of life, so within a few weeks things had started to deteriorate, although in different areas than that of the crossroads. For example, my relationship was reborn and was going from strength to strength, yet I was starting to experience dramas and difficulties in my workplace, which hadn't been present before. In Susie's case, in contrast to her previous pregnancy, this one was unfolding as a breeze with no complications or even the slightest discomfort, yet the dreaded rash was back with a vengeance. After all those months of hard work only to be rewarded with a mere few weeks of peace, was just more than we could take. We wanted to demonstrate our lives working to prove (to ourselves and others) that our faith in spirituality was not unfounded, yet we were simply unable to do so. Things were going wrong – again. We were angry, confused and overwhelmed by our perceived failings, yet initially we were completely incapable of facing these feelings honestly. We sat in this depressing energy for several weeks, churning and fuming.

At the same time Susie and I were meeting at least weekly to transcribe onto disk all of Virgil's original channelling sessions. Inadvertently we were revisiting the techniques and theory of the course. Again it was promising so much, yet according to our measures, true success eluded us and we of course believed it was our fault – we were just too stupid. I can still recall the day when, for both of us, our feelings hit rock bottom and our depression and moods matched perfectly, despite the fact that our physical triggers were very different. We were having a break from the arduous task of transcribing the tapes and were sitting at Susie's kitchen table on a cold miserable day drinking warm drinks and eating chocolate (as women tend to do when they are depressed). We were feeling very sorry for ourselves, lamenting how many years we had dedicated to our spiritual growth and cleaning up our act, spending hard earned money on books, courses and the like, only to be seemingly more uncertain than most people who were not involved in spirit. We talked about a few of our friends who had no interest in spiritual development or conscious creation, yet were manifesting fantastic lives in every aspect that they desired – relationships, career, travel, money, while we continued to struggle day-to-day with our same desires. I can remember both of us fighting back tears, embarrassed yet overwhelmed by the pain of thinking this course - and therefore, yet again, spirituality - had abandoned and failed us. It was truly a devastating moment.

We sat confused and dismayed in that energy for some time, trying to establish why. Both of us were on the brink of admitting something lurking deep within us, it was written in our eyes. We both knew it as we exchanged glances, but we were holding back, skirting around the subject. Nonetheless we continued to dissect our feelings and thoughts until eventually the truth came out. It is a testament not only to our friendship but our belief in non-judgement that we were able to speak of our worst feelings and therefore birth them into the physical in a conscious way. For both of us, it was the most difficult thing to admit consciously let alone verbalise to each other and it came from the depths of self and from feeling. It was that deep down, we were expecting the lives of others not in spirit to be shaken in the future. We anticipated they would get a tap on the shoulder from spirit calling them to the pathway – worse still, we believed this calling would come in the form of some kind of pain, struggle, or tragedy to necessarily wake them from unconsciousness. We were both appalled by our insights into our own feelings – feelings that had been simmering since just after our last session with Virgil – the session detailing the existence of a core belief.

In short, the tumultuous feelings pervading all aspects of our lives could be surmised as: We were expecting pain in the lives of ourselves and others because that essentially was the way of spirit. Feelings rising from this belief took on many guises; abandonment, unworthiness, betrayal, and lack of safety to name a few. The evidence of it was everywhere, since no matter how dedicated our effort, we were simply incapable of manifesting our heart's desire. Add the sense of shame to the mix because it seemed like we were wishing struggle upon people – which wasn't our intention at all. It was just as Virgil had said; our core belief was something we considered not so much as a belief, but rather as a fact about the reality we lived in. The important thing here is that it came forward in feeling, yet while we were immersed within it, we were completely unable to identify our core belief in the terms described above. Rather we had felt it for many weeks, festering, complaining, and feeling jealous of others, and sorry for ourselves, all because our hearts desire seemed far away. In that moment however, we knew that we were on to something. Immediately we set up the space for a channelling session with Virgil. He was now able to expand on the notion of core belief for us because we had not only identified it in feeling, but we had positively wallowed in it. This immersion in feeling of what had long been ignored (our core belief), gave rise to the final conscious birthing of it into the physical via our admissions at that kitchen table. As we had finally embraced this aspect via feeling it opened the doorway for it to be, not so much healed, but consciously worked with as an ally rather than a dictator.

The following is Virgil's explanation of Susie's and my core beliefs. What was ours may not be yours, but the concept is constant to all. It is that old familiar feeling that is always with you, yet continually denied. When you look back on your journaling it should be a constant thread linking all of your responses to various physical dramas back to the same source. To us, once grounded, it was glaringly obvious that it had been present right back from Lesson One in the recording of our ego thoughts. Virgil was right: there is nothing hidden – we just refuse to see – the entire course process was nothing more than to open our eyes to what was there all along. Virgil states categorically to Susie in several chapters of her inherent fear and distrust of the physical realm – at the time it was so obvious that we didn't even bother to discuss it with him. Honestly, Susie and I had always considered the physical to be a really difficult journey for Soul and this notion was espoused and confirmed by just about all of our spiritual books and teachers as a fact, too. It was as much a part of our spiritual truth as the Earth is a part of our physical truth; we just never questioned it, let alone thought we could change it.

It was a difficult channel for me to keep my ego self out of initially. In the beginning, Susie's voice was often caught in her throat as she was holding back tears and this naturally affected my emotions also. I believe this is why in the early stages of the channel Virgil states quite emphatically that he can feel Susie's pain, because of course, it was something that I shared with her and my own pain was very close to the surface too. As always, once we got started the connection strengthened as I embraced and surrendered to Virgil's energy. Even today as I re-read this channel I am still encouraged and awestruck by his wisdom. I can hardly believe that these words came out of my mouth – even though they did not originate within my mind. I am still amazed that I was able to assist in Virgil grounding them. We have found that periodically reviewing this chapter in particular, is helpful in reinforcing the lessons of the course. Now, over to Virgil.

Sally...

Good Afternoon Susie, I am present and ready for our session, please begin.

Hi Virgil, I trust that you have been listening to Sally's and my discussions this afternoon?

Indeed I have.

Okay, basically they concerned our feelings that we have once again been let down by spirit despite our strong commitment and significant efforts. I feel completely devastated. What are we missing?

(Virgil begins in a controlled but very intense manner) I can feel your pain, I can feel your confusion; it is like you don't know whether to shake your fist at Spirit in anger or pray and plead for your torment to cease. You need to know why it is all going wrong, yet the answers continue to elude you and it is frustrating. Add to this others, not consciously pursuing the grounding of spirit in their lives seemingly have the life you desire, then that frustration becomes embellished in deep resentment and pain. The culmination of the past months of the course which led you to observe your life against a new conscious expectation of joy has accessed an aspect of self that lies deep within both you and The Channel – in your very D.N.A in fact. This is a great day for you and one that has the potential to change your paradigm forever.

From now on, as I speak to you Susie, I am also speaking to The Channel. Your prevailing blueprint, from which stems the basic broad creation of your life is grounded and limited by a compelling core belief in the insecurity, the difficulty, the unsupportive, and painful environment that is the physical realm period. I would characterise it as a wounding to purpose that could be summarised as, *I fear life*. That in itself is not an unusual paradigm to work with in this day and age; however, your response to this as it has manifested physically in your life is the reason you have been bound by it so fully and why it appears that spirit has failed you in your efforts to overcome it.

For instance, your purpose in flesh is to evolve the human condition and you have come in with the most suitable blueprint to facilitate the greatest good in this area. However, in seeking spirit you have sought refuge from the physical, when your greatest purpose was instead to ground spirit and thereby immerse it in your physical life and evolve it from the inside out. The more you intellectually learned of the love and peace of spirit, the more you developed a disdain and discomfort in the conditions of the physical. The more you ascribed to this belief in the physical, the more it manifested. Therefore your life seemed to follow a pattern around greater spiritual awareness coupled with greater challenges in your physical life. This led to a separation of the spiritual and the physical as two distinct pursuits, rather than a marrying of the two.

To rationalise this general theme of your life you resorted to looking at your issues in hindsight and deciding that you were growing, even though it was in pain. This pain began to represent your link to spirit and your sense of connectedness to something greater occurring in your life. From that point on, your whole purpose in pursuing spiritual matters was not in joy, freedom, and confidence, but in trying to fix the things going wrong in your life. By then your whole paradigm bore witness to a life of hardship, so the only way growth could be manifested, despite your surface intention, was via this limited construct. Your intentions were always unconsciously modified to fit into this core belief because that is the foundation from which your creations stem. It is time now to expose this fault in this basic premise of your life.

The reason you are so perplexed when you witness another's wonderful life is that it contrasts with everything you believe in your core. The ego then rationalises that their 'time' will come (at the hands of spirit no less), for you consider that no one is immune from 'spiritual growth', that is, in your terms, hardship. You have become so tired of trying to produce long lasting happiness that you have recently added to this basic core, the notion that true spiritual growth comes not in the manifestation of good things, but instead in your internal ability to deal with grace all that is hurtful. Pain is not an aspect of spiritual growth unless you believe it to be and to seek pain as a measure of connectedness to spirit is a tragedy. We are now able to work consciously with your paradigm and refocus on evolving your life through a love of the spiritual rather than through a fear, or aversion, or judgement of the physical, if this makes sense to you.

It does Virgil. So how do we do that?

There can be no one lesson, affirmation, or course for that matter to teach you to actualise such a change in focus. Recognition and expansion of the feelings emerging from your core belief, rather than suppression, is by far the most important phase of this undoing, so I applaud you to have come this far. However in finishing the course, instead of completing a journey as you have assumed, you have in fact now begun a new one. Your new intention needs to consistently support a focus of essence over form, that is, feeling over ego judgement in each moment. You have reached the point where you have the ability to take full responsibility for consciousness and therefore your life. You are now intimately aware of your most basic core belief which is essentially the paradigm you have chosen to evolve. There can be no more excuses, no more keeping the truth hidden from your awareness, no more victimhood.

You have wallowed in these feelings for some time now so you are quite familiar with them, which is essential, but you need to embrace them further as you progress. Whenever these feelings arise, no matter what the trigger, they are coming forth to expose where your core belief is starting to exert an influence in your creation activities. You merely need take notice and allow your feelings to guide you away from the form and directly into essence – the self. The point from which you create your living environment is in the present, although this exists within the context of an expanded blueprint or paradigm that affords you a myriad of probabilities. Cease looking for a weighing of events, or 'right' action, and instead allow feeling to guide you inward.

Essentially this movement of feeling energy is natural, but has previously been rationalised by the ego after the trigger event as giving rise to some sort of spiritual universal test. Spirit does not test you – period. Instead you are constantly offering yourself the opportunity to evolve your core belief and free yourself from outmoded patterns. The prior unconscious nature of your belief structure has led you to rely on the limited ego to analyse your life events in hindsight which gives rise to much confusion for all the reasons already grounded in the course.

To begin, simply immerse in the feeling about being in this reality and become familiar with the manner in which it manifests in the physical, including the guises it takes. This might then clarify the reason you continue to rely on pulling in old karmic relationships in order to grow, as opposed to being present in the moment and responding to feeling. You only need old karmic patterns if you are unconscious of your present life purpose and true self image. The more aware you become of your spiritual identity and power, the less those encoded karmic patterns will be needed to serve your growth. To this end, your difficulties have not arisen because you are incapable of manifesting peace, but rather because at your core you simply do not believe it is possible to experience consistent happiness here.

You should now understand how your core belief, as an accepted 'fact' of this reality, was bound to alter even your most powerful positive thought affirmations. The energy of positive affirmation follows a natural urge toward physical fulfilment via manifestation, but first it must be measured against or compared with the basic premise of the foundation belief structure – i.e. your core belief. When the two do not align energetically, the new affirmation simply can never birth physically for it lacks the support of its creator – YOU. The contradictions of thought and feelings have taken their toll physically and emotionally, but you can sever this pattern, starting now.

You retreated into spirituality as an escape from the pain you were manifesting, but instead found a place where not only did your thoughts and aspirations not consistently materialise, but they were frequently flaunted in front of you only to be yanked away. Spirituality encouraged you to dream and believe in the highest visions for self, yet the opposite vision was often your companion. It is time to align all your energy consciously and thereby know the pathway to the highest vision, but you still have to choose it. **Your ideal life will never be bestowed upon you – know this, for if it were you would never accept responsibility for consciousness, which is the ultimate goal of this phase of your evolution, individually, and en masse.**

Now you will cease to measure your spiritual success or otherwise by comparing your physical life against others. Instead you will immerse yourself in your own feeling and thereby learn to understand the power of being present and conscious in each moment of your own life. Know that all souls are working within their own paradigm, communicated via the feelings and made physical by their own core belief. Do not attempt to be so arrogant that you could in any way determine what is at the foundation of another's creative source. As this is quite unknowable to you from your current vantage point, then it follows that if you compare physical lives as a measure of spiritual progress, you may well be comparing apples and oranges, for the source of the physical is the true key.

You were expecting others' lives to be shaken by spirit only because, to you, an apparent absence of struggle equates to an absence of spiritual intervention, not because you wished for struggle per se. You perceive that pain is an opportunity for spiritual growth, and indeed it can be, but equally it can just be an experience of pain. It has been necessary for you to associate spiritual growth with pain because of the paradigm or core belief you were working with. On one hand, on the surface, you embraced all the beauty of the doctrines of spiritual growth, yet due to your core belief continued to manifest struggle. Your surface expectations and actual life were contradictory. You had no desire to relinquish the spiritual doctrine as it is clearly your calling in this life frame, but were unable to relinquish the struggle because it appears to 'happen' to you. The ego therefore seeks to reconcile the contradiction to maintain order and sanity (in its terms) and embellishes a doctrine that supports both; i.e. growth through pain. Growth through pain is only sourced from spirit where the pain can be evolved and therefore eliminated from the evolutionary cycle, such as the nature of the course.

The weeks gone have proved a difficult process for you, but you are now standing at a doorway which when entered, will reveal the one source of all the struggle and you can consequently begin to eliminate it. Previously, you have been working through your painful so-called lessons and tests in the hope that one day they will be over and your perfect life will materialise. You have been waiting to bear witness to other peoples lessons (in your terms – pain), so that you can evidence spirit working in their lives and then come to their rescue. Due to your direct association of pain and struggle evidencing spiritual intervention, bearing witness to it has somehow brought you closer to spirit. Only knowing at a feeling level that pain and struggle is not of spirit will bring you closer to spirit. You do not need to grow through pain, yet you do not believe this at your core as perfectly illustrated by the events and feelings leading to this discussion. It is time for you to take the reins directing your life away from a universal force that delivers lessons for your own good and firmly return them to your own hand. Begin by feeling the core belief and making it an ally rather than an enemy.

How should we take control of the reins, Virgil? I always equate control with ego, so in considering that, I feel like I will be operating more from an ego stance. It seems somewhat ironic as the whole course has been about exposing and undoing that.

There is a danger here. There is a necessary balance of sharing between the feeling tone and the ego's perceptions – both are critical. This is why we have undergone the processes of learning the ego's reality, then getting in touch with the feeling body. The grounding of all the that the course contains and continuing to work with it as a way of moving through your life, will enable you to consistently ascertain the difference between denial of true feeling, via ego thoughts, and being in communion with source, via the feeling tone.

Now is the time to trust and work with your creations so you can learn to engage the joys, as well as the challenges, in order to expose and eliminate patterns that no longer serve you. Don't automatically look for drama or struggle to work with the core belief. For some the correcting circumstance could be in the opening of the heart from the joy of a birth experience, for others it may be trauma – but there is no collective rule. Its nature is determined merely by your own personal belief constructs. You need to learn to see through and beyond your core belief in pain to its polarity of grace and love. You need to learn that growth with love is a choice in every moment regardless of physical circumstances and is present in every aspect of your life. Imagine the enormous growth inherent in manifesting your heart's desire, the confidence this would inspire as a spiritual being incarnate in flesh, deeply in tune with one's entire reality.

You need to immerse yourself willingly and in peace in the natural ebb and flow of your life. You need to understand when the time to go within is upon you, not through retreat or coercion, but due to feeling a genuine need to reflect. Couple that with knowing when to be outwardly mobile and active, preparing the physical in readiness for the birthing of all that you know you have created, is imminent. You currently perceive the joy of your life as an aside to your spiritual growth, an opportunity for a rest from the arduous lessons imposed upon you. If you learn to adjust your paradigm, your vision will clear to expose the inherent growth that exists in every circumstance of your life, regardless of form. When you are able to do so, you will equate your spiritual development with pleasure and you will be able to minimise or cease to choose pain.

So when we have the moments of joy we should take heart in them, and understand that we have also created them. Is that what you mean?

Indeed, but also reflect on what has inspired this joy. Focus upon the decisions you made that ultimately gave rise to the experience. Importantly, look for opportunities that bring you closer to spirit within the joyful times. Don't wait for pain to consciously bring spirit into the fold of your life via the feeling tone. Keep the communication line open as an active and ongoing choice. You learn to recognise growth in pure happiness and no longer rely solely on your ability to recognise growth in pain. Your desire to have a spiritual hue to your life will not change. You need to actively ground growth in the context of joy or you will continue to manifest it only in the way you do now. This reality is far more fluid and pliable than your current experience would have you believe. The fact that you exist at all in your present form is merely a belief about this reality, it is even down to that seemingly most permanent level that you can learn to manipulate this existence. Time and space cannot be compromised at this stage as they are a fundamental aspect of the current mass core belief, and as part of the mass consciousness you are consequently bound by it. Therefore, everything you attempt to create will be measured against this 'fact' and will simply be unable to birth if it is not in alignment. Eventually, even such powerful mass core beliefs will be more pliable and fluid; however, that is a topic for future books.

Virgil, can I just recap? Sally's and my core belief is essentially a fear of life; a belief that the physical reality is unsupportive, hostile, involves struggle and pain, while our spirit's reality is full of all the love and joy, thus causing us to separate our two realms. I understand this because I have certainly felt that now for weeks, unarticulated though until today. I can see that it's always been there, too, as for many years both of us have said we are never reincarnating back to the physical world and have been incredulous when we've been told by spiritual readers that we actually chose to come in for this life time, when we apparently didn't have to. It seems our spiritual pursuits have been around getting the physical over and done with and just heading back to the safety of spirit. It has been a difficult paradigm to work with Virgil; it's separated us from 'normal' people, both within and outside of spiritual circles. Is it what we've come into transmute or has it been carried over from other life times?

You have set up conditions in your life to manufacture this faulty perception of reality so you can evolve it. You can then assist others in evolving their own faulty perceptions, which is actually the overall blueprint of your current life frame. You have not picked this up, in your terms, from other life frames. You have layered upon it from previous existences, which is partly why the paradigm appears so intrinsically as an aspect of self and this reality rather than merely a belief about it. However, unlike previous life frames, you have decided to evolve it in this here and now, where it is very timely to do so. It is in time with a potentially enormous leap in the evolution of mass consciousness and it was your ultimate aim to contribute to this phase in some way. I sense that you have difficulty in understanding why you would choose such a difficult paradigm, in your terms, to work with.

Yes, I do.

So you ask, 'Why didn't I choose to come through with a perfect picture of this world as my foundation belief?' (Virgil leans forward intently). Susie, you have an ability, a level of mastery gained through lifetimes of experience that you do not recognise at this point, to overcome and evolve all that is considered 'dark' in this reality and so, too, does The Channel. You have chosen this life frame to complete an inner cycle, to expose and balance a polarity that you carry to make whole what is fractured. You, in time, will learn of your potential to assist others, and then will understand why the journey has taken this direction. There are collective implications in your greater plan, for so many individuals on this planet carry fear of spiritual abandonment as a result of previous existences in Atlantis and Lemuria. A variation of this core belief is compelling and common to many, many individuals incarnate here at this time. However, you only need focus on dealing with your own life in this now. Any other focus is a distraction. You are currently only aware of one aspect of this polarity– that is the ego pain associated with unconscious manifestation of the core belief.

You are learning that there are gifts within, that are yet to be recognised. The joy and pleasure of this physical ego existence can be many and should be enjoyed. The gifts of becoming a conscious creator and assisting to evolve the collective are vastly more rewarding, when compared to unconsciously creating a comfortable ego existence via a more supportive core belief. At this significant point of earthly evolution you have the potential, moreover the need, to become a conscious creator of the mass change. In times past, when such change was spreading the Earth, you were an unconscious participant and fell from grace so to speak, along with the majority of those also present. Your purpose cannot be denied, as it stems from your deepest essence. That is why through all the struggle, you could not abandon your spiritual search, so entrenched was your need to learn to become conscious. Does this make sense to you?

(Whew) It does. I think at this stage I needed to hear that it was all going to be worth it because maybe it hasn't felt like that so far.

Be conscious in every moment of your life, knowing that the point of creation exists in the present. Conscious awareness of your core belief does not make it redundant; it just means when you are being presented with an opportunity to evolve it, you will recognise it. Through feeling you can 'flip the coin' of the experience and thereby automatically meet the circumstances from the vantage of Soul and grow through joy. As I have said, karmic encoding is the method you currently use to expose your issues. When you can navigate your life consciously, according to your inner guide, you will render such third dimensional tools, such as karma, redundant.

You will be able to identify resistance to your dreams and aspirations as it emerges and through feeling, know what actions will actually bypass or minimise that resistance. You must begin to trust that if your intention is strong, the highest vision will materialise as you continue to respond in feeling over form. I have never said anything other than the course was a process not a destination. The course was designed as a microcosm of your life, to enable you to open your eyes and provide you with a practical way forward. Your life is fluid and moving, not a destination to be lusted after and you are the master of your own experience. Remember that you are Soul incarnate in flesh, and humanity in all its expressions is an intricate part of your present journey. Humanity is evolving and seemingly imperfect. You will continue to witness this seeming imperfection in your lives because you are immersed fully in the collective of this mass dream – you can no longer deny your collective responsibilities either. Your feeling awareness, however, will eventually evolve to the point where you can recognise the perfection within all the surface manifestations.

This does not mean you will rejoice when others are in pain, or remain aloof and untouched by tragedy when it strikes. You will have a greater knowing, that only comes through feeling body awareness, of the perfection within any situation. This will ensure you do not escalate inevitable human drama into something that binds you through karma going forward. It is not to think we are feeling, or think circumstances are perfect through rational or irrational judgement. It is viewing all circumstances, be they global or personal only from the vantage of the feeling they trigger. There is no political message for you, no moral high ground to learn, no spiritual doctrine to prove, only a knowing that in responsibility for those feelings lies your salvation. Live the course and the awareness will come. Then immerse yourself fully and as an ongoing choice in *Your Beautiful Life.*

Be Blessed

Epilogue: Living Your Beautiful Life

Welcome to a new way of working with your life. Knowing your core belief from the perspective of the rational mind will make immediate improvements to your day to day encounters, particularly your relationships. However, as you continue to explore it within the framework of feeling essence rather than form, it becomes a powerful tool to purify and empower and will profoundly impact your awakening into conscious creation. From feeling, what was once considered an 'enemy' or perhaps a shadow stalking your happiness, can be now anchored as a genuine ally to open you to a deeper awareness of self. It is valuable to embrace all you have learned about yourself from the course, including your knee-jerk response and defence patterns as well as the feelings you project or internalise. It is also helpful to seek comfort and counsel in the company of others who share your hard won insight, so you can reflect your new awareness in support. Surrender to the process you have now initiated, for it truly does light the path of least resistance. You are standing at the threshold of a new beginning and we wish you every success as you journey deeper into the realm of your Soul and claim your purpose, love and self.

The Separation Enigma

When each of us decided at a Soul level to embark upon the illuminated pathway to conscious creation, the choice instantly manifested our separation from source. The shock of this moment entrenched a deep wounding to the self that blocks aspects of Soul from coming in to our conscious awareness. A sense of loss or lack in our life prevails, not to hurt us, but instead to drive us inward in order to find our pathway to illumination. The process is one of deep empowerment and responsibility and the gift of the journey is the magnificent wisdom of your own Soul made conscious. Most of us though, search outside in the physical to fill the void, which might temporarily surrogate our pain and turmoil, but does not heal it. We must find our healing and love within, and the course of your life is supporting this unfailingly.

Soul cannot be limited by definition and imposed rules, however at the same time, it is critical for our ego minds to grasp the journey before us if we are to grow with grace. The separation story referred to is one that most of us know well and while it is compelling, it is hardly tangible. The following notions are our attempt to translate the ethereal enigma of separation from source into something we can all work with in our day to day lives. It is by no means meant as an absolute doctrine, but rather should be treated as something to be evolved within your own inner truth, in your own way, guided by your unique journey. This chapter combines channelled material together with our ego world experience, gained from years of walking this path with Virgil.

Love, Purpose and Self – the Keys to Conscious Creation

The moment we adopted the illusion of separation from the God/Goddess as real, an instant wounding to one of three main facets of Soul sovereignty anchored within our being. Each one of us carries trauma associated with separation from source in either our sense of ***love***, ***purpose*** or ***self-identity***. A lack of empowerment rooted in any one of these planes of awareness, results in an inability to ***hold our light***, our ***presence*** or our ***truth***. The process of reclaiming what appears lost, and then manifesting it in our physical lives, is the way in which we become enlightened and evolve into conscious creation. We have not been left here to flounder – far from it. Instead, we have the support of each other to mirror our healing and ascension process in unity. We must however clear our vision in order to see it, know it, and ensure we contribute positively within it. Feeling awareness, coupled with an acceptance of our unique life story as it is made physical by our core belief, offers us a powerful way in which to lift the veils of judgement, and meet each other within the beauty, solidarity and oneness of purpose that we all contain and yearn to live.

Separation Wounding and Core Beliefs

From the outset, I need to caution you that we are delving into an area of earth *physical* existence when we consider the notion of wounding and core beliefs. They form not to separate but to unite. They can be evolved because they are illusion and so are no more of an aspect of your eternal self than death is. The inner self is infinite and perfect, yet within temporal reality such truth is camouflaged by the illusions of time and judgement. Core beliefs form to open doorways to the inner self, where illusion can be transcended to enable the gifts of the eternal self to be restored to awareness, in a manner that is uniquely our own. We write our entire story it seems - even the means to return home!

Working through our wounding should not be confused with notions of karma, of paying dues, or working though 'issues' from past lives. Put simply, it is our most fundamental truth of self as it appears in this now; however it is not a reflection of our true identity. It is what we have long been searching for, in vain however, due to the constant urge to project it outside ourselves or hide it deep within. It motivates all human conditions and gives rise to all unconscious response. In accordance with free will, we have countless choices in the manner we can manifest the effects of our wounding, and the fact that we project it within such varied physical guises, is partly why complete awareness of it has been so elusive. Core beliefs seek to unify the separation, by lighting a pathway inward to enable us to transcend the illusion and pain of our separation trauma. Therefore, core beliefs must be embraced as the master healers they are, rather than as master manipulators.

The earth plane is an expression of polarity, and core wounding is *bound* to be manifested within this broad blueprint. However, *always* the Universe seeks balance in the unification of separation, and core beliefs are no exception. Our wounding divides to form core beliefs in order to reflect our reality of polarity and in doing so will manifest either the yin or yang principle within our healing process. Immediately following separation, each half of the whole seeks the other for healing and unification. In this way we are irresistibly drawn to balance, healing and completion and are never without our sign posts or indeed support to direct us home. In physical life we label them anything from love, lust, attraction, hate, disgust and repulsion, but essentially, within those manifestations we are only seeking consciousness and oneness. In any relationship where we are challenged and pushed, both our terror and our eternal safety reside in equal measure. The choice in what we embody is entirely our own and will align directly to our ability to transcend the physical trigger and embrace the feeling truth within. In awareness we will recognise an ally, no matter how disagreeable their tactics, actions or motives. In ignorance, we will behold an adversary, amid judgement that will bind and disempower us.

As we reflect upon and own the feelings emerging from our highly charged events and interactions, we can learn more of ego purification and so lift the veils of illusion. The notions of essence over form, or feeling over judgement are powerful tools supporting our ascension process. Ego purification is the *only* weapon the spiritual warrior needs, for in the allowance of it, all of our suppressed gifts, talents and inner-knowing rise to consciousness to be used in integrity and service. Where we couple with another who is also working in conscious awareness we can experience infinity. In contrast, where we insist on operating in judgement we will experience an intensification of the separation trauma that we already know too well.

No matter how compelling the physical expression of our core belief and wounding, it is merely detail, and obsessing over form will only stifle feeling energy and so limit healing potential. The physical detail does need to be vented in our journals, but only in order to support the ego's need to be heard and so enable the inner pathway to be revealed. For this reason, we will only contemplate core beliefs and wounding in feeling terms as we explore the pathway leading within.

Identifying Your Core Belief

In identifying your core belief, it is important to precede your statement with "I" which was the true purpose of the "I Technique" provided in the course. Many of you will align with notions such as failure, betrayal, abandonment and more. These are all valid manifestations of core beliefs but are not core beliefs in themselves. Core beliefs cannot be changed by external conditions for they transcend logic, judgement *and* physical form. For example if you consider "I am a failure" as a core belief, you would be automatically compelled to fix it from the outside in, perhaps seeking ego success. In articulating your core belief you must get underneath the physical expression of it in feeling, so that it makes sense at a Soul level. In our failure example, we would delve into what is driving it out into the world. Specifically, what wound is *manifesting* the perception of failure to get your attention, and why? Soul cannot fail, or betray, or miss out, or be unworthy. It can however, hold fear that blocks your recognition of your own true power and unlimited identity. Of itself, fear is unreal, but the illusion of it prevents you from knowing your inner beauty, and the pain of that is indeed compelling.

Susie and Sally's core belief is "I fear life". It is a broad belief that encompasses an extensive potential in manifestation experience – as all core beliefs do. Clearly, for both women, the instant of separation from source anchored a fear of not being able to consciously create in empowerment in the physical realm. This ***fear*** blocks potential and talents as there is nothing wrong with Soul, per se. The potential blocked, then manifests as struggle and pain and so fear is further grounded in the physical and the process then compounded. No core belief can identify an imperfection of Spirit because this is impossible. However, it should point to a lack of faith or fear around an aspect of holding your light in this dense Earth realm. In Sally and Susie's case, it pinpoints a wounding to ***purpose*** blocked by their fear of ever truly being able to create in an empowered, conscious manner.

Below is a list of feelings that manifest when we are ensconced within the illusion of separation from source – as we all are. These should not be confused with actual core beliefs, but instead recognised as doorways to uncover them.

Unworthiness
Rejection

Lack of support
Abandonment
Judgement
Betrayal
Separation
Isolation
Inferiority
Superiority
Jealousy
Insecurity
Injustice
Anger
Control
Restriction
Sacrifice
Wounded inner child
Failure

I am sure you could add more conditions simply by revisiting your course journals. Within the manifestation of these lower expressions, a common feeling thread exists that will lead directly to your own core belief. In accordance with the yin/yang principle, the remedy to transcend these expressions to their higher love frequency exists in the embodiment of your core belief and following it through to the other side. If however, you continue to project or internalise the source of such manifestations, then the experience of them will intensify in degree until you surrender to your own innate wisdom. Trust yourself now and follow the journey to completion.

Core beliefs do not clear (except in the instant of ascension) because they are not an enemy to be expelled, but an ally to be embraced. When owned and worked with, they will take you to deeper and deeper levels of purification, where you will consciously know initiation is rising, because you feel it in every fibre of your being and see its effects manifested all through your physical reality. Begin to consider your core belief as an advocate, serving to heal any or all of these conditions in your life, rather than as a tormentor creating them. As your focus evolves, your core belief will become the brightest light in your life, leading you inward to purification and ascension. The challenges it presents will still be powerful, however you will now have the inner resources to navigate them to higher awareness. Furthermore, this awareness cannot be hijacked by anything outside of you. In essence the core belief teaches you to hold your light amid ego chaos - another mark of the spiritual warrior.

I repeat. The cause of all angst lies in the illusion of separation – a bond you all share. The core belief draws your attention to gift you with the insight to transcend all of these painful conditions in your life, so you can heal and ascend. This is our true purpose; ascension through empowerment.

Core Beliefs - Defined

You are an infinite eternal being that can never be defined. Therefore, I caution you that the following characteristics are in no way meant to define who you are, what you do, nor even what your 'issues' are. They are instead characteristics that rise from misguided ego defences designed to buffer you from genuinely experiencing the feeling of your life when you are pushed, challenged and triggered. They are conditioned responses used to hide your inner truth from yourself as well as others; hence they are based in illusion. However the illusion is sourced and nurtured absolutely from within and therefore can only be transcended from the inside out – or in other words, from the experience of it beyond ego judgement and within the sanctity of feeling.

We have previously stated that our wounding has given rise to struggle in one of three planes of manifestation either in – ***purpose***, ***love*** or ***self-identity***. Our pain or fear cloaks aspects of self that can empower and heal and so core beliefs emerge to trigger awareness and turn our focus within.

The following pages examine and differentiate core beliefs according to five distinct formats:

Characteristics: The *feelings and physical manifestations* that frequently rise when our core beliefs are triggered directly. Generally, the more acute the condition, the longer or more resolute we have been in avoidance.

Patterns of Ego: Here we identify common ego *responses* that we often employ in an attempt to obliterate or 'fix' painful feelings. Not all of them may apply to you, but the overall theme should be familiar.

Shadow Wisdom: This refers to the *gift within* self that is trying come in to conscious awareness in your life. It is the process of integration of balance as the yin/yang truth manifests in a tangible manner physically.

Support: This section suggests the course lesson or other approach that will assist you to work *with* the core belief rather than against it.

Key Phrase: Each core belief aligns with a key phrase that crystallises the gift of the journey from illusion to awareness. It represents your sacred vision and in the embodiment of it in your life via anchoring your core belief wisdom, then empowerment often accompanied by new beginnings, will birth. It is also a useful 'mantra' to open feeling when you are facing deeper ongoing initiation.

Our lists are not exhaustive or explicit and you should always follow your own inner guide in accepting what feels right for you.

Core Beliefs

I Fear Life – wounding to Purpose

Characteristics:

Hold a pervasive sense of loss amid even the most bountiful times.

Hold a feeling of deep insecurity and a sense of abandonment.

Minimal self-empowerment or confidence.

Aversion to feeling at any level - might be seen as aloof or confident but are actually insecure and yearning for connection.

Indecisive.

Resentful.

Fear the spot light.

Feel spiritually weak or inferior.

Often plagued by intense feelings of not wanting to be here, which can deteriorate to depression or hopelessness and so may contemplate or manifest mental problems if left unchecked.

Patterns of Ego:

Defences against feeling are first, to withdraw inward, then shut down and in extreme cases permanently retreat from life.

Often attracted to substances that numb.

Looking for rules to abide by to give them some control over their life.

Tendency to internalise blame rather than project it outwardly.

Flight rather than fight, which may appear in ego terms as a lack of commitment.

Disconnected from the physical world and will be drawn to substances that shut it out.

Diligent and loyal to whatever support they are offered, spiritually or physically.

Crave security but dream of adventure.

Self-sacrifice with a tendency to please others and so are easily let down.

Driven to search for meaning in life.

Attach themselves to others and surrender their identity.

Shadow Wisdom:

When the core belief is transcended the union of the inner and outer world occurs which will initiate enormous change. Conscious creation is restored to the self, gifts and talents rise to the surface and strong purpose is *finally* birthed. Rather than hide within spirit, they are able to anchor spirit in the physical and so learn to appreciate life and the freedom it can contain, rather than feel they are at the mercy of it, without power or influence.

Support:

As these people tend to clutch at spirit and hide from the physical, the chapter on responsibility is the most relevant. Fear of life results in feeling powerless to influence the outside world, yet in responsibility one is urged to actually challenge circumstances from the inside out. Taking responsibility upholds the truth that your spirit is within every manifestation you encounter. That focus unites both planes of awareness, allowing strong foundations to anchor that support you to plant your feet in your Earth journey as a holy expression of self- mastery. Purpose that has for too long been an inner contemplation begins to be embodied and owned. In transcending their core belief they cease hiding their light and instead draw it in to transform the physical.

Key Phrase: I Empower

I Fear Self – wounding to Purpose

Characteristics:

Usually emotionally mild, but can be unexpectedly volatile when even slightly provoked.

Feeling is projected outside of themselves and on to the physical trigger.

Emotional response from charged events is often far more intense than the situation itself.

Often feel trapped in obligation and routine as they yearn for expansion.

Consistently searching for cause and effect in the physical as the source of any anxiety.

Fear of failure and need to demonstrate success.

Intolerant of 'fools'.

Confident in the physical realm and are aware of their strengths, but fearful of loss.

Frequently dissatisfied with what they have - cup half empty.

Tend to retreat into externalised judgement to avoid inner feeling responsibility.

Can tend to appear untouchable emotionally.

Patterns of Ego:

Failure and judgement are the main defences erected against feeling - not only of self, but of others and life itself.

Tendency to always look for new external experience, in direct alignment to their inability to look within for experience.

Fight instead of flight and can appear aggressive as they defend their judgement.

Any inner discord is externalised via control, perfectionism and order as they define it.

They confuse inner awareness and work with outer intent and physical action.

Perfectionists and sometimes too critical or intolerant.

Shadow Wisdom:

The true Soul joy and potential of these people is hidden below ego judgement concerning right and wrong obligations, burdens and blame. The sense of dissatisfaction, failure and loss that ensues becomes more intense until they surrender to the inner self and are finally guided by it toward *genuine* fulfilment and joy. These people need to own and express their uniqueness and discover what nourishes them at a deeper level, rather than pursue ego obligation that rarely inspires, and then judge outcomes against strict measures of success or failure. The yearning for inner connection is truly driving their search in the outer realms, but it can only be fulfilled from following and honouring inner guidance and discovering their inner passion. This passion will reveal new abilities that will ignite purpose and empowerment on the inner and the outer.

Support:

As their ego thoughts are often brutally judgemental, those with the core belief "I fear self" need to cease projecting them externally and instead follow them to their source within. Regular commitment to recording ego thoughts in their journal is important so they can choose feeling and so expose and yield to their own innate wisdom that hides within, which is truly gentle outside of ego influence. These people also resonate with nature in all forms and can learn to own their feeling and so awaken their ability to influence the physical with their unique beauty, instead of their judgement and anger. They crave change and in the surrender of ego judgement and 'right' action, their true power to influence change, can emerge.

Key Phrase: I Surrender

I Am Unloved – wounding to Love

Characteristics:

Abides within a pervading sense of grief, loss and regret
with roots in the past.

Exhibits a sense of victimhood, desperation and unworthiness.

Prone to emotional hypersensitivity and volatility.

Tormented by unmet expectation in relationships and
frequently disappointed.

Cup is half empty.

Attach themselves to people and possessions for a sense of security and identity.

Neediness and a history of profound loss (death, orphan or similar).

Seen as naïve and easily exploited.

Poor self-esteem, except in the area of outward appearances where they are usually confident.

Driven by a consuming desire to be loved that triggers genuine grief when not met.

Patterns of Ego:

Victimhood and attack are alternated as defences against feeling a lack of love. The form of attack however, is usually either externalised or internalised, not both.

Withdraws inward for protection from feeling.

Craves attention that in extreme cases can lead to bouts of hypochondria or 'crying wolf'.

In need of constant reassurance and approval.

Always needing more love and so are prone to excess in food, spending or substances as surrogates to love.

Vulnerable to self-destructive patterns/behaviours due to unfulfilled longing.

Tendency to sabotage relationships because any and all problems are not seen as challenges directly, but instead as evidence of being unloved.

Generous with material objects as an expression of love.

Emotionally volatile due to inability to express their angst in an empowered way.

Lack of balance in relationships.

Shadow Wisdom:

These people feel empty and are often tormented by their past, especially the conditions that gave rise to their sense of being unloved, which the ego cannot reconcile. They are fixated in looking outward, in particular to others to fill the void within. People with a core belief of 'I am unloved' must relinquish their attachment to their past physical trauma, because it aligns their focus with manifestation, rather than source. They must begin to seek evidence of love that is inherent in all their challenges and joys, and cease to confine love to only specific manifestations and circumstances. They have an enormous capacity to love, but are unable to access this from within and so can neither hold, nor reflect that love in their life. They can only heal within when they turn inward to embrace their own source of love, and trace its gifts even back to their past turmoil, for it is there if they seek it. When they can transcend their ego patterns of attachment and expectation, they will learn that their inability to let go has been the true source of their pain and the real barrier to love. With nothing to externalise, they will be forced to look within where their true beauty, compassion and freedom is waiting for them to manifest as they set their love free and let go.

Support:

Understanding the difference between ego and soul expression when it comes to love, is at the heart of healing for these people. Ego love is needy, imperfect and conditional so they will never be fulfilled from outside. This journey is characterised by bouts of intense grief from lack of love and constant searching, which sooner or later must turn within. They must redefine the notion of love existing outside of them as a conditional and transitory objective to be procured, and instead anchor it at the source of who they are. These people struggle to see themselves worthy of Spirit as a whole, and so see it as something that sits outside them, intangible and elusive. This is a direct reflection of how they perceive love in other forms. Therefore Chapter Five is particularly challenging and for this reason they should work with those concepts often from the perspective of feeling awareness, in order to reconnect to love.

Key Phrase: I am Love

I Am Alone - wounding to Love

Characteristics:

Rejection, separation, unworthiness are prime feeling forces.

Hide a great emotional capacity which is difficult or impossible to express or acknowledge.

Often overtly judgemental with a critical slant.

Can appear to lack emotional commitment in relationships.

Comfortable in solitude and much less so in crowds.

Intensely vulnerable but controlled and masked by an impenetrable exterior.

Rejection often stems from severance of connection to parent in childhood via death, adoption, rejection, separation or abandonment.

If both parents were physically present, then rejection will have been overt and even cruel emotionally.

Fear emotional pain and manifest not only an island within the self,but in extreme cases erect a fortress against feeling.

Will live and die according to their ideas of right and wrong on many levels.

Patterns of Ego:

Attack is the favoured defence of the "I am alone" core belief. The attack is rarely aggressive, but is instead simply the choice to stubbornly uphold an opposition stance that invalidates others in the process.

Being logical thinkers, they have a tendency to deny feeling amid rigid beliefs and analysis if they are triggered emotionally.

They like to take physical action to fix their angst when triggered in order to avoid feeling any loss or pain.

Often hide in excessive work and attention to physical responsibility, while completely avoiding emotional needs of themselves and consequently also those who depend on them.

Emotion is always close to the surface requiring enormous energy and judgement to keep it under control.

These people lack compassion for triggers manifesting in their intimate reality, particularly relationships, yet extend it in a genuine heartfelt way to strangers or social causes.

Less aware of their inner depth beyond ego morality.

Shadow Wisdom:

These people feel like something is missing from their lives, though they could probably not admit it. They too, have a strong attachment to past trauma, but they have a tendency to rationalise the pain away rather than feel it. Yet if allowed it would expose a well hidden vulnerability, lost amid a judgemental, sometimes harsh exterior that fools no one but themselves. In allowing their vulnerability, they will learn the depth of Soul *compassion* not only for others but eventually for themselves. In so doing, they heal their wounding to love and begin to be able to express feeling willingly, as they embrace the fact that within their vulnerability lies a great and true spiritual strength and power.

Support:

These people wear compassion on their sleeve, however they struggle to extend this to those they love because it would trigger intense feeling in their own world, which creates a fear of being overwhelmed. They need to work with the lesson 'feeling is just feeling' because it transcends judgement and so enables their inner world to be validated. These people fear feeling, which is why they need to work consistently with allowing it and so open the doorway to self-acceptance and self-worth at an intimate level. Within their vulnerability lies great strength which can be channelled for life changing effects.

Key Phrase: I Feel

I Am Disconnected – wounding to Self

Characteristics:

A constant sense of being ungrounded and without foundation dominates their life.

Present larger than life personalities and are often charismatic, dynamic achievers on one level, yet disempowered and lost on another.

Feel invisible on the inner realm that could be articulated as "I am a lost soul".

In contrast, they easily manage their strong sense of self in the day to day outer ego world.

Carry within a strong sense of exclusion and a feeling of belonging nowhere.

Often feel like a fraud because of the confident air they project, which is in fact an outer defence against a consuming sense of self-doubt.

Lack balance and the ability to reconcile it.

The embodiment of "separation" on all levels.

Patterns of Ego:

Often attract people in need of nurturing and aid, with self-interest barely acknowledged.

Strength in achievement and action and strong planners, yet when life serves up the unexpected challenges they struggle to own them.

Perceived by others as being superficial, lacking depth and sometimes even 'flaky'.

Always searching in the outer world for a means to ground their inner presence.

Plagued by a strong sense of it all being taken away and often manifest illness that cannot be traditionally diagnosed and treated.

Often subject of envy as they appear to have it 'all' in their physical life.

Easily distracted, often blind to their impact on others and unable to hold their light amid emotional power plays.

Need assurance and acceptance.

Shadow Wisdom:

The wounding to self creates an abyss between the inner knowing and the outer ego experience, where the illusion of separation is manifested completely. The investment of energy in to external focus subjugates inner sovereignty to such a degree, that its influence is reduced to a mere flutter. The result is a deep sense of insecurity and loss of inner identity, coupled with a need to control the outer world in order to feel safe. In the diminished sense of self, growth must be triggered almost exclusively from the outside in. This creates unnecessary drama and turmoil which further ingrains the need to control. As the inner self's influence is acknowledged as it manifests within these trials, then eventually the link between each awareness will be strengthened. Then, spiritual and personal growth can be undertaken in ease, with less angst and trepidation. Within surrender to inner wisdom, no matter the camouflage, a new found security is anchored and the need to control gives way to a sense of allowance. Growth in grace rather than drama becomes empowered.

Support:

These people need to regularly journey to the point of stillness so they can begin to acknowledge the depth that resides there. They need to focus everyday on psychic protection and anchor their being in nature, which will reflect their light until they are ready to claim it. Commitment to this level of self will be initially challenging as it will feel contrived or disingenuous, however it is essential. They must relinquish expectation in order to ground awareness that the sacred connection to spirit can be lost when one is unable to hold their light, but is never truly severed. The exercise of 'flipping the coin' is an effective way to engage both sides of their psyche and empowers them to begin to acknowledge and honour their unassailable connection to self.

Key Phrase: I Connect

I Am Invisible – wounding to Self

Characteristics:

These people struggle to hold their light and often feel less, inferior and/or without voice.

They are usually endowed with special talents, but are plagued with doubts about their value, skill and abilities.

Overly sensitive to the needs of others, they are prone to surrogate and take on too much in false obligation that usurps their own needs.

Quiet and unassuming, but still waters run deep.

They judge their inner voice as self-indulgent or self-centred and so suppress their needs.

People often feel sorry for them as they are perceived as not living their full potential. Appearances are deceptive because beneath their surface humility, they often nurture unique gifts and talents that rise from deep creativity, yet they may lack the ambition, confidence or means to develop it further.

They are guarded about their inner and outer life.

Giving and considerate and frequently taken for granted.

Patterns of Ego:

Often lack a voice in their family life and relationships and struggle to hold their light when challenged, particularly by authority figures.

They always strive for 'right' action and external validation, as though they need an external road map to success.

Flexible to the point where they will put themselves last.

When they are in their inner world they can enjoy their talents immensely, however they see this beautiful joy as an aside to life, rather than a link with their true creative self and therefore genuine Soul communication.

They tend to scrutinise and compartmentalise their life circumstances into defined roles that they then measure according to ego expectation. As this choice ignores their inner wisdom, they frequently return empty handed or disempowered and a sense of failure can prevail.

Encouraging, supportive and in awe of others, while rarely giving their own talents value.

Shadow Wisdom:

These people make easy targets for projection, but will take on so much before their inner light bursts forth. Strong and deep, they need to embrace the inner beauty willingly as a unique and reliable way to journey their life. They are so accommodating that they need to be pushed to near breaking point at an ego level, in order to open the flood gates to their being and hold their light in self-expression. They are immensely powerful when they allow their ego to express what lies within. In their heart they long to be recognised for their gifts and talents and the more they stand in their light willingly, less and less failure triggers will need to manifest, in order for them to own their true power. They learn the value of holding their light amid the ego world and so prepare to return to oneness via ascension and not be suffocated and made invisible in the process. They do honour their inner self and talents, but they need to express them in freedom in the ego world, rather than trying to conform to expectations or indeed fulfil the needs of others. When this occurs, their light is brilliant.

Support:

These people need to embrace their voice, expression and presence and instill it in to the outer world in a way that makes an impression and moves energy. They evolve more rapidly from action and so investing in crossroads experience and immersing themselves fully in a robust and fearless manner in the *ego* world, is their way forward. By this approach their inner strength and resolve, which is powerful, can manifest freely. Crossroads initiates a need to come out of hiding, to explore themselves in new environments, which is as challenging for them as it is rewarding. For this reason, these people can quite easily navigate their core belief without the need to engage the yin/yang principle of a relationship. Where relationships do form within these two polarities, they are often less plagued by traits of attraction and opposition that gives rise to so much ego drama in the other core belief pairs.

Key Phrase: I Embody

The Course of Your Life – A New Beginning

Arriving at this point of self-awareness in your life will open a doorway within, where your own wisdom and strength can emerge to light the way. You now have the tools and ability to begin to work with your life in a far more conscious way. It will not always be easy for there is no 'quick fix' and your life is continually evolving. In working with your core belief you simply own the feelings within, while acknowledging the manifestations outside. Within this awareness, you will clearly recognise that change and growth is trying to enter your life and work positively to ground it, rather than resist it. When you find yourself in the midst of your core belief feelings and familiar patterns and triggers, simply return to feeling and allow them to be your guide. You don't have to take action or know the pathway in the instant of your experience - time is not a measure for Spirit. In moments of deep angst, I have felt enormous relief in the knowledge I can just 'be' and allow the journey to complete me, as opposed to feeling the pressure to complete the journey. Always keep your intent clear and free of ideas concerning physical outcomes. Be always mindful of essence over form and allow the will of your higher self and feeling tone to work through you. In feeling, clarity will come and the doing will be much easier as a result.

Surrender the notion of a universal force acting outside of you creating your life – it is false. Begin now to acknowledge your hand in all your experiences and focus on being immersed in them, rather than merely an observer who is judging them. Be present in each moment of your life via a consistent focus on what you are feeling. Physically, there simply is no preferred destination or lost opportunity - there is however the ever present feeling tone urging your focus inward. In this way *Your Beautiful Life* seeks completion via manifestation, challenging you to higher consciousness by clearing the blocks that blind you to your potential.

The rules you follow from now on are of your own making, so consider them carefully. Are they sourced from within or do they resemble the old demands of ego? Are they familiar truths belonging to others? Allow your pathway forward to be truly, uniquely your own. We welcome you to our Soul group of feeling focus and wish you every success in living *Your Beautiful Life*.

Please log into our website **www.yourbeautifullife.com.au** if you require any further clarification. There is a great deal of support and assistance available to you – for truly you are worth it.

With Love

Virgil, Sally and Susie

Moving Beyond Limitation

It is my greatest hope that in the completion of this course, you will have come into awareness that everything you need to free yourself from the bonds of physical tribulation is contained within **you**. I hope that you can accept the truth that this Earth plane is indeed a grand teacher that supports you to master the self, and in that process ascend into the love and light that is both your inescapable destiny as well as your birth-right. You are never without, apart or separate from the support, guidance and love that you all seek, for it exists, albeit expertly camouflaged, within the manifestation of your ordinary life in every moment. While I understand that it is often difficult to recognise the love and support within the trials that you undertake, simply knowing and then maintaining the conscious awareness that it is there, can be sufficient to draw your focus to the inherent clarity amid the chaos. The process of seeking your eternal, inextinguishable connection to truth within any apparent darkness will assist you to open to your own light as never before – and your own light is your only true guide.

Any darkness that you perceive in your reality is indeed a part of you and so cannot act independently of your own ***higher*** will, no matter what judgements you may entertain. Therefore, there is nothing that can occur that is outside of your ability to transcend. The darkness within, regardless of the way in which it manifests physically, is always seeking the light of consciousness for it seeks its true being. This truth is a microcosm of the larger purpose of *your* life, in that you too are seeking your source light. Therefore, this is what gives rise to all of your choices, all of your responses and consequently all of your future experience. In the conscious acceptance of all that you experience, a knowing will emerge of the deeper truth of what is trying to anchor within the illusion. Avoid identifying too heavily with the notion that you must be healed, for you are indeed transcending the illusion that you are in need of anything at all. You are awakening into your own unassailable truth and knowing; you do not need to be ***fixed*** in order to experience who you are, you only need to accept your own grace.

As the layers of illusion are transcended, the truth of your profound power will be revealed in direct alignment. It occurs effortlessly, as a spiral of alchemy, where the old is transformed by the next wave of vision and intent that you are able to *hold*. At the most fundamental level, your intent energises your power centre and it is critical that this be purified in direct alignment to the Earth shift in frequency. This is the true purpose of your Earth walk. Before now though, you have been cowering from your power – yet the time is upon you my friends, to own it in integrity. The preparation has been long I understand, the journey arduous. However the consequences for misusing your power in ignorance is what you would call karma, which is actually a safety net that ensures you meet the conditions of your intent and responses so that you can learn their reality. The consequence of misusing this intent consciously has far more absolute and penetrating conditions than you could ever comprehend or indeed would want to. For this reason, your Earth walk is truly incalculable in its value and support. Please honour her every day as she transmutes the consequences of your misguided intent so as to save you from harming yourself in the same way. In other words, she has carried the burden of your learning so that you will never truly be a victim of your own ignorance, as you reclaim spiritual truth. She is ready to return your sovereignty to yourself however.

Most of you would be aware that since the completion of our book *Your Beautiful Life* the frequency of the Earth has shifted to fifth dimensional vibration. In real terms, this means the evolutionary paradigm has shifted away from tests and power plays that *compel* you to act in a new way, to one of *conscious* purification of intent and power, as a precursor to *conscious* initiation and eventually ascension. The most important shift that our course aimed to anchor was the change from being at the mercy of an external force, to accepting that we do indeed create **all** of our experience. The grounding of this most important and undeniable truth as the way in which you meet your life, is the single most important awareness you can hold, since all deeper re-alisations rise from this foundation. Avoid projecting your power and intent outside of you, for if you do you will be operating apart from the support and growth that characterises the coming into fifth dimensional awareness.

You will never own your power by projecting it outside of yourself. Without ownership there can be no ego purification and without purification there is no ascension. For this reason, nurture and contribute to like-minded groups, where you can reflect a truth that supports growth through purification rather than struggle and hence anchor this paradigm more fully in your own life to affect the collective consciousness and the entire vibrational shift.

Another important aspect of fifth dimensional awareness is the surrender of identification with specific roles that may inadvertently define you. Understand that you are not a political party, a religion, a race or even a gender for that matter. Yet, within the choice of camouflage you have adopted, a doorway to truth *always* exists. Attachment to roles will not serve you in this new world because they limit. You can embrace them, love them, but you cannot be attached to them or allow them to define you. If you are attached to any notions as a definition of self, especially where it is something you glorify or conversely suppress, then there is an illusion connected to that identity that must be transcended. Truly it is that simple - and that difficult. Focus on what triggers you, no matter how you may dress it physically, and your purification can be revealed. Your life is important, your choices are meaningful and what you cast aside runs amok. Yet within your daily life, you must begin to understand that you are working towards a greater gift and a greater process than merely learning to work with spiritual tools or rules or manifestation desires. Such old notions of spirit representing an external doctrine that can be learned are grounded in third dimensional thinking and as such must be evolved to higher awareness along with everything else. The past need not be discarded, your wisdom and talents not diminished, but they do need to blossom into fifth dimensional frequency. The wandering Soul is returning to the heart of Source, but you must raise the vibration of all the treasures you have collected along the way, so they are worthy of the grand self that you truly are.

This is the new paradigm that I wish you to focus on. You are here at this time because you have anchored the necessary foundations to enable you to take an evolutionary leap and return to unity – and you are returning with new gifts and talents earned from the adventure you have undertaken. You can only make the transition back to Source through heart expansion. As the heart opens it *breaks* – but it is actually breaking limitation, which is then reflected in your outward environment in all manner of ways. Often you lament the outer manifestations, sometimes becoming more attached as you mourn illusion and ignore their truth. It is attachment that causes pain, not the event itself. Please work with this truth. If the process of purification, via opening a deeper heart chamber hurts you, it is only because of notions such as attachment, expectation and/or a sense of powerlessness – all of which are manifestations of limitation that must be relinquished in order to hold your power. A 'broken' heart can lead you to embrace more love if you have the awareness and courage to follow it home. It is the solution; it is the way to make sense of nonsense. You have 'free will' in the manner you manifest your pathway home, but you will only discover the light of evolution within heart awareness. Keep your heart open amid courage and fearlessness, for truthfully nothing is ever lost. Any trigger of the heart at this time is an act of support and love urging you home. Again, in your groups you could reflect this support to each other. You are never, ever left to flounder and you are more loved and cherished than you can fathom from your current awareness.

Live your heritage of support and love in every now moment of your life. Infuse your groups with the intent of purification and ascension. Let go of the old paradigm and raise the vibration of anything you do to reflect the new frequency that is upon you, caressing you to new depths that in turn manifest new heights. Reach for the stars and reach for the heart of Source. It will not be denied to you for it is who you are, who you have always been and who you must now make physical.

Be blessed,

Virgil

Testimonials

'This course was like a sniper in the night that hit me with a direct shot to the core of my Being. I was completely unprepared for the impact it would have on my operating paradigm of consciousness and the shattering affect it would have on my ego. This course has finally opened the door for my soul to step into the spotlight and shine! I AM FREE!'

- Tim

'What is so profound with completing this course is that it is something that remains, grows, and evolves; a true shift occurs.'

- Juliet

'I was becoming increasingly absorbed in Sally's and Susie's lives as they put words to the tumult that had been within me – unidentified and without voice for a very long time. Upon completion I was filled with relief and life and the most amazing feeling of freedom. Why my life had not been working came rushing at me with an "of course!" after weeks of it hovering around my periphery.'

- Bronwyn

'The course of discovering our beautiful lives has been one of many challenges and many joys. Now as I sit here years later it is still evolving and constantly changing, allowing me the awareness of my life, I so longed for.'

- Rebecca

'This course moves beyond all of that 'do the weekend workshop' and 'all will be well'. It integrates all parts of yourself and opens you up to live your life in feeling. This awareness extends into everyday life helping you understand that you are the perfect creator of your own life.'

- Nikki

'One of the important things that sets this course apart is that it teaches us not to invalidate the ego. In doing so, we uncover our unique core belief that shapes our life currently, so that we can recognise its illusionary nature and re shape our existence into the beautiful life we have always wanted.'

- Elisabeth

'Your Beautiful Life awakened in me the ability to see through the illusions of the ego world I was so deeply absorbed in. It has fundamentally changed and improved, the way I respond to my life.'

- Angelique

For the first time I know how I create my reality (past and present) and how my choices affect it. My life is becoming clearer as I explore what I have learnt and trust in my feelings.

- Deb

Mother
Reborn into light - a soul's journey
SALLY MACKAY

'*Mother*', speaking through Sally Mackay, provides alternative commentaries on many compelling spiritual concepts to align with the emerging consciousness shift of our present age. She explores:

Reincarnation

Your 'baggage' is nothing more than your beliefs and not karmic or reincarnation debt as many suppose.

Karma

How can you deal with issues from an unconscious past life? How is that empowering? Rather than be a victim of an angry God, one becomes a victim of your own self … and we all understand there is no escaping the Self.

Death

All 'undoings' of past 'wrongs' must be undertaken on the Earth plane. It is incorrect to consider that one could learn of enlightenment through some afterlife spiritual class room.
If this were the case, then Earth would hardly be necessary.

Purpose

Your purpose is inseparable from your own process of becoming into full conscious awareness. It is not something you do as much as it is something you are.

The Power of Now

If you yearn for some 'thing' in the future, then you must be affirming lack in the now and so the lack you focus on, rather than the object of your desire, will manifest into your future.

Mother also clarifies modern notions on *Birth*, *Spirit Guides*, *Fear*, *'It's Meant to Be'*, *Guilt and Compassion* and other misconceptions of Spirituality.

Be non-attached to what you think you know and allow your true inner awareness to emerge and so guide you experientially.

With love, Mother.